Hot Chefs
HIP CUISINE

Participating chefs have generously agreed that all royalties will be donated to UNICEF.
UNICEF acknowledges with gratitude this generous contribution in support of the world's children.

Editor **Melisa Teo**
Culinary Consultant **Freddy Schmidt**
Designer **Annie Teo**
Production Manager **Sin Kam Cheong**
Editorial Assistant **Inci Sarp**
Spanish Translator **Florence Lei**

First published in 2002 by
Editions Didier Millet
121 Telok Ayer Street
#03-01, Singapore 068590
Tel: (65) 6324 9260
Fax: (65) 6324 9261
E-mail: edm@edmbooks.com.sg
www.edmbooks.com
Printed in Singapore

Text © Sandi Butchkiss and Melisa Teo
© 2002 Editions Didier Millet

All rights reserved. No portion of this book may be reproduced, stored in a retrieval system, or transmitted in any form or by any means, without permission from the Publisher.

ISBN: 981-4068-36-5

Hot Chefs
HIP CUISINE

AUTHORS
Sandi Butchkiss and Melisa Teo

CHEFS
Alain Passard, Alain Solivérès, Albert Adrià, Andoni Luis Aduriz,
André Jaeger, Charlie Trotter, Cheong Liew, Claude Troisgros,
Diego Chiarini, Ferran Adrià, Freddy Schmidt, Frédéric Anton,
Gordon Ramsay, Guy Martin, Guy Savoy, Heinz Winkler, Jacques Chibois,
Jacques and Laurent Pourcel, Jean-Georges Vongerichten, Joël Antunes,
Kiyomi Mikuni, Marcus Samuelsson, Marc Veyrat, Martin Berasategui,
Michel Troisgros, Mitsuhiro Oda, Nadia Santini, Peter Doyle,
Sam Leong, Sergi Arola, Susur Lee, Tetsuya Wakuda and Yoshihiro Murata

EDITIONS DIDIER MILLET
Singapore · Paris · Bali · Kuala Lumpur

Contents

Introduction   6

Alain Passard • Arpège, Paris   14
Alain Solivérès • Les Elysées, Paris   18
Albert Adrià • El Bulli Taller, Barcelona   22
Andoni Luis Aduriz • Mugaritz, Errentería   26
André Jaeger • Die Fischerzunft, Schaffhausen   30
Charlie Trotter • Charlie Trotter's, Chicago   34
Cheong Liew • The Grange, Adelaide   38
Claude Troisgros • Claude Troisgros, Rio De Janeiro   42
Diego Chiarini • Senso, Singapore   46
Ferran Adrià • El Bulli, Roses   50
Freddy Schmidt • The Oriental, Singapore   56
Frédéric Anton • Le Pré Catelan, Paris   60
Gordon Ramsay • Gordon Ramsay, London   64
Guy Martin • Le Grand Véfour, Paris   68
Guy Savoy • Restaurant Guy Savoy, Paris   72
Heinz Winkler • Residenz Heinz Winkler, Aschau   76
Jacques Chibois • La Bastide Saint-Antoine, Grasse   80
Jacques and Laurent Pourcel • Le Jardin Des Sens, Montpellier   84

88   Jean-Georges Vongerichten • Jean Georges, New York
92   Joël Antunes • Joël, Atlanta
96   Kiyomi Mikuni • Hotel De Mikuni, Tokyo
100   Marcus Samuelsson • Aquavit, New York
104   Marc Veyrat • Auberge De L'Eridan, Veyrier Du Lac
108   Martin Berasategui • Martin Berasategui, Lasarte Guipuzcoa
112   Michel Troisgros • Troisgros, Roanne
116   Mitsuhiro Oda • Belfry Garden, Hiroshima
120   Nadia Santini • Dal Pescatore, Mantova
124   Peter Doyle • Celsius, Sydney
128   Sam Leong • Jade, Singapore
132   Sergi Arola • La Broche, Madrid
136   Susur Lee • Susur, Toronto
140   Tetsuya Wakuda • Tetsuya's, Sydney
144   Yoshihiro Murata • Kikunoi, Kyoto

148   **Basic Recipes**
150   **Glossary**
153   **Addresses**
154   **Photo Credits**
158   **Recipe Index**

Introduction

Common kitchen tools do not, for most cooks, include syringes and hypodermic needles. Nor are Fisherman's Friend lozenges and seawater regular features on dinner menus. But things are changing.

Professional cooks have grown discontented with merely tasty, failure-proof formulae. Diners too have come to expect—or even demand—a great deal more than sustenance from their food. These days, not only should the presentation of a dish be aesthetically accomplished, but the combination, flavour, texture, temperature and aroma of its ingredients are expected to surprise. And with the increasing sophistication of an audience for whom preparations such as foie gras sushi have become almost routinely acceptable fare, making a statement in the culinary world is becoming more and more difficult.

Even top European chefs whose efforts are endorsed by Michelin's *Red Guide* are seeking new inspiration. Not satisfied with just serving classic French food in

RIGHT: The two-Michelin-star La Broche in Madrid showcases Sergi Arola's creative cuisine.
LEFT: Troisgros' trendsettting kitchen design.

PREVIOUS PAGES
PAGE 1: Kitchen activity at La Broche on a typical night.
PAGE 2: The reception at New York's Jean Georges.
PAGES 3 AND 5: Silver cutlery designed by Vivianna Torun for Georg Jensen.
PAGE 4: Foie Gras Ganache by Marcus Samuelsson of Aquavit in New York.

ABOVE (FROM TOP): Laurent Pourcel from Le Jardin Des Sens in Montpellier; Freddy Schmidt, Executive Chef of The Oriental Hotel in Singapore; Jean-Georges Vongerichten of Jean Georges in New York. OPPOSITE, TOP: Brothers Ferran and Albert Adrià debriefing their crew in El Bulli's stylish kitchen before dinner service. OPPOSITE, BELOW: Sergi Arola planning his menus for the new season.

three-Michelin-star environments, a handful of top Parisian chefs are experimenting.

Guy Martin of the historic Le Grand Véfour was duly rewarded when critics applauded his attempts at sidestepping expectations—most significantly, blurring the lines between the sweet and savoury; they christened his workplace 'the upside-down kitchen'.

After turning out the perfect roast year after year, Arpège's Alain Passard announced his plans to go vegetarian despite resistance from the Parisian public. He is currently savouring the payback of his foresight and daring, and has a long waitlist of guests.

In Spain, culinary clichés are treated to a shakedown every day. With their experiments, Brothers Ferran and Albert Adrià are stirring up enough controversy for the food world to flock to their restaurant El Bulli in Roses when it opens every summer. The brothers are fascinated with gadgetry. Using the syringe and needle, they create bread bubbles that pop into mouthfuls of olive oil. With the siphon, they transform fresh seawater from the Mediterranean into effervescent garnishes for the freshly harvested crustaceans.

Fisherman's Friend, according to Ferran, 'offers the fifth taste' (after sweet, salty, sour and bitter). He introduced it into El Bulli's menu dégustation, which is made up of no less than 30 miniscule courses. From warm gelatine noodles to piping-hot soup that dips dramatically in temperature within one mouthful, every course is an event at El Bulli.

The same will to go beyond expectations is shared by chefs across the continents. In Australia, Tetsuya Wakuda continues to intrigue and impress with his delicate French-based, Japanese-inspired compositions. He has mastered the cooking of ocean trout—crusting with konbu and slow-poaching in grapeseed and olive oil until it turns melt-in-mouth tender, or tossing lightly smoked cubes in black truffle and olive paste. But the chef's dedication to delivering exceptional taste didn't stop there. Rather than leave the supply of fish to chance or risk having other chefs beat him to the best pick at the markets, Tetsuya had Tasmanian fish farmers Petuna cultivate ocean trout in optimum growing conditions for his exclusive use.

Even the most conservative Asian chefs, entrusted with a culinary legacy to protect, are feeling the urge to break the stereotype. Yoshihiro Murata may be the third-generation heir to one of Kyoto's most respected ryoteis (traditional

Japanese kaiseki restaurants), but his strict upbringing and training in his native cuisine only served to stimulate further his curiosity with regard to foreign cultures, ingredients and cooking styles. He is responsible for the century-old Kikunoi which epitomises the art of traditional kaiseki; but he adopts a more creative approach at Roan Kikunoi where the menu unapologetically combines truffles, foie gras and champagne with uni, bonito and sake.

In Brazil, a new strain of French cuisine has emerged as a result of Claude Troisgros' encounters with indigenous ingredients and techniques. While brother Michel is taking care of the family business back in France and showing his

ABOVE: A dramatic spice rack adorns El Bulli's Barcelona test kitchen.
BELOW: Troisgros in Roanne has retained its three Michelin stars for over three decades.
BELOW, LEFT: Susur Lee's namesake restaurant in Toronto.
OPPOSITE: The dining room at El Bulli Taller in Barcelona where the Adrià brothers' experimental cooking gets the taste test.

own creative style in their revered three-Michelin-star establishment, Claude is putting to good use his training by French masters such as Paul Bocuse. Combining classical French techniques with Brazilian produce, and drawing inspiration from native specialities, he has single-handedly pioneered Tropical French Cuisine.

Claude's spirit of improvisation is shared by chefs around the world. While they cannot be categorised by nationality, age or ethnic roots, they are united by a deep passion for food. They understand the complex blend of art and science, and strive continually to surprise. Their credentials are noteworthy and their recipes are both inspired and sensibly satisfying.

Thirty-four such individuals are featured in the following pages. Depicted are their roots, visions and inspirations and a glimpse of the surroundings within which their privileged guests get to enjoy highly inventive cuisines. They have contributed to this book the recipes for their signature dishes. With a little practice you will be able to enjoy the rare thrill of reproducing them in your own home.

ABOVE: Le Jardin Des Sens is designed to indulge the five senses.
LEFT: 'Enfant terrible' Marc Veyrat (centre) and his brigade at Auberge De L'Eridan.
OPPOSITE, ABOVE (CLOCKWISE FROM TOP): Vegetables on the Grill (recipe on page 53) by Ferran Adrià of El Bulli in Roses; The Apple for Sweet Dreams at Night (recipe on page 115) by Michel Troisgros of Troisgros in Roanne; Avocado Bavarois and Langoustine and Caviar Tarama with Pistachio Oil (recipe on page 17) by Alain Passard of Arpège in Paris; Composition of Tomato, Eggplant, Basil Flowers and Olive Oil (recipe on page 122) by Nadia Santini of Dal Pescatore in Mantova.
OPPOSITE, BELOW: Chilled Tomato Soup with Devilfish Medallions (recipe on page 79) by Heinz Winkler of Residenz Heinz Winkler in Aschau.

Arpège
Paris

RIGHT: Arpège occupies the former site of Alain Senderens' three-Michelin-star Archestrate.
ABOVE: The dining room is adorned with Lalique glass panels inspired by those found in old-fashioned railroad dining cars.

Alain Passard

When Alain Passard announced that Arpège, one of Paris' elite three-Michelin-star restaurants, was turning vegetarian, he stunned the culinary world. Some thought him foolhardy. Surely, a restaurant needed more than just fruit and vegetables to sustain its customers' interest and keep the Michelin inspectors impressed? Some attributed the move to diet- or health-consciousness. But according to Passard, after three decades spent perfecting the cooking of red meat (slowly, over the lowest possible heat, in hardly any liquid to keep it tender, juicy and flavourful), the challenge no longer thrilled him. So he moved away from the red (and most of the white) and looked to greener pastures for culinary inspiration.

Two years later, Passard's extraordinary vegetarian creations have made him famous all over again. A glance at his garden-focused menu will show it lacks neither imagination nor appeal. Consider the inventiveness of a gratin of celeriac and sweet chestnuts with black truffle fondue; vegetable couscous flavoured with argan oil (made from nuts grown in Morocco so exceptionally delicious that goats climb trees for them); and celery root layered with chestnut purée—or the surprising after-dinner dessert of a big red, stuffed and candied tomato.

Meat and seafood addicts will still find, among the vegetarian creations, Passard's signature meat dishes such as the Dragée de Pigeonneau with moist farm pigeon rolled in crushed almonds, as well as a number of seafood dishes, including lobster sautéed in mustard and garnished with baby red onions, scallops roasted in bay leaves, and nasturtium-filled sea urchins.

◀ CARROT PURÉE WITH ORANGE AND LEMON CONFIT, AND SPINACH WITH SESAME OIL Serves 4

INGREDIENTS

Orange Zest Confit
Zest from 2 oranges, grated; juice from 2 oranges

Lemon Brunoise Confit
4 tsp sugar; 40 ml/1⅜ fl oz/⅛ cup water; 20 g/¾ oz/⅛ cup lemon brunoise (flesh only)

Lemon Zest Confit
4 tsp sugar; 40 ml/1⅜ fl oz/⅛ cup water; zest from 1 lemon, grated

Carrot Purée
120 g/4¼ oz carrot, peeled; 20 g/¾ oz salted butter

Spinach with Sesame Oil
300 g/10½ oz spinach; 30 g/1 oz butter; sesame oil

Garnish
1 tsp toasted sesame seeds

PREPARATION

Add the grated orange zest to the orange juice and bring to the boil. Lower the heat and simmer for 10 to 15 minutes. Remove from the heat and set aside until the mixture is completely cool. Transfer into an airtight container and refrigerate until required.

Dissolve the sugar in the water to make a light syrup. Add the lemon brunoise and bring to the boil. Lower the heat and simmer for 10 to 15 minutes. Remove from the heat and set aside until the mixture is completely cool. Transfer into an airtight container and refrigerate until required.

Dissolve the sugar in the water to make a light syrup. Add the grated lemon zest and bring to the boil. Lower the heat and simmer for 10 to 15 minutes. Remove from the heat and set aside until the mixture is completely cool. Transfer into an airtight container and refrigerate until required.

Steam the carrot until it is well-cooked. Process the steamed carrot in a blender to obtain a smooth purée, then add the orange zest and lemon brunoise confit, and salted butter. Mix well.

Blanch the spinach, then refresh with iced water immediately. Sauté the spinach in the butter, then flavour with some sesame oil and 2 tsp of lemon zest confit.

PRESENTATION

Divide the spinach among 4 plates. Place 1 quenelle of carrot purée on each plate. Drizzle some of the spinach's cooking juice around and sprinkle some toasted sesame seeds over to serve.

▶ AVOCADO BAVAROIS AND LANGOUSTINE AND CAVIAR TARAMA WITH PISTACHIO OIL Serves 4

INGREDIENTS

Avocado Bavarois
200 ml/6¾ fl oz/⅞ cup avocado purée; juice from ½ lemon; sea salt; 100 ml/3⅜ fl oz/⅜ cup whipped cream

Langoustine and Caviar Tarama
100 g/3½ oz raw langoustines, heads and shells removed, chopped; 70 g/2½ oz/⅞ cup Aquitaine caviar; 4 tsp olive oil; 100 ml/3⅜ fl oz/⅜ cup whipped cream

Garnish
4 tbsp smoked herring roe; 3 dashes of pistachio oil; sea salt; lemon juice

PREPARATION

Pass the avocado purée through a fine-mesh sieve. Add the lemon juice and season to taste with sea salt. Fold in the whipped cream gently until the mixture reaches a light consistency. Keep refrigerated until required.

Mix the chopped langoustines, caviar and olive oil. Add the whipped cream and mix gently until the mixture reaches a light consistency. Keep refrigerated until required.

PRESENTATION

Fill 4 Martini glasses with 1 tbsp of smoked herring roe each. Top each serving with 1 quenelle of avocado bavarois and 1 quenelle of langoustine and caviar tarama. Drizzle some pistachio oil over and garnish with a small pinch of sea salt. Spritz some lemon juice over to serve.

Les Elysées
Paris

RIGHT: Les Elysées' imposing vaulted glass ceiling was designed by Gustave Eiffel.
ABOVE: Hotel Vernet is the preferred accommodation for many celebrities visiting Paris.
BELOW: The Salon Bleu, an English-style bar across the hotel's lobby from Les Elysées, offers an aperitif before or cigars and Cognac after a sumptuous meal.

Alain Solivérès

Born in the south of France, Alain Solivérès embarked on a lifelong romance with traditional Mediterranean flavours and picked up an intimate understanding of olive oil, vinegar, peppers, and other herbs and seasonings in his home kitchen in Béziers. These insights provide the inspiration for his cuisine today and the menu at the two-Michelin-star Les Elysées is a personal tribute to this heritage.

Leading food critics attest that this 39-year-old's Mediterranean cuisine is exceptional and pay the highest compliments to creations such as the soup of cherries marinated in kirsch, the fresh herb dumplings, and the flourless chocolate tart with basil and olive oil sorbet. Spelt, a wheat from Provence, cooked with zucchini flowers and crayfish in a rich stock, is one of Solivérès signatures. It has attracted countless visitors to this landmark restaurant located in the historic Hotel Vernet.

Only a few steps away from the Arc de Triomphe and the Avenue des Champs-Elysées, Hotel Vernet was established in 1913. With its limestone façade decorated with scarlet awnings and black, wrought-iron balconies, it looks more like a private town house than a boutique hotel favoured by the likes of fashion icon Inès de la Fressange. Its palatial, Louis XVI-style interior, with design elements by Gustave Eiffel, creator of the Eiffel Tower, offers fitting hospitality to admirers of Solivérès' fine cooking.

▲ ROASTED SEA BASS WITH SWISS CHARD, ARTICHOKES, CÈPES AND POTATO RAVIOLIS Serves 4

INGREDIENTS

Roasted Sea Bass

8 artichokes; 8 Swiss chard leaves, cut into diamond-shaped pieces;
8 fresh cèpes, quartered (those from Auvergne preferred);
15 g/½ oz black truffles, crushed; olive oil;
sea salt; freshly ground black pepper;
20 g/¾ oz butter;
4 (180 g/6⅜ oz each) sea bass fillets;
8 tbsp mushroom stock (recipe on page 148)

Potato Ravioli

40 g/1¾ oz Bellota ham, diced finely;
8 white button mushrooms, diced finely;
4 cloves garlic, sliced; 4 shallots, sliced;
olive oil; sea salt; freshly ground black pepper;
2 tbsp grated Parmesan cheese;
120 g/4¼ oz veal brain, cooked and chopped;
8 Pompadour potatoes, peeled and washed;
groundnut oil

PREPARATION

Preheat the oven at 180°C (356°F).
Trim the artichokes and slice the edible centre evenly.
Season the Swiss chard, artichokes, cèpes and crushed black truffles to taste with the olive oil, sea salt and freshly ground black pepper.
Brush some butter on 4 sheets of aluminum foil.
Season the sea bass fillets to taste with sea salt and freshly ground black pepper, and place each portion of fish on a sheet of aluminum foil.
Top the fish with the Swiss chard mixture, spoon some mushroom stock over and wrap the fish in the foil.
Bake for 7 minutes until the fish is cooked.

Stir-fry the diced Bellota ham and mushrooms, and sliced garlic and shallots in some olive oil.
Season to taste with sea salt and freshly ground black pepper.
Add the grated Parmesan and veal brain, and mix well.
Pat the potatoes dry with kithen tissue, then slice them very thinly.
Spoon some of the ham mixture onto the centre of a potato slice, then cover the filling with another slice of potato to make a ravioli. Repeat this process with the remaining filling and potato slices.
Pan-fry the raviolis on both sides in groundnut oil until they are crispy and golden brown in colour.
Keep warm until required.

PRESENTATION

Unwrap the baked seabass carefully and pour the baking juices into a small pan.
Reduce the baking juices to a thicker consistency. Add some olive oil to the reduced baking juices and season to taste with sea salt and freshly ground black pepper.
Place each sea bass fillet with its toppings in the centre of a plate.
Spoon the baking juices over the sea bass and garnish with some crispy potato raviolis to serve.

▼ SPELT RISOTTO WITH BLACK TRUFFLES Serves 4

INGREDIENTS

Spelt Risotto

Butter; 4 bone marrows, diced;
240 g/8½ oz/1¼ cups spelt; 8 shallots, sliced;
200 ml/6¾ fl oz/⅞ cup dry white wine;
sea salt; freshly ground black pepper;
4 litres/8 pts 7¼ fl oz/17 cups chicken stock (recipe on page 148);
40 g/1⅜ oz black truffles, chopped;
4 Swiss chards, chopped;
8 tbsp grated Parmesan cheese;
4 tbsp whipping cream

Garnish

4 tbsp veal jus (recipe on page 149);
extra virgin olive oil;
40 g/1⅜ oz black truffles, sliced

PREPARATION

Warm some butter in a saucepan and sauté the diced bone marrows, spelt and sliced shallots until the shallots turn translucent. Deglaze the mixture with the white wine and simmer until the white wine evaporates. Season to taste with sea salt and freshly ground black pepper.
Add enough chicken stock to cover the mixture, then cover the pan.
Lower the heat and let the mixture cook slowly, stirring occasionally.
When the chicken stock is almost dry, add more stock.
Repeat this process with the remaining chicken stock until the spelt is cooked.
Add 160 g/5⅝ oz of butter and mix well.
Add the chopped black truffles and Swiss chard, then sprinkle the grated Parmesan over. Mix well.
Season to taste with salt and freshly ground black pepper if necessary.
Stir in the whipping cream just before serving.

PRESENTATION

Divide the spelt risotto among 4 warm soup plates.
Drizzle some veal jus and extra virgin olive oil over.
Garnish with some black truffle slices to serve.

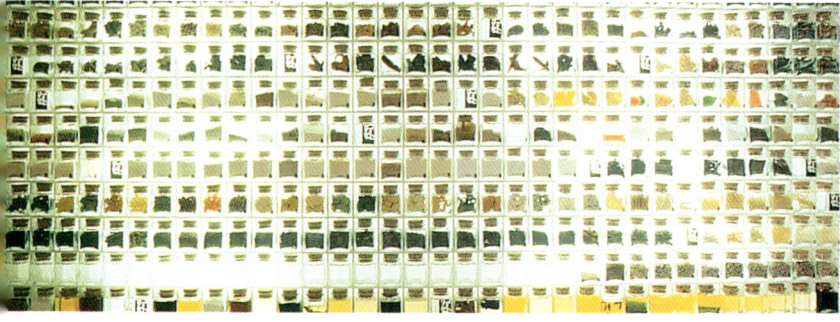

LEFT: El Bulli Taller's stylish spice rack.
BELOW: El Bulli's research laboratory is dedicated to the art and science of gastronomy.
BELOW, LEFT: The test kitchen.
BELOW, EXTREME LEFT: The Adrià brothers' alcove in Barcelona.

El Bulli Taller
Barcelona

Albert Adrià

He may face the challenge of creating dramatic finales that will stand their ground against brother Ferran's exceptional cooking, but Albert Adrià prefers to be called a cook who works with sweets, rather than a pastry chef. He spends most of his time at the El Bulli Taller, the brothers' test kitchen in Barcelona, researching and developing new recipes and cooking techniques, which are then unveiled every summer at their revered restaurant in Roses.

Adept at avoiding culinary clichés, he applies the same ingenuity to his desserts and petit fours as does Ferran to savoury cooking. So, while Ferran puts Parmesan into his siphon, Albert tips in yoghurt. Both are preoccupied with the textural properties of gelatine, so Ferran experiments with consommé and makes fettucine, and Albert toys with curry in gelatine-based desserts. Dark chocolate gets paired with wasabi, white chocolate with truffle oil. All forms of chocolate—cake, mousse, sorbet, caramel—come together in a sculpture impressive in both taste and architecture. Desserts are never dull at El Bulli.

Michel Guérard's health-conscious cooking philosophies are also deeply embedded in Albert's own kitchen practices. Keeping his desserts light and tasty, avoiding excessive fat, sugar and calories, Albert creates dishes that aim to not only emphasise the ingredients' inherent properties, but also to transcend them.

Between them, the brothers have successfully blurred the lines that separate the pastry and savoury kitchens, inventing new tastes, textures and techniques appropriate to the exotic ingredients found on El Bulli's three-Michelin-star menu.

YOGHURT SORBET WITH ASPARAGUS AND ORANGE Serves 4

INGREDIENTS

Yoghurt Sorbet

25 ml/⅞ fl oz/⅛ cup syrup; 3 tsp glucose; ¼ tsp stabiliser; 250 ml/8½ fl oz/1 cup yoghurt; 125 ml/4¼ fl oz/½ cup milk; 125 ml/4¼ fl oz/½ cup cream

Caramelised Asparagus Sauce

75 g/2⅝ oz green asparagus, blanched and refreshed in iced water; 50 g/1¾ oz/¼ cup sugar; 50 ml/1¾ fl oz/¼ cup water

Orange Sauce

A pinch of gelatine powder; 1 gelatine leaf; 100 ml/3⅜ fl oz/⅜ cup orange juice

Orange Reduction

100 ml/3⅜ fl oz/⅜ cup orange juice; 3 tsp sugar

Muscat Gelatine

A pinch of gelatine powder; 1 gelatine leaf; 100 ml/3⅜ fl oz/⅜ cup Muscat wine (those from Saint Emilin in Spain preferred)

Garnish

4 asparagus tips, thinly sliced; 8 orange segments; 1 tbsp powdered orange zest

PREPARATION

Combine the syrup, glucose and stabiliser in a pot and mix well.
Heat the mixture to 85°C (185°F) and add the remaining ingredients.
Mix well, then remove from the heat and let it stand for 12 hours.
Process the mixture in an ice cream maker set to sorbet specifications.
When ready, keep frozen until required.

Pass the asparagus through a juice extractor to obtain 50 ml/1¾ fl oz/¼ cup of asparagus juice.
Heat the sugar with the water until the mixture reaches the consistency of caramel without colouring.
Add the asparagus juice and cook for 2 minutes, then mix well.
Remove from the heat and pass the mixture through a fine-mesh sieve. Set aside.

Heat the gelatine powder and leaf in some orange juice until they are completely dissolved.
Mix in the remaining orange juice.

Combine the sugar and orange juice in a pan and reduce the mixture over low heat until it reaches the consistency of caramel.

Heat the gelatine powder and leaf in some Muscat wine until they are completely dissolved.
Add the remaining wine and mix well.
Divide the mixture among 4 moulds and allow the gelatine to set.

PRESENTATION

Unmould each portion of Muscat gelatine onto the centre of a plate and spoon some orange sauce around. Arrange 2 orange segments and some sliced asparagus tips on each portion of gelatine, then drizzle the orange reduction over. Top this with a scoop of yoghurt sorbet. Make a small incision on the sorbet, then spoon some asparagus sauce over. Sprinkle the powdered orange zest over to serve.

CHOCOLATE WITH APRICOT SAUCE Serves 4

INGREDIENTS

Flourless Chocolate Sponge Cake

250 g/8⅞ oz couverture chocolate (with 64 per cent cocoa); 60 ml/2 fl oz/¼ cup egg yolk; 90 g/3⅛ oz/½ cup sugar; 250 ml/8½ fl oz/1 cup egg white

Chocolate Mousse

125 ml/4¼ fl oz/½ cup milk; 150 ml/5 fl oz/⅝ cup cream; 50 ml/1¾ fl oz/¼ cup egg yolks; 40 g/1⅜ oz sugar; 100 g/3½ oz couverture chocolate (with 70 per cent cocoa)

Chocolate Sorbet

400 ml/13½ fl oz/1⅔ cups water; 40 g/1⅜ oz sugar; 35 g/1¼ oz/½ cup cocoa powder; ¼ tsp stabiliser; 160 g/5⅝ oz couverture chocolate (with 70 per cent cocoa)

Chocolate Caramel

120 g/4¼ oz/⅔ cup sugar; 120 g/4¼ oz/scant ½ cup glucose; water; 3 tbsp cocoa paste

Cocoa Caramel

50 g/1¾ oz/¼ cup sugar; 2½ tsp glucose; 95 ml/3 fl oz/⅜ cup water; 3 tbsp cocoa paste

Others

Apricot coulis

PREPARATION

Preheat the oven at 160°C (320°F). Melt the couverture chocolate in the microwave set on low heat.
Beat the egg yolk with 30 g/1 oz/⅛ cup of sugar, then gently mix in the melted couverture chocolate.
Beat the egg white with the remaining sugar until the mixture forms a soft peak.
Gently incorporate this into the chocolate mixture.
Pour the batter into a flexipan baking mould and bake it in the oven for 6 to 7 minutes so that it remains uncooked in the centre.

Combine the milk and cream in a saucepan and bring to the boil.
Add the egg yolk and sugar and mix well.
Melt the couverture chocolate in the microwave set at low heat.
Add the melted chocolate to the milk and cream mixture, and mix well.
Process the mixture in a blender until smooth. Strain and pour it into a container.
Refrigerate the mixture so that it will set into a mousse.
Keep refrigerated until required.

Combine the water and the sugar in a pot and bring to the boil.
Remove from the heat and add the cocoa powder and stabiliser. Mix well.
Melt the couverture chocolate in the microwave set at low heat. Add the melted chocolate to the water, sugar and cocoa mixture. Mix well and set aside to cool. Process the mixture in an ice cream maker set to sorbet specifications. When ready, keep frozen until required.

Warm the sugar and glucose with a little water in a pan over low heat, without stirring.
When the mixture reaches 163°C (326°F), remove from the heat.
Add the cocoa paste and some water.
Mix well until the cocoa paste is completely dissolved and the mixture has the consistency of thick caramel.

Warm the sugar and glucose with 20 ml/⅝ fl oz of water in a pan over low heat, without stirring.
When the mixture reaches 163°C (326°F), remove from the heat. Add the cocoa paste and remaining water.
Mix well until the cocoa paste is completely dissolved and the mixture has the consistency of thick caramel.

PRESENTATION

Cut the flourless chocolate sponge cake into 4 pieces and place each piece in the centre of a plate.
Top with the chocolate mousse. Spoon some apricot coulis and cocoa caramel on the side.
Top the chocolate mousse with 1 tsp of chocolate sorbet. Create volume with the chocolate caramel.

Mugaritz
Errenteria

RIGHT: Basque culture and produce are prominently featured on Mugaritz's menu.
ABOVE: Mugaritz is one of San Sebastián's rising stars.

Andoni Luis Aduriz

One of Martin Berasategui's star pupils, who listened hard and diligently applied himself to the task, Andoni Luis Aduriz is now a well-respected, award-winning chef in his own right, and an ardent advocate of Basque flavours and produce. 'Here at Mugaritz,' says Aduriz, 'our dishes are all ingredient-driven and although they may look simple on the surface, they are extremely complex underneath.'

His approach to cooking falls somewhere between the strictly classical style of Santi Santamaria and the wildly experimental, and much-copied, style of Ferran Adrià of El Bulli. He joins a pack of young Spanish chefs such as Sergi Arola, Adrià's protégé, who is looking for 'the third way', which will further enhance Spain's stature in the culinary world.

Yet with a repertoire of creations such as a stark white slab of turbot floating on a pale yellow broth gilded with bits of candied pomelo, and bite-size bonbon filled with spiced pear, olive oil and a granita of local Basque cheese, Aduriz may be on to something even newer than the Nueva Cucina Vasca pioneered by his mentor, Berasategui, that decades ago made San Sebastián the Michelin-star capital of Spain.

▶ GRILLED TURBOT WITH WARM CITRIC VINAIGRETTE AND CRYSTALLISED ZEST Serves 4

INGREDIENTS

Syrup
100 g/3½ oz/½ cup sugar;
100 ml/3⅜ fl oz/⅜ cup water

Crystallised Zest
1 lemon; 1 grapefruit;
1 orange; 1 tangerine; 1 lime

Warm Citric Vinaigrette
60 ml/2 fl oz/¼ cup grapefruit juice;
60 ml/2 fl oz/¼ cup lemon juice;
60 ml/2 fl oz/¼ cup tangerine juice;
60 ml/2 fl oz/¼ cup lime juice;
60 ml/2 fl oz/¼ cup passionfruit juice;
2 heads of garlic, peeled;
600 ml/1 pt 4¼ fl oz/2½ cups olive oil;
4 g/⅛ oz gelatine leaves

Grilled Turbot
4 pcs (200 g/7 oz each) turbot fillet;
salt; 3 tsp olive oil

Garnish
Sea salt

PREPARATION

Combine the sugar and water in a casserole and bring to the boil. Mix well.
Set aside to cool until it is approximately 30°C (86°F).

Cut off the top of each fruit and peel the zest with a knife to make a 0.4-cm- (0.16-inch-) thick strip.
Squeeze the juice from the fruit and set aside for the warm citric vinaigrette.
Blanch the zest separately, then strain and set aside to cool. Repeat this step 3 times, using fresh water each time. Combine each type of zest with some syrup and cook separately for 1 minute each.
Remove from the heat and leave the zest in the syrup to cool.
Cut the zest into 0.4-by-0.4-cm (0.2-by-0.2-inch) squares and return to the syrup. Set aside.

Pour all the juices into a casserole and bring to the boil. Set aside.
Mince the garlic and fry it in the olive oil until it turns light brown in colour.
Add the fried garlic to the fruit juices in the casserole, cover and store it in a cool place for 12 hours.
Strain the mixture and discard the solid ingredients.
Soak the gelatine leaves in cold water for a few minutes.
Heat about 2 tsp of the fruit juice mixture and add the gelatine leaves.
Remove from the heat and stir until the gelatine dissolves completely.
Stir this into the remaining fruit juice mixture.

Season the turbot fillets lightly with the salt, then pan-fry them in olive oil, until the skin turns crispy and golden brown in colour.
To serve, preheat the oven at 80°C (176°F) and bake the turbot for 8 to 9 minutes.

PRESENTATION

Divide the crytallised zest among 4 soup plates and top each portion with 4 tsp of warm citric vinaigrette.
Place a turbot fillet in the centre of each plate and sprinkle some sea salt on the turbot's skin to serve.

▼ CHAR-GRILLED FOIE GRAS WITH RICE 'BOMBA' AND SEAWEED STOCK Serves 4

INGREDIENTS

Grilled Foie Gras
2 slices (500 g/1 lb 1⅝ oz each) foie gras,
cleaned and deveined;
50 ml/1¾ fl oz/¼ cup sunflower oil

Rice 'Bomba' and Seaweed Stock
10 ml/⅜ fl oz extra virgin olive oil;
50 g/1¾ oz onions, chopped;
1 litre/2 pts 1⅞ fl oz/4¼ cups chicken stock
(recipe on page 148);
100 g/3½ oz/½ cups rice 'bomba'
(short grain rice from Murcia in Spain;
if unavailable, use other short grain rice);
100 g/3½ oz seaweed; salt

Garnish
Rock salt

PREPARATION

Preheat the oven at 130°C (266°F). Pan-fry the foie gras in the sunflower oil until they are crispy and golden brown in colour on both sides. Place the pan with the cooked foie gras in the oven for 9 minutes.
Remove from the heat and set aside to rest for 9 minutes. Char-grill the foie gras [try to keep them about 20 cm (8 inches) above the flame] for 5 minutes (expect some fat from the foie gras to drip on the charcoal if using an open grill, so sprinkle some salt on the fire to prevent the fire from rising and burning the foie gras).

Warm the olive oil in a casserole and sauté the chopped onions until they are soft and golden brown in colour. Add some chicken stock, then lower the heat and add the rice. Simmer for 5 minutes.
Add the remaining chicken stock and cook for 20 minutes.
During the last 5 minutes of cooking, add the seaweed and bring to the boil.
Remove from the heat and set aside to rest for 10 minutes.
Strain and season the stock to taste with salt.

PRESENTATION

Cut each piece of foie gras into 2, then place each portion in the centre of a warm soup plate.
Keep the plates covered, while you get the rock salt and stock, so as to retain the foie gras' smoky flavour.
Sprinkle a few salt crystals on each piece of foie gras and cover the plate when you are done.
Spoon some rice 'bomba' and seaweed stock around each piece of foie gras to serve.

Die Fischerzunft
Schaffhausen

ABOVE: Die Fischerzunft, housed in a refurbished 14th century building, used to be a meeting place for the fishermen's guild.
LEFT: The restaurant sits on the banks of the Rhine and offers diners a romantic view of gliding swans.

André Jaeger

André Jaeger was born into the restaurant business. When he was 10 years old and at boarding school in the Black Forest, his parents sold their small family restaurant and bought Die Fischerzunft, a well-respected restaurant in the town of Schaffhausen. There was never any doubt in Jaeger's mind that he would spend his life as a chef, and until his mid-twenties he worked hard to hone his skills, first in schools and then in hotel kitchens, and always in the classic techniques.

The turning point came in 1971. Working at The Peninsula in Hong Kong, he was exposed to the Asian way of thinking about food and stimulated by Asia's vast array of exotic tastes, flavours and aromas. This was the time when many people all over the world were becoming increasingly conscious of health and diet, and careful about what they ate. Inspired by the notion of combining the best of West and East to create something both healthy and delicious for the people back home, Jaeger took his 'less fattening butter and heavy cream, more light and fresh vegetable juices, spices and herbs' recipes to Switzerland. Soon he was able to buy Die Fischerzunft from his father.

Today Die Fisherzunft has two Michelin stars to its name, and Jaeger continues to express the balance of Yin and Yang— contrast and complement, light and dark, warm and cool, masculine and feminine. His cuisine combines the foreign and the familiar in a harmonious blend.

MADRAS CURRY MARINATED LAMB CHOPS IN FILO PASTRY WITH LAMB GRAVY, AND GREEN PAPAYA SALAD AND BOUTIQUE GREENS WITH THAI VINAIGRETTE

Serves 4

INGREDIENTS

Madras Curry Marinated Lamb Chops in Filo Pastry
- 200 g/7 oz butter;
- 2 tbsp Madras curry paste;
- 8 (40 g/1 3/8 oz and 2 bones each) lamb chops;
- 2 large sheets filo pastry; salt

Lamb Gravy
- 455 g/1 lb lamb bones, chopped into small pieces;
- 455 g/1 lb oxtail, chopped into small pieces;
- 1 carrot, cut into pieces;
- 1 small stick celery, cut into pieces;
- 3 shallots, peeled; 1 head of garlic, peeled;
- a few sprigs of thyme and rosemary;
- 1 small tomato; 300 ml/10 1/8 fl oz/1 1/4 cups red wine;
- 1 litre/2 pt 1 7/8 fl oz/4 1/4 cups water;
- 1 tsp balsamic vinegar; 50 g/1 3/4 oz butter; salt

Thai Vinaigrette
- 3 tbsp Thai fish sauce; 2 tbsp lemon juice;
- 1 tbsp sesame oil; 6 tbsp extra virgin olive oil;
- 1 tbsp chopped coriander

Green Papaya Salad and Boutique Greens
- 8 young corn; 4 French beans, sliced thinly;
- 1/4 green papaya, cut into thin strips;
- 2 chillies, seeds removed and cut into strips;
- 2 tbsp chopped peanuts; 1 tbsp chopped coriander;
- 4 handfuls of mixed salad greens

Garnish
Carrot strips

PREPARATION

Preheat the oven at 200°C (392°F). Melt the butter over low heat in a saucepan and mix in the curry paste. Marinate the lamb chops in half of this mixture for at least 10 minutes before cooking.
Stick both sheets of filo pastry together by brushing some of the remaining curry paste mixture on 1 side of 1 filo sheet, then placing the other sheet over. Cut this into 4 strips, each about 6 cm (2.3 inches) wide.
Season the marinated lamb chops to taste with salt. Arrange 2 lamb chops in such a way that their bones, when put together, look like deer horns. Wrap a strip of filo pastry around the lamb and bind with some butcher's string. Repeat this process with the remaining lamb chops and filo strips.
Bake the lamb chops for 7 minutes, then remove from the heat and set them aside to rest for 5 minutes.

Preheat the oven at 200°C (392°F).
Roast the lamb bones and oxtail in the oven until they turn golden brown in colour.
Add the carrot, celery, shallots and garlic and roast for 3 minutes.
Transfer the ingredients to a stockpot and add the thyme, rosemary, tomato and red wine and simmer until the red wine is almost dry. Add the water and cook over low heat for 3 hours, skimming away the material that floats to the surface and adding more water if necessary.
Strain the liquid and pour it into a small saucepan and reduce it to about 400 ml/13 1/2 fl oz/1 2/3 cups.
Add the balsamic vinegar and stir in the butter. Season to taste with salt.
The gravy should have a thick consistency.

Combine the Thai fish sauce, lemon juice, sesame and olive oils, and chopped coriander in a big bowl and mix well.

Cut each young corn into 4, lengthwise.
Combine the young corn, sliced French beans, green papaya strips, chilli strips, and chopped peanuts and coriander. Mix well. Add half the Thai vinaigrette and toss well.
Add the remaining vinaigrette to the boutique greens. Toss well.

PRESENTATION

Untie the lamb chops. Arrange some green papaya salad on 4 plates, then place a serving of lamb chops on top of each salad. Tuck some boutique greens between the lamb chop bones and garnish with carrot strips. Spoon some lamb gravy around to serve.

▲ CINNAMON PIGEON, LIQUORICE FOIE GRAS AND PEAR CRISPS WITH PEAR AND BLACK BEAN CHUTNEY Serves 4

INGREDIENTS

Cinnamon Pigeon
300 ml/10⅛ fl oz/1¼ cups mushroom soya sauce;
2 tsp cinnamon powder;
2 pigeons; oil

Pear Crisps and Pear and Black Bean Chutney
2 pears, peeled and halved;
1 onion, peeled and sliced; 1 tbsp butter;
½ tsp black bean paste;
zest from ¼ orange, cut into thin strips

Liquorice Foie Gras
4 slices (30 g/1 oz each) foie gras;
1 tbsp liquorice powder; salt

Garnish
1 sprig rosemary

PREPARATION

Mix the mushroom soya sauce with cinnamon powder and marinate the pigeons in this mixture for 48 hours. Keep refrigerated during this time.
About 30 minutes before serving, preheat the oven at 200°C (392°F).
Remove the pigeons from the marinade and arrange them on a baking tray.
Brush them with oil and bake for 7 minutes. Remove from the heat and set them aside to rest for 10 minutes before separating the breast meat from the bones. Slice the meat evenly.

Preheat the oven at 80°C (176°F). Using a slicer, cut the pears lengthwise into paper-thin slices.
Remove the seeds and reserve the best 8 slices for garnishing. Cut the remaining slices into long, thin strips and sauté them with the sliced onion in melted butter over low heat for 10 minutes until they are soft (add a little water to quicken the process if necessary). Add the black bean paste and half the orange zest strips, and cook for another 2 to 3 minutes. Remove from the heat and set aside.
Arrange the 8 slices of pear on a baking tray lined with baking paper and bake them in the oven for 3 to 4 hours until they are dry and crispy (these should be prepared ahead).
Store the pear crisps in an airtight container until required.

Preheat the oven at 200°C (392°F).
Arrange the foie gras slices on a baking tray and bake them for 4 minutes.
Dust the foie gras to taste with liquorice powder and salt.

PRESENTATION

Spoon some pear and black bean chutney on 4 plates and top with the foie gras slices. Arrange some pigeon slices around. Garnish with the pear crisps, rosemary leaves and leftover orange zest to serve.

RIGHT: The bar at Charlie Trotter's; the restaurant's magnificent wine list has been the recipient of *Wine Spectator*'s Grand Award for many years.
BELOW: The North Dining Room is designed for diners seeking privacy.

Charlie Trotter's
Chicago

Charlie Trotter

After 15 years in the pursuit of excellence, Charlie Trotter states that he has only just begun to scratch the surface. Yet, his restaurant continues to astound and impress with its inspired culinary creations receiving numerous awards and accolades. Organic produce and pristine ingredients supplied by a network of over 90 purveyors provide the basis of Trotter's ever-changing cuisine. The delicate flavours, impeccable techniques and artistic yet spontaneous presentations provide feasts for the palate, the eyes and the soul. There are no firm guidelines or rules for the food or the chef. Beauty is the defining philosophy.

Trotter, a native of Chicago, brings the force of his unique background to the US culinary scene. A political science and philosophy graduate from the University of Wisconsin, Madison, Trotter began cooking professionally in 1982. Since then, he does not appear to have looked back. His ventures have expanded to include a Culinary Foundation for students in need, other humanitarian efforts, and Trotter's To Go, a prepared-food market, as well as a restaurant opening in London in 2003. We wait with bated breath to see what this dynamic chef will do next.

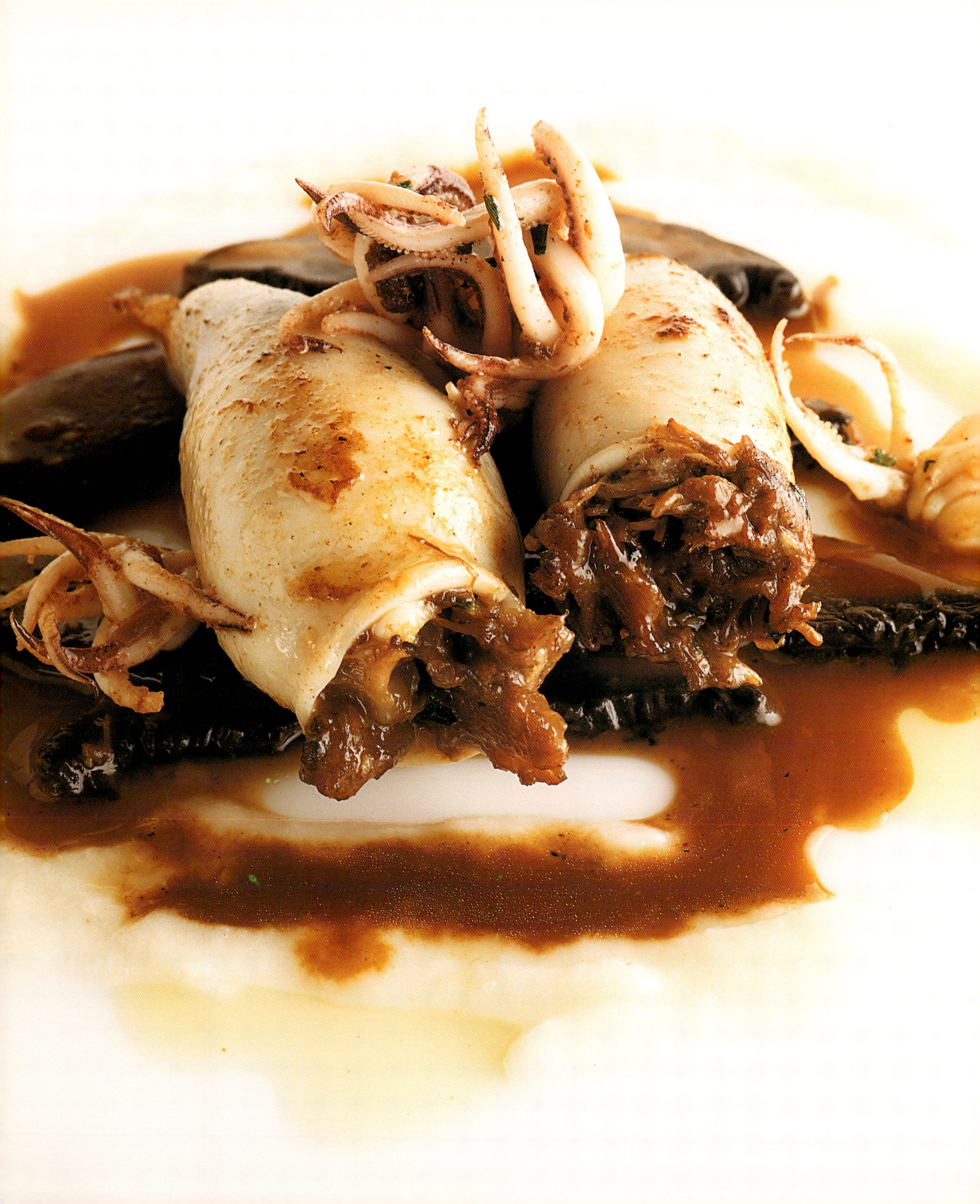

◀ OXTAIL-STUFFED BABY SQUID, ROASTED CREMINI MUSHROOMS AND SALSIFY PURÉE WITH OXTAIL BRAISING JUICES AND MUSTARD OIL   Serves 4

INGREDIENTS

Oxtail Braising Juices
- 2 tbsp grapeseed oil; 8 oxtails;
- 50 g/1¾ oz/½ cup chopped carrots;
- 50 g/1¾ oz/½ cup chopped celery;
- 100 g/3½ oz/1 cup chopped Spanish onion;
- 3 tbsp tomato paste;
- 500 ml/1 pt 1 fl oz/2⅛ cups red wine

Oxtail-stuffed Baby Squid
- 2 tbsp chopped fresh coriander;
- 1 tbsp minced jalapeno;
- 1 tsp freshly squeezed lime juice; salt; pepper;
- 8 baby squids; 1 tbsp butter

Salsify Purée
- 2 stalks salsify;
- 500 ml/1 pt 1 fl oz/2⅛ cups milk; salt; pepper

Roasted Cremini Mushrooms
- 400 g/14⅛ oz/3 cups cremini mushrooms;
- 35 g/1¼ oz/⅓ cup chopped Spanish onion;
- 1 clove garlic; 1 sprig thyme or rosemary;
- 2 tbsp olive oil;
- 180 ml/6 fl oz/¾ cup mushroom stock (recipe on page 148) or water; salt; pepper

Garnish
- Mustard oil (recipe on page 149)

PREPARATION

Heat the grapeseed oil in a large saucepan and sear the oxtails.
Remove the oxtails from the pan, add the chopped carrots, celery and onion, and cook until they caramelise.
Add the tomato paste and cook for 5 minutes. Deglaze with red wine and return the oxtails to the pan.
Add enough water to cover the oxtails and bring to a slow simmer. Cover and allow it to simmer for 2 to 3 hours or until the meat falls off the bone easily (you may need to add more water during the braising process). Remove the oxtails from the saucepan and strain the braising liquid through a fine-mesh sieve.
Simmer the liquid over medium heat for 30 minutes until it reaches a rich, sauce-like consistency.

Remove the oxtail meat from the bone, pull into small pieces and place in a small saucepan. Add the coriander, jalapeno and lime juice and warm over medium heat for 2 to 3 minutes. Season to taste with salt and pepper. Clean the baby squids and separate their tentacles. Season the squids and tentacles with salt and pepper. Stuff the squids with the oxtail mixture. In a medium pan, sauté the squids with butter for 2 to 3 minutes, turning occasionally to ensure both sides are cooked evenly. Add the tentacles and sauté for 1 minute.

Peel the salsify, cut into 5-cm (2-inch) pieces and place in a medium saucepan with the milk immediately. Simmer for 30 minutes until the salsify is tender. Remove the salsify from the liquid and process in a blender with some braising juices to obtain a smooth purée. Season to taste with salt and pepper.

Preheat the oven at 160°C (320°F).
Slice the cremini mushrooms into 0.6-cm (0.25-inch) pieces and place them in an oven-proof pan.
Toss them with the onion, garlic, thyme or rosemary, and olive oil.
Add the mushroom stock or water and season to taste with salt and pepper.
Cover and cook in the oven for 30 to 40 minutes, until the mushrooms are tender.
Remove from the heat and set the mushrooms aside to cool in their cooking juices.

PRESENTATION
Place a few slices of roasted cremini mushrooms in the centre of each plate.
Top the mushrooms with 2 stuffed squids and a few tentacles. Spoon the salsify purée followed by some hot braising juices around the plate. Drizzle a few drops of mustard oil around to serve.

▼ BRAISED VEAL TONGUE WITH SWEET CORN EMULSION   Serves 4

INGREDIENTS

Sweet Corn Emulsion
- 8 ears sweet corn, husks removed;
- 1 Spanish onion, peeled and chopped;
- 1.9 litres/4 pts/8 cups water;
- 1 tsp lemon juice;
- salt; freshly ground black pepper;
- 80 g/2⅞ oz butter

Vegetables
- 130 g/4⅓ oz/1 cup sweet corn kernels;
- 2 tsp butter; salt; freshly ground black pepper;
- 1 tsp minced shallot;
- 500 g/1 lb 1⅝ oz young spinach, cleaned;
- 2 tsp sherry wine vinegar

Crayfish
- 20 crayfish, cleaned, shells removed and deveined;
- 1 tsp butter; 1 tsp minced shallot; 1 tsp lemon juice;
- 2 tsp shellfish oil (recipe on page 149);
- salt; freshly ground black pepper

Braised Veal Tongue
- 1 braised veal tongue (recipe on page 149);
- salt; freshly ground black pepper

Garnish
- 16 asparagus tips, blanched and quartered;
- shellfish oil (recipe on page 149);
- 2 tsp small sage leaves, cut into a fine chiffonade;
- freshly ground black pepper

PREPARATION

Remove the kernels from the corn and place the kernels, cobs and onion in a large saucepan.
Cover the corn cobs with water and simmer over low heat for 1 hour.
Strain liquid through a fine-mesh sieve and return it to the saucepan.
Simmer over medium heat for 40 minutes until about 500 ml/1 pt 1 fl oz/2⅛ cups remain.
Add the lemon juice and season to taste with salt and freshly ground black pepper.
Just before using, whisk in the butter and process the mixture with a hand-held blender to create froth.

Sauté the corn kernels with 1 tsp of butter over medium heat for 4 minutes until the corn kernels are tender.
Season to taste with salt and freshly ground black pepper.
Sweat the minced shallot in 1 tsp of butter over medium heat for 1 minute.
Add the young spinach and sherry wine vinegar, and cook for 2 to 3 minutes until the spinach is barely wilted. Season to taste with salt and freshly ground black pepper.

Sauté the crayfish in the butter and minced shallot.
Cook over medium heat for 3 minutes until the crayfish is barely cooked.
Add the lemon juice and shellfish oil. Toss well.
Season to taste with salt and freshly ground black pepper.

Slice the braised veal tongue into 12 portions, each about 1 cm (0.5 inch) thick.
Season to taste with salt and freshly ground black pepper.

PRESENTATION
Place some wilted spinach in the centre of each plate and arrange 3 slices of veal tongue over the spinach.
Arrange some of the crayfish, corn kernels and asparagus tips around, then spoon some sweet corn emulsion froth over.
Drizzle a little shellfish oil around the plate.
Garnish with sage leaves and freshly ground black pepper to serve.

LEFT: Gourmets visiting Australia are putting The Grange on their must-do list along with the Great Barrier Reef and Ayer's Rock.
BELOW: The Grange at the Hilton in Adelaide is named after the acclaimed Penfolds Grange Hermitage wine.

The Grange
Adelaide

Cheong Liew

The Grange, the fine-dining room at the Hilton Hotel in Adelaide, Australia, has been the domain of Cheong Liew since 1995. Born in Malaysia, Cheong was raised by a family of 'food people', who owned poultry, fish and vegetable farms as well as a restaurant in the city. Though he did dabble in some kitchen work back home, he had to pick up professional cooking in order to make ends meet when he first moved to Adelaide 30 years ago.

Mixing French techniques and Asian flair with Australian ingredients, in the seventies he was one of the first to define his style as 'East meets West'. Now he has moved on, and prefers the terms 'World' or 'Friendship' cuisine. He doesn't believe in following recipes word-for-word. Instead, he prefers to pick out the best bits and adapt them to create new dishes. 'My cuisine is about understanding and appreciating cuisines of different countries, then cooking with my heart,' Cheong explains. A typical dish proves the point: roasted red snapper, leek fondue, snow pea vine shoots with green chilli, coriander and calamari shavings. And his desserts, such as Russian praline tourte with pear purée or white chocolate mousse with mandarin liqueur and red bean pâté, are equally multicultural.

The American magazine *Food & Wine* named Cheong one of the '10 hottest chefs alive', alongside Ferran Adrià, Susur Lee, Marc Veyrat and Gordon Ramsay. Patricia Wells, Food Editor of *International Herald Tribune*, proclaimed Liew's prowess in the kitchen, attributing to him an uncanny talent for combining balance, strength, harmony and nutritional value. He was inducted into the Hall of Fame during the American Express Awards with good friend and fellow chef Tetsuya Wakuda from Sydney, The Grange has received their prestigious 'Best Restaurant in the Five-star Category' award on numerous occasions.

FOUR DANCES OF THE SEA Serves 6

INGREDIENTS

Soused Snook

2 (300 g/$10\frac{1}{2}$ oz each) sashimi-grade snook fillets; 1 tbsp sea salt; 1 tbsp sugar; 50 ml/$1\frac{3}{4}$ fl oz/$\frac{1}{4}$ cup mirin; 100 ml/$3\frac{3}{8}$ fl oz/$\frac{3}{8}$ cup rice vinegar (or cherry vinegar); 50 ml/$1\frac{3}{4}$ fl oz/$\frac{1}{4}$ cup rice wine; 6 slices avocado

Wasabi Mayonnaise

1 egg yolk; 1 tsp wasabi powder; 1 tbsp rice vinegar; 100 ml/$3\frac{3}{8}$ fl oz/$\frac{3}{8}$ cup warm peanut oil; 50 ml/$1\frac{3}{4}$ fl oz/$\frac{1}{4}$ cup syrup

Octopus with Aioli

2 kg/4 lb $6\frac{1}{2}$ oz octopus tentacles; 200 ml/$6\frac{3}{4}$ fl oz/$\frac{7}{8}$ cup olive oil; 40 g/$1\frac{3}{8}$ oz/scant $\frac{3}{8}$ cups black olives, crushed; 4 cloves garlic, crushed; $\frac{1}{4}$ bay leaf; $\frac{1}{2}$ red chilli; juice from $\frac{1}{2}$ lemon

Aioli

6 cloves garlic; 1 big red chilli; 4 coriander roots; 1 egg yolk; 100 ml/$3\frac{3}{8}$ fl oz/$\frac{3}{8}$ cup olive oil; $\frac{1}{2}$ tsp sea salt; juice from $\frac{1}{2}$ lemon

Raw Cuttlefish with Squid Ink Noodles

180 g/$6\frac{3}{8}$ oz sashimi-grade cuttlefish; 300 g/$10\frac{1}{2}$ oz squid-ink taglarinni pasta, cooked and chilled

Asian-style Dressing

$\frac{1}{2}$ tsp sesame oil; $\frac{1}{2}$ tbsp oyster sauce; 1 tbsp balsamic vinegar; 2 tbsp sunflower seed oil; 1 tbsp light soya sauce; 1 tbsp mirin; freshly ground black pepper

Rempah Mixture

20 g/$\frac{3}{4}$ oz fresh galangal; 10 g/$\frac{3}{8}$ oz fresh turmeric; 15 g/$\frac{1}{2}$ oz ginger; 6 candlenuts; 1 red chilli; 6 to 10 shallots, chopped finely; 3 cloves, chopped finely; 15 g/$\frac{1}{2}$ oz belachan

Spiced Prawn

6 large king prawns, shells removed; a pinch of salt; a pinch of sugar; a pinch of finely grated lime zest; 40 ml/$1\frac{3}{8}$ fl oz/$\frac{1}{8}$ cup coconut cream; 60 ml/2 fl oz/$\frac{1}{4}$ cup peanut oil; 50 ml/$1\frac{3}{4}$ fl oz/scant $\frac{1}{4}$ cup tamarind juice; 40 g/$1\frac{3}{8}$ oz light palm sugar

Banana Leaf Glutinous Rice Sushi

200 g/7 oz/scant $1\frac{1}{8}$ cups glutinous rice, soaked in water for 1 hour; 4 tsp peanut oil; 1 tsp sea salt; 80 ml/$2\frac{3}{4}$ fl oz/$\frac{1}{3}$ cup coconut cream; 1 large fresh banana leaf

Garnish

6 sprigs chervil; 6 sprigs parsley

PREPARATION

Remove the snook's outer skin membranes, lay the fillets skin-side down and sprinkle the sea salt and sugar over evenly. Marinate the fillets for 2 hours, then mix the cured snook fillets with mirin, rice vinegar and rice wine, and marinate for another 1 hour or longer.
Slice the fillet diagonally, at a 45-degree angle, into 18 slices, preparing 3 slices per person.
Cut each slice of avocado into 2 and set aside.

Whisk the egg yolk with the wasabi powder and rice vinegar to mix well.
Add the warm peanut oil and whisk until the mixture thickens.
Add the syrup and mix well. Keep refrigerated until required.

Peel off the octopus' skin, leaving the suckers intact. Pat the tentacles dry with kitchen tissue.
Bring the olive oil to the boil, then add the crushed olives and garlic, bay leaf, red chilli and lemon juice, and fry until the olives are cooked. Carefully gather the small ends of the tentacles and gently lower the tentacles into the pot. Seal them on all sides very quickly and remove from the heat immediately.

Pound the garlic, chilli and coriander roots into a fine and smooth paste using the mortar and pestle.
Combine the paste with the egg yolk in a bowl and whisk with a fork.
Slowly add the olive oil and whisk until the mixture reaches the consistency of mayonnaise.
Season with sea salt and lemon juice.

Clean the cuttlefish thoroughly, wiping off any ink marks with a damp cloth.
Chill it for 30 minutes, then slice it at a very low angle. Shave the white 'insides' of the cuttlefish very thinly and gather enough slices to form a white rose.
Keep the cuttlefish roses and squid-ink taglarinni pasta covered and refrigerated until required.

Combine all the ingredients in a bowl and mix well.
Keep refrigerated until required.

Grate the fresh galangal, turmeric, ginger and candlenuts. Pound the chilli to a paste.
Process all the ingredients in a blender to obtain a smooth paste.

Cut the prawns into half, lengthwise and remove the veins. Sprinkle the salt, sugar and lime zest over and mix well. Sauté the rempah mixture and coconut cream in the peanut oil and stir-fry the mixture over lower than medium heat, stirring very slowly constantly until half the oil starts to separate from the solids.
Add the prawns, tamarind juice and light palm sugar and stir-fry until the prawns are cooked.

Mix the soaked glutinous rice with the peanut oil and sea salt, and steam for 15 to 20 minutes.
When the rice is cooked, mix in the coconut cream. Roast the banana leaf with a hot iron or a frying pan.
Trim off the hard stems and edges. Spoon the cooked rice on the banana leaf and roll it into a sushi 'log', approximately 3 to 4 cm (1.2 to 1.6 inches) in diameter.
Wrap the 'log' in aluminium foil and char-grill the sushi for about 3 to 4 minutes on each side until the edges of the sushi rice are slightly brown and emit a smoky aroma when unwrapped.

PRESENTATION

Prepare 6 plates. On each plate, place 3 slices of the soused snook on 2 pieces of avocado and spoon some wasabi mayonnaise on the side. Garnish with a sprig of chervil.
Toss the chilled squid ink pasta in 6 tbsp of Asian-style dressing, then divide the pasta into 6 small portions.
Place a portion of pasta next to each portion of snook and arrange a cuttlefish rose on top.
Slice the octopus, using the suckers as intervals.
Divide the slices among 6 plates and arrange the slices next to the cuttlefish and pasta on each plate.
Spoon a little aioli on top of each serving. Garnish each portion with a sprig of parsley.
Cut the glutinous rice sushi into 6 pieces, each about 4 cm (1.6 inches) long.
Place a spiced prawn on each sushi. Spoon some of the prawns' spice mixture on top of the sushi.
Place the sushi next to the octopus to serve.

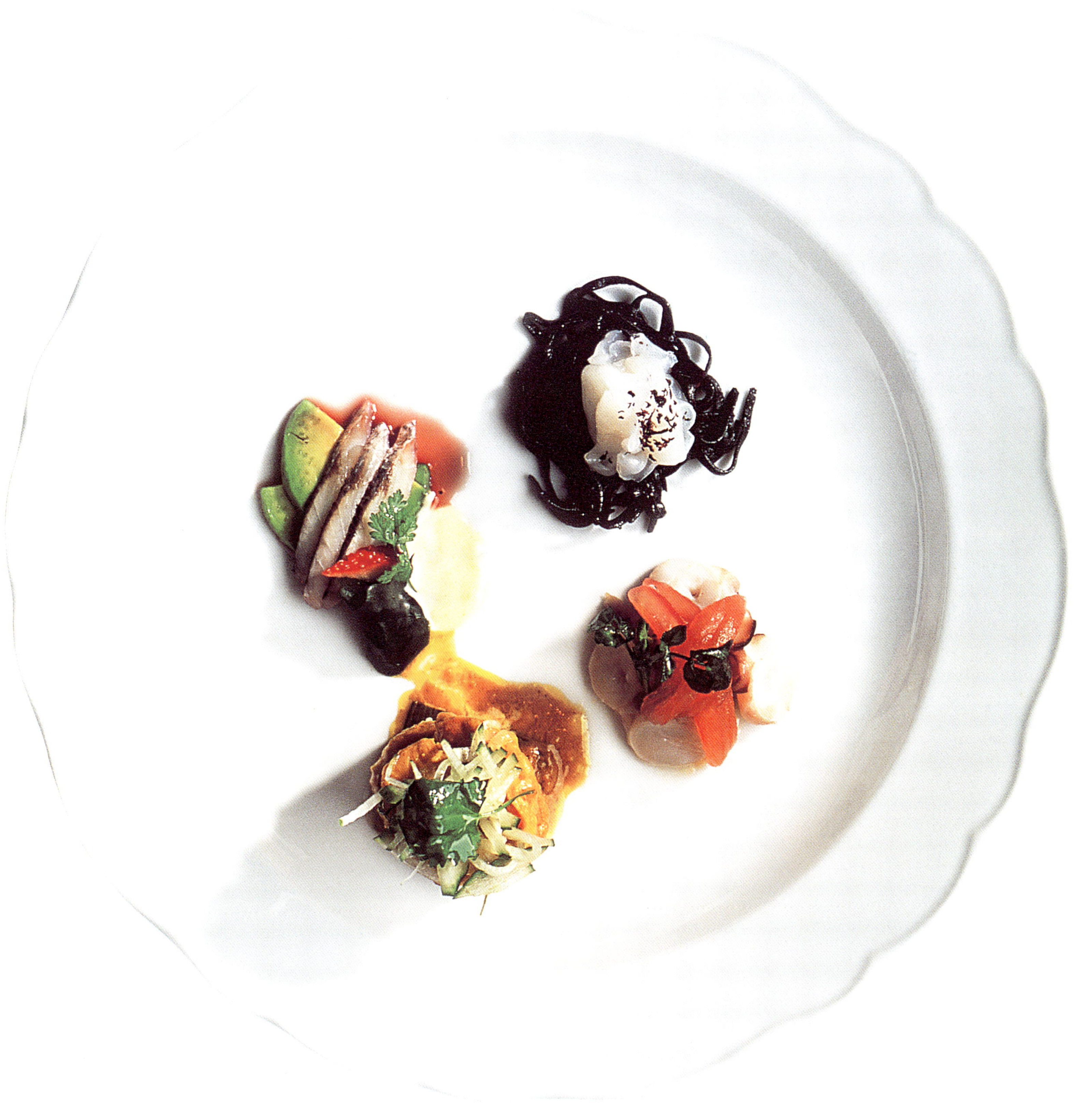

Claude Troisgros
Rio de Janeiro

BELOW: Claude Troisgros' eponymous restaurant in Rio de Janeiro has captured the culinary world's admiration.
RIGHT: Claude Troisgros is a disciple of Paul Bocuse. When Troisgros was only seven years old, Bocuse had him sign a contract promising to apprentice in his kitchen.

Claude Troisgros

Claude Troisgros was turning out the perfect beurre blanc before he knew how to spell the words. Grandson of Jean-Baptiste, son of Pierre, nephew of Jean and brother of Anne-Marie and Michel Troisgros, he has a family name that is part blessing and part curse for a chef born in France. While he didn't have to fret over which career path to choose, his performance in the kitchen was bound, so long as he was in Europe, to be under the constant scrutiny of gastronomes, Michelin inspectors and the media. But that's not the reason why Troisgros opened a restaurant and two French bistros in Brazil.

After serving an apprenticeship with Paul Bocuse, he worked in Paris at Taillevent, and then travelled to London and the Connaught, to Munich and Tantris, before accepting a job offer from Gaston Lenôtre at Le Pré Catelan restaurant in Rio de Janeiro. He fell in love not only with the country but also with Marlene Pereira da Silva, who became his wife, and he stayed on in Brazil. He now juggles his businesses in Rio with consultancy contracts in New York and Miami.

Troisgros' cooking philosophy comprises 'something acidic, something crispy and something green in every dish'—the first ingredient to whet the appetite, the second to alert the ears to the experience and the third to please the eye and refresh the palate. His creations, such as the Big Ravioli, encasing a smooth mousseline of taro and served with a cream sauce scented with white truffle oil, boldly fuses French cooking techniques with Brazil's ingredients. Like the other culinary legends in his family, Troisgros swears by the spirit of improvisation and is responsible for the evolution of 'Tropical French Cuisine'.

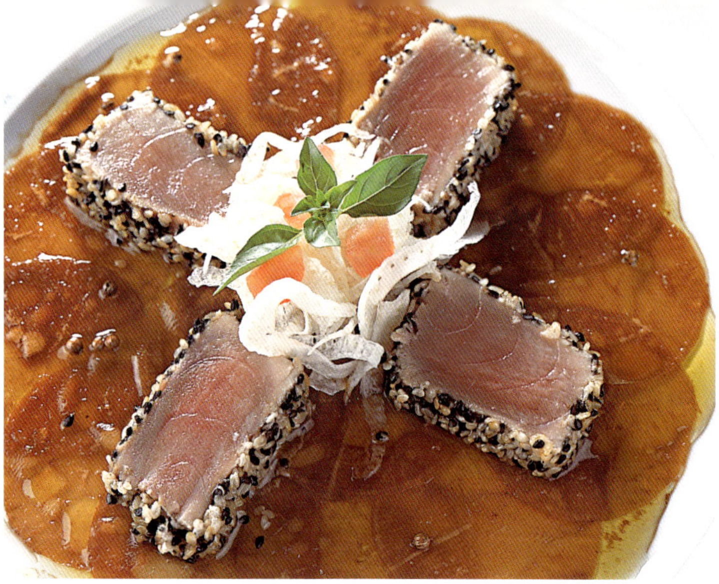

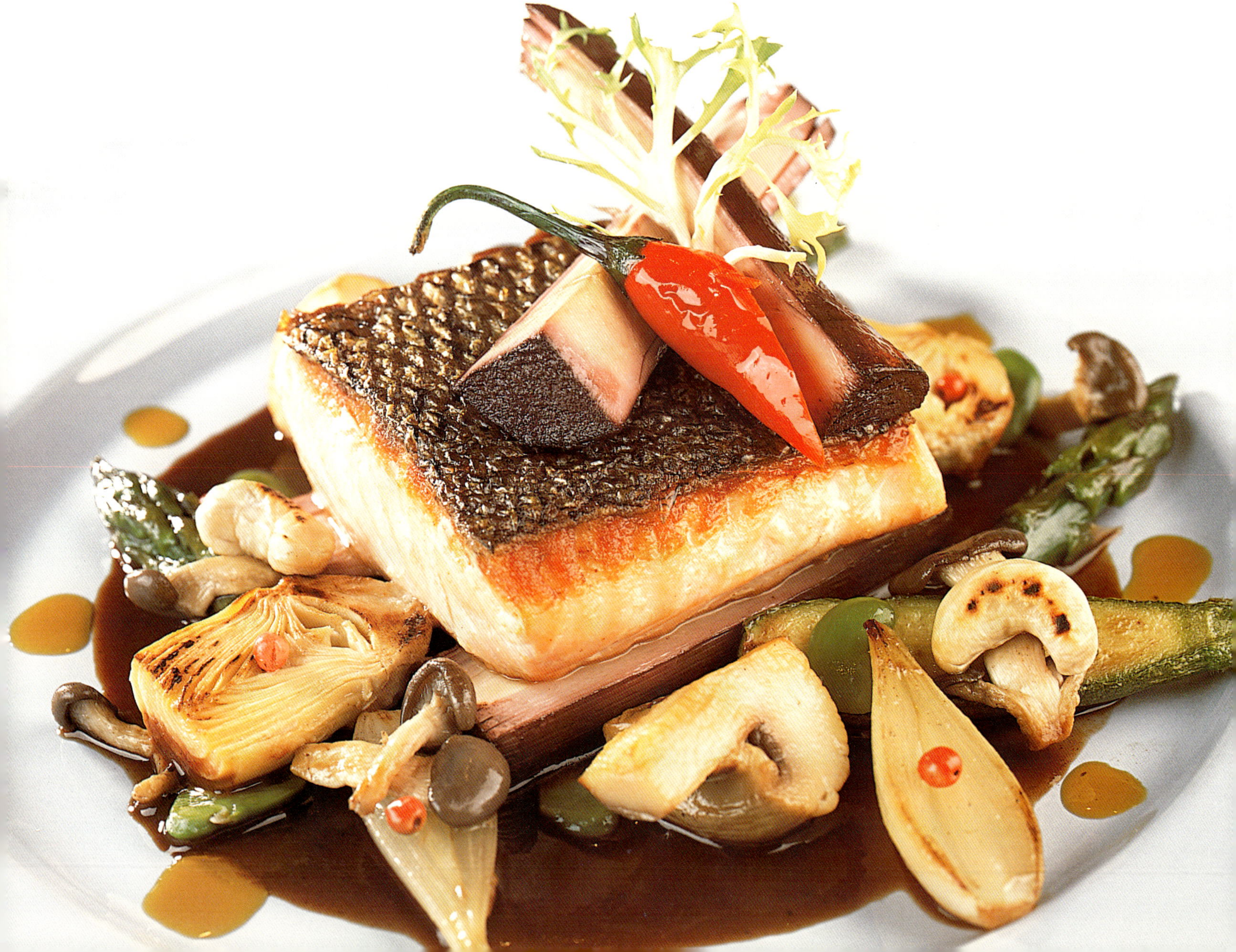

◀ BLACK AND BLUE TUNA WITH MARINATED DAIKON AND SESAME OIL VINAIGRETTE Serves 4

INGREDIENTS

Marinated Daikon
170 g/6 oz daikon, peeled and sliced thinly;
2 tbsp grated ginger; 4 cloves garlic, peeled;
juice from 4 limes; 4 tbsp soya sauce;
130 ml/4⅓ fl oz/½ cup sesame oil; salt

Sesame Oil Vinaigrette
4 cloves garlic; 1 tsp black peppercorns;
1 tsp coriander seeds; 4 tbsp soya sauce;
2 tbsp grated ginger; juice from 4 limes;
salt; 60 ml/2 fl oz/¼ cup sesame oil

Black and Blue Tuna
60 g/2⅛ oz/1⅛ cups white sesame seeds;
60 g/2⅛ oz/1⅛ cups black sesame seeds;
455 g/1 lb tuna fillet;
salt; pepper; 2 tbsp olive oil

Garnish
1 fennel bulb, cut into thin strips;
2 tomatoes, diced; 4 sprigs basil;
60 ml/2 fl oz/¼ cup sesame oil

PREPARATION
Combine all the ingredients in a mixing bowl and toss well.
Allow the mixture to marinate for at least 24 hours before serving.
Keep refrigerated until required.

Process all the ingredients, except the sesame oil, in a blender to obtain a smooth purée.
Add a quarter of the sesame oil and allow the mixture to marinate for at least 24 hours before serving.
Keep refrigerated until required.

Mix the white and black sesame seeds. Cut the tuna fillet into 3.8-by-2.5-by-1.3-cm (1.5-by-1-by-0.5-inch) pieces. Season to taste with salt and pepper, then coat the sides of the tuna with the sesame seed mixture.
Warm the olive oil in a pan and sear all the coated sides of the tuna, leaving the middle uncooked.
Transfer the tuna onto a plate lined with kitchen tissue to absorb the excess oil.
Set aside to cool, then refrigerate for at least 1 hour before serving.

PRESENTATION
Divide the marinated daikon slices among 4 plates and overlap the slices to form a circle as shown.
Spoon the sesame oil vinaigrette over and place the tuna slices on the daikon circles.
Garnish each portion with some fennel strips, tomato cubes, a sprig of basil and some sesame oil to serve.

◀ PAN-FRIED SALMON, SAUTÉED VEGETABLES AND HEARTS OF PALM WITH SWEET AND SOUR RED WINE SAUCE Serves 4

INGREDIENTS

Red Wine Stock
600 ml/1 pt 4¼ fl oz/2½ cups red wine (syrah preferred);
50 ml/1¾ fl oz/¼ cup balsamic vinegar;
1 cinnamon stick; 1 star anise; 1 tbsp sugar;
1 tbsp crushed white peppercorns

Hearts of Palm
8 [each 4 to 5 cm (1.6 to 2 inches) long] fresh hearts of palm

Sweet and Sour Red Wine Sauce
200 g/7 oz butter;
100 ml/3¾ fl oz/⅜ cup heavy cream; salt; pepper

Sautéed Vegetables
4 young zucchinis; 4 young onions, cooked;
4 artichokes, cooked;
150 g/5¼ oz/1¼ cups fava beans;
200 g/7 oz/6⅔ cups white button mushrooms;
12 green asparagus spears, cooked;
150 g/5¼ oz/1½ cups honshimeiji mushrooms;
12 roasted cashew nuts; butter; salt; pepper

Crispy Salmon
4 (180 g/6⅜ oz each) salmon fillets;
salt; pepper

Garnish
4 red chillies; 12 red peppercorns;
curly endive leaves

PREPARATION
Combine the red wine, balsamic vinegar, cinnamon stick, star anise, sugar and crushed white peppercorns in a stockpot and bring to the boil for 10 minutes. Strain and set aside.

Cook the hearts of palm in the red wine stock for 15 minutes or until the hearts of palm are al dente.
Remove from the stock and set aside.

Reduce the red wine stock to a glaze and strain.
Add the butter and heavy cream to the clear stock and mix well. Season to taste with salt and pepper.

Sauté all the ingredients in some butter until they are cooked.
Season to taste with salt and pepper.

Season the salmon fillets to taste with salt and pepper. Pan-fry the salmon fillets, skin-side facing downwards. When the skin turns crispy and golden brown in colour, turn the salmon over and finish cooking, taking care not to overcook the fish.

PRESENTATION
Spoon the sweet and sour red wine sauce on 4 plates, arrange the sautéed vegetables on the sauce and place a crispy salmon fillet on each portion of vegetables. Top each salmon fillet with the hearts of palm, 1 red chilli and some curly endive leaves, then sprinkle the red peppercorns around to serve.

LEFT: The owners of Senso aim to create dining experiences that will appeal to the five senses and, possibly, the sixth.
LEFT BELOW: Besides an elaborate wine list, Senso also stocks the widest range of grappa in Singapore.
BELOW: Senso's central courtyard is dressed up with candlelit tables, antique sculptures and lush foliage for al fresco dining in the evenings.

Senso
Singapore

Diego Chiarini

Chef and part-owner of Italian restaurant Senso in Singapore, the youthful and charismatic Diego Chiarini is bent on delivering the most exciting Italian dining experience outside his homeland: from cuisine to accompanying music to even the sculptures and artwork that grace his restaurant. This passion has translated into a global Senso franchise, with sister restaurants so far in Geneva, Shanghai and New Delhi.

Since leaving his family's farm in north Italy over a decade ago, Diego has worked in distinguished Italian kitchens in the world's most fashionable cities, including the Royal Monceau Hotel in Paris, the Four Seasons Hotel in Milan, Hotel de Paris in Monaco, and Bice restaurant in Tokyo's Four Seasons Hotel. Besides lecturing at the Bice Cooking School in Tokyo, Chiarini has also taught at the Le Cordon Bleu in Paris.

What little free time he gets is spent studying the history, geography and traditional culture of Italian cuisine. He analyses recipes from his collection of antique cookbooks and revives them for Senso's menu, infusing them with his own experience. Among his current favourites is Manzo, a beef fillet served with cinnamon and honey that was first eaten in 1529 by the aristocracy of northern Italy. In turn, distinguished guests, touched by his talent for blending nutritiousness with historicity, have bestowed upon him a string of 'Best of' awards in France, Japan, and, most recently, Singapore.

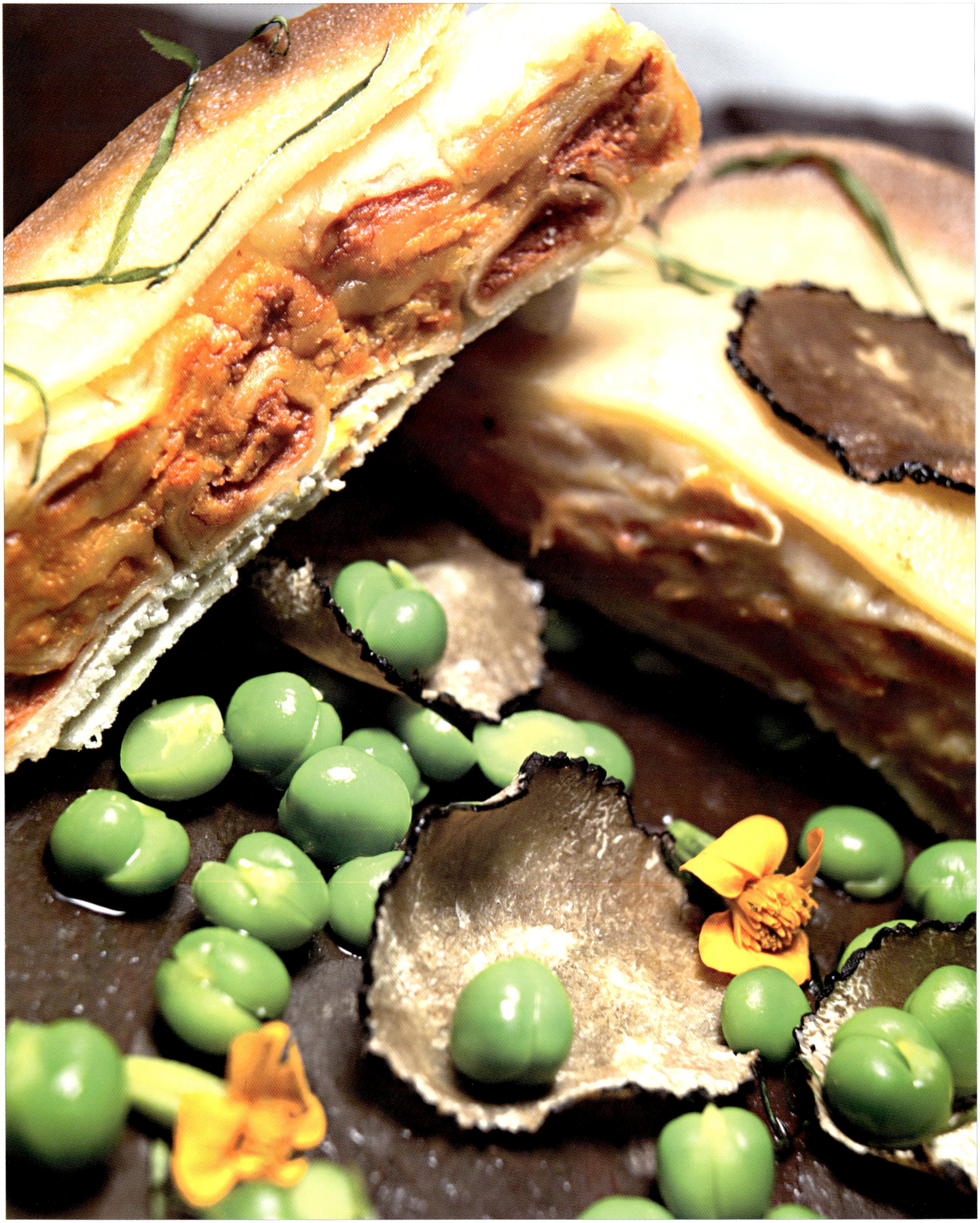

◂ OVEN-BAKED VEGETARIAN RAVIOLI-STUFFED BREAD, GREEN PEA AND BLACK SUMMER SCORZONE TRUFFLE SAUCE Serves 4

INGREDIENTS

Vegetable Filling

20 g/$\frac{3}{4}$ oz carrots; 20 g/$\frac{3}{4}$ oz leek; 20 g/$\frac{3}{4}$ oz potatoes; 20 g/$\frac{3}{4}$ oz pumpkin; 20 g/$\frac{3}{4}$ oz eggplant; 20 g /$\frac{3}{4}$ oz spinach; 10 g/$\frac{3}{8}$ oz garlic; 20 g/$\frac{3}{4}$ oz cauliflower; 40 ml/1$\frac{3}{8}$ fl oz/$\frac{1}{8}$ cup extra virgin olive oil; 1 egg

PREPARATION

Dice all the vegetables. Transfer the cut vegetables into a pot, add the olive oil and toss well. Cover the pot with a lid and braise the mixture over very low heat until the vegetables are well cooked and very soft. Mash the mixture with a fork, then add the egg. Mix well.

Cheese Filling

100 g/3$\frac{1}{2}$ oz/$\frac{1}{2}$ cup ricotta cheese; 20 g/$\frac{3}{4}$ oz Parmesan cheese; 10 g/$\frac{3}{8}$ oz fresh thyme; 1 egg yolk

Combine the ricotta and Parmesan cheese with the thyme leaves and egg yolk in a mixing bowl. Mix well.

Oven-baked Vegetarian Ravioli-stuffed Bread

110 g/3$\frac{7}{8}$ oz/$\frac{7}{8}$ cup white flour '0'; 110 g/3$\frac{7}{8}$ oz/$\frac{7}{8}$ cup white flour '00'; 1 egg; 40 ml/1$\frac{3}{8}$ fl oz/$\frac{1}{8}$ cup warm water; 400 g/14$\frac{1}{8}$ oz fresh plain bread squares; salt; pepper

Preheat the oven at 180°C (356°F). Mix both types of flour, egg and warm water and work the mixture with your fingers until it becomes a soft dough. Leave it in the fridge for 2 hours to rest. On a floured surface, roll the dough out very thinly and cut out 3-by-3-cm (1.2-by-1.2-inch) squares for the ravioli skin. Prepare raviolis with both fillings and seal the sides with water. You should be able to make about 32 raviolis altogether. Poach the raviolis in boiling, salted water for 4 minutes or until they are al dente. Roll the bread squares out thinly and cut each into a circle with a 12-cm-(4.8-inch-) diameter ring mould. Prepare 8 circles. Top a bread circle (with ring mould still around the bread) with 4 of each type of ravioli, then cover them with another bread circle. Repeat this procedure with the remaining ingredients to make 3 more servings. Transfer the ravioli timbales (with ring moulds still intact) onto a baking tray and bake for 8 minutes until the bread turns crispy and golden brown in colour.

Green Pea and Black Summer Scorzone Truffle Sauce

300 g/10$\frac{1}{2}$ oz/2$\frac{1}{4}$ cups green peas; 50 g/1$\frac{3}{4}$ oz black summer Scorzone truffles; 2 tsp chopped garlic; 50 ml/1$\frac{3}{4}$ fl oz/$\frac{1}{4}$ cup extra virgin olive oil; 30 ml/1 fl oz/$\frac{1}{8}$ cup dry white wine

Poach the green peas for few seconds, then peel them. Slice the truffles thinly.
Sauté the chopped garlic with the olive oil, add the sliced truffles, white wine and reduce the heat. Simmer for a few minutes until the bubbling nearly stops, then add the peeled green peas and toss gently.

PRESENTATION

Cut each ravioli-stuffed bread into 2 and arrange on a plate as shown. Spoon the sauce around to serve.

▾ CANDIED ZUCCHINI FLOWERS WITH MIXED BERRY SORBET AND SAUCE Serves 4

INGREDIENTS

Candied Zucchini Flower

8 zucchini flowers; 1 egg white; 30 g/1 oz/$\frac{1}{8}$ cup sugar

PREPARATION

Preheat the oven at 80°C (176°F). Toss the zucchini flowers in the egg white and sprinkle the sugar over. Arrange the zucchini flowers on a baking tray and bake them for 3 hours until they are crispy and still vibrant in colour.

Mixed Berry Sorbet

20 ml/$\frac{5}{8}$ fl oz/4 tsp water; 20 g/$\frac{3}{4}$ oz/4 tsp sugar; 2 tsp glucose; 150 g/5$\frac{1}{4}$ oz/1$\frac{1}{2}$ cups mixed seasonal wild berries; juice from $\frac{1}{2}$ lemon

Combine the water, sugar and glucose in a saucepan and bring to the boil, then remove the pan from the heat. Set aside to cool. When cool, combine the syrup and the mixed seasonal wild berries in a mixing bowl, then add the lemon juice. Mix well and transfer the mixture into an ice-cream machine set to sorbet specifications. When the sorbet is ready, keep refrigerated until required.

Mixed Berry Sauce

2$\frac{1}{2}$ tbsp sugar; 10 g/$\frac{3}{8}$ oz butter; 100 g/3$\frac{1}{2}$ oz/1 cup mixed seasonal wild berries; 30 ml/1 fl oz/$\frac{1}{8}$ cup balsamic vinegar

Heat the sugar and butter in a saucepan until the mixture reaches the consistency of caramel.
Add the seasonal wild berries, toss well and cook for 3 minutes. Add the balsamic vinegar and cook for another 5 minutes over low heat.

Garnish

4 sprigs mint

PRESENTATION

Fill each candied zucchini flower with some mixed berry sorbet. Arrange 2 flowers on 1 plate and spoon some sauce on the side. Garnish with the mint sprigs to serve.

LEFT: El Bulli's dining room, designed in rustic, Catalan style, has welcomed many well-known chefs and other celebrities who come to witness Ferran Adrià's cooking.
RIGHT: The bull, El Bulli's namesake, fronts the kitchen where Adrià's unorthodox cooking fantasies are realised.
BELOW: Stunning views of the Mediterranean make up for the gruelling three-hour drive from Barcelona to Roses.

El Bulli
Roses

Ferran Adrià

Foam is not 'out' as some critics claim. It is just overexposed. The siphon, designed to transform liquid into froth, had lost its novelty value by the time Ferran Adrià's hands were on it. Seemingly destined to little more than spluttering clouds of cream on sundaes, the gas-jet device, a symbol of culinary creativity in the late nineties, owed its dramatic comeback to Adrià's phobia of predictability in his cuisine. With the siphon, he set off a series of taste explosions by using underrated ingredients such as seawater. A long string of admirers followed suit. Foam culture spread far afield from El Bulli, Adrià's three-Michelin-star restaurant, which overlooks the Mediterranean coast.

Adrià's goals are consistent: topple conventions and play up the senses. That's why guests at El Bulli are told to hold up rosemary sprigs or vanilla pods to their noses while they eat, so that aroma, an often neglected sensation, comes to the fore. To experience the impact of temperature on taste, Adrià's guests are made to drink up shot-glass portions of pea soup, which start off warm and end up chilled. Even gelatine, normally served cold to maintain its form, is flash-heated with a salamander to offer a new taste sensation while preserving its shape. Recently, Adrià has taken to blindfolding his guests so that taste will be the focus when eyes and mind are released from the distractions of environment and conversation.

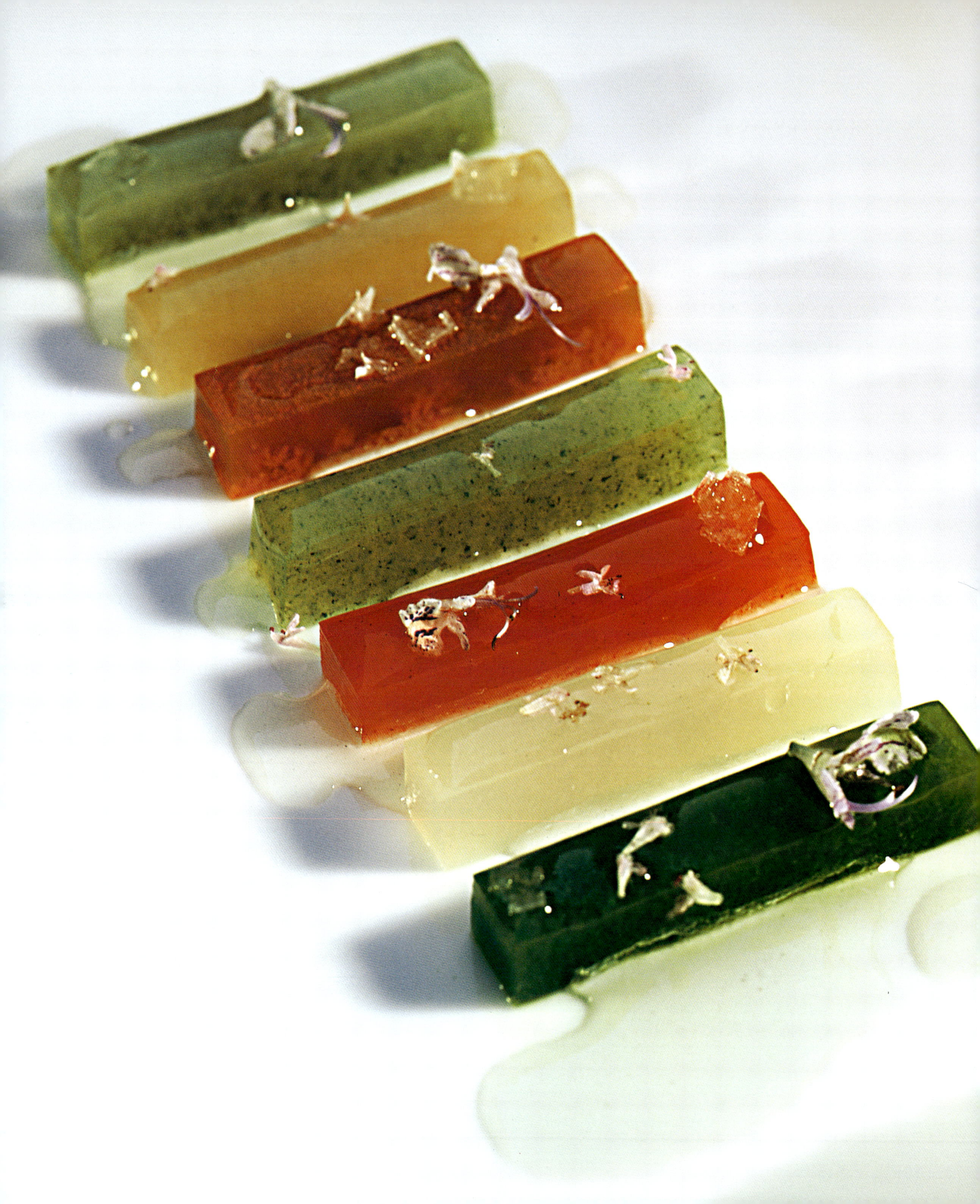

◀ VEGETABLES ON THE GRILL Serves 10

INGREDIENTS

Warm Red Capsicum Gelatine
200 g/7 oz red capsicum, cleaned and seeds removed;
salt; a pinch of gelatine powder

Warm Green Capsicum Gelatine
200 g/7 oz green capsicum, cleaned and seeds removed;
salt; a pinch of gelatine powder

Warm Onion Gelatine
4 big onions, peeled and covered in salt for 2 hours;
salt; a pinch of gelatine powder

Warm Celery Gelatine
½ stick celery, peeled;
salt; a pinch of gelatine powder

Warm Daikon Gelatine
300 g/10½ oz daikon, peeled, cut into pieces and cooked until very soft;
salt; a pinch of gelatine powder

Warm Carrot Gelatine
400 g/14⅛ oz carrots, peeled;
salt; a pinch of gelatine powder

Warm Asparagus Gelatine
1 or 2 asparagus, trimmed;
salt; a pinch of gelatine powder

Coal Oil
3 kg/6 lb 9⅞ oz wood;
500 ml/1 pt 1 fl oz/2⅛ cups sunflower oil

Garnish
40 thyme flowers;
40 rosemary flowers;
40 rock salt crystals

PREPARATION

Pass the capsicum through a juice extractor to obtain 150 ml/5 fl oz/⅝ cup of juice.
Season to taste with salt.
Mix the gelatine powder with some capsicum juice and heat the mixture gently to dissolve the gelatine.
Add the remaining juice slowly and mix well.
Pour the mixture into a rectangular dish so that it will rise to 1 cm (0.4 inch) high from the base of the dish.

Pass the capsicum through a juice extractor to obtain 150 ml/5 fl oz/⅝ cup of juice.
Season to taste with salt.
Mix the gelatine powder with some capsicum juice and heat the mixture gently to dissolve the gelatine.
Add the remaining juice slowly and mix well.
Pour the mixture into a rectangular dish so that it will rise to 1 cm (0.4 inch) high from the base of the dish.

Clean the onion, grill or scorch them in a hot pan, then soak them in water for 4 hours.
Drain off the water, then squeeze the onion in a muslin strainer to obtain 150 ml/5 fl oz/⅝ cup of juice.
Season to taste with salt.
Mix the gelatine powder with some onion juice and heat the mixture gently to dissolve the gelatine.
Add the remaining juice slowly and mix well.
Pour the mixture into a rectangular dish so that it will rise to 1 cm (0.4 inch) high from the base of the dish.

Blanch the celery in boiling water, then refresh it with iced water immediately.
Pass it through a juice extractor to obtain 150 ml/5 fl oz/⅝ cup of celery juice.
Season to taste with salt.
Mix the gelatine powder with some celery juice and heat the mixture gently to dissolve the gelatine.
Add the remaining juice slowly and mix well.
Pour the mixture into a rectangular dish so that it will rise to 1 cm (0.4 inch) high from the base of the dish.

Squeeze the cooked daikon in a muslin strainer to obtain its juice.
Do this twice to obtain 150 ml/5 fl oz/⅝ cup of daikon juice.
Season to taste with salt.
Mix the gelatine powder with some daikon juice and heat the mixture gently to dissolve the gelatine.
Add the remaining juice slowly and mix well.
Pour the mixture into a rectangular dish so that it will rise to 1 cm (0.4 inch) high from the base of the dish.

Pass the carrot through a juice extractor to obtain 150 ml/5 fl oz/⅝ cup of carrot juice.
Season to taste with salt.
Mix the gelatine powder with some carrot juice and heat the mixture gently to dissolve the gelatine.
Add the remaining juice slowly and mix well.
Pour the mixture into a rectangular dish so that it will rise to 1 cm (0.4 inch) high from the base of the dish.

Blanch the asparagus and refresh it in iced water immediately.
Pass it through a juice extractor to obtain 150 ml/5 fl oz/⅝ cup of asparagus juice.
Season to taste with salt.
Mix the gelatine powder with some asparagus juice and heat the mixture gently to dissolve the gelatine.
Add the remaining juice slowly and mix well.
Pour the mixture into a rectangular dish so that it will rise to 1 cm (0.4 inch) high from the base of the dish.

Burn the wood until the fire extinguishes on its own, then infuse the ashes in the sunflower oil for 12 hours.
Keep the container covered during this time.
Pass the oil through a muslin strainer before using.

PRESENTATION

When the gelatine has set, cut them all into 5-by-1-by-1-cm (2-by-0.4-by-0.4-inch) pieces and arrange them on the plates as shown.
Just before serving, put the plate under intense heat (under a salamander or a heated oven) until the gelatine is warm but not melted.
Garnish each portion with 2 tsp of coal oil, 4 thyme flowers, 4 rosemary flowers and 4 salt crystals to serve.

CAULIFLOWER COUSCOUS Serves 4

INGREDIENTS

Cauliflower Couscous
- 2 small cauliflowers;
- olive oil

Gingerbread
- 100 g/3⅓ oz gingerbread with honey;
- 60 ml/2 fl oz/¼ cup extra virgin olive oil;
- a pinch of five-spice powder

Campari Gelatine
- 60 ml/2 fl oz/¼ cup Campari;
- a pinch of gelatine powder

Vinegar Reduction
- 200 ml/6¾ oz/⅞ cup red wine vinegar;
- 2 tsp sugar; ½ tsp glucose

Lamb Gravy
- 1.2 kg/1 lb 10⅜ oz lamb neck;
- 50 ml/1¾ fl oz/¼ cup olive oil;
- 30 g/1 oz onion, peeled and chopped roughly;
- 20 g/¾ oz garlic, peeled and crushed;
- 250 ml/8½ fl oz/1 cup dry white wine;
- 1.5 litres/3 pts 2¾ fl oz/6⅓ cups water;
- a pinch of dried oregano;
- 1 bay leaf; a pinch of black peppercorns

Lamb Sauce
- 200 ml/6¾ oz/⅞ cup lamb gravy; salt; cornflour

Garnish
- 8 mint leaves;
- 16 rosemary flowers;
- zest from 2 lemons (avoid white part), grated;
- 8 small basil leaves;
- zest from 2 oranges (avoid white part), grated;
- 2 Conferencia pears, peeled and diced into 0.5-cm (0.2-inch) cubes;
- 4 juniper berries, halved;
- 8 chervil leaves;
- 8 soft almonds;
- 2 Granny Smith apples, peeled and diced into 0.5-cm (0.2-inch) cubes;
- 8 strands saffron, lightly toasted;
- 8 fennel leaves, tied in 4 bunches;
- 20 g/¾ oz ginger, peeled and diced into 0.2-cm (0.1-inch) cubes;
- 4 tsp muscovado sugar

PREPARATION

Clean the cauliflowers' leaves and shred thinly.
Separate the florets from the stems with a small knife and chop the florets to the texture of couscous.
Blanch them, then plunge them into salted iced water right after.
Strain and dry on kitchen tissue. Set aside.
Just before serving, sauté the cauliflower couscous in some olive oil.

Preheat the oven at 150°C (302°F).
Crumble the gingerbread on a baking tray to resemble chopped almond seeds.
Bake the gingerbread until it is dry. Remove from the heat and set aside to cool.
When cool, toss it with the olive oil and five-spice powder. Set aside.

Heat the Campari, add the gelatine powder and, stirring continuously, bring the mixture to the boil.
Remove from the heat and keep the mixture in a cool place.
When the gelatine has set, cut it into 0.2-cm (0.1-inch) cubes.

Combine the red wine vinegar, sugar and glucose in a saucepan and reduce the mixture over low heat until it reaches the consistency of caramel.

Preheat the oven at 180°C (356°F).
Cut the lamb neck into small pieces and arrange the pieces on a baking tray.
Drizzle the olive oil over and roast in the oven, stirring occasionally, until the pieces are evenly cooked.
Remove some of the grease from the tray and add the onion and garlic and roast until they are cooked.
Remove all the grease from the tray and deglaze with the dry white wine.
Bake until the wine evaporates completely and the lamb neck turns golden brown in colour.
Remove the ingredients to a pot and add the water, dried oregano, bay leaf and black peppercorns.
Cook over medium heat, stirring occasionally, and bring to the boil.
Lower the heat and simmer for 1 hour. Remove from the heat.
Discard the pieces of lamb neck and set the mixture aside to cool.
When cool, skim off the fat, then reduce the sauce until it reaches the consistency of gravy.
Process the mixture in the blender to obtain a smooth purée.

Reduce the lamb gravy by half and season to taste with salt. The sauce should be thick enough to coat the back of a spoon without dripping. Thicken with cornflour if necessary. Warm it up just before serving.

PRESENTATION

The ingredients should be arranged on each plate to resemble the face of a clock.
Place 1 tsp of gingerbread topped with a mint leaf, a rosemary flower and a small pinch of grated lemon zest at the positions of 12 and 6 o'clock.
Place 1 tsp of gingerbread topped with a basil leaf, a rosemary flower and a small pinch of grated orange zest at the positions of 3 and 9 o'clock.
Place 1 tsp of Campari gelatine cubes at the positions of 11, 1, and 4 o'clock.
Place a cube of pear topped with half a juniper berry and a chervil leaf at the positions of 2 and 7 o'clock. On each side, place a soft almond.
Place a cube of apple topped with a strand of saffron and a bunch of fennel leaves at the positions of 11 and 5 o'clock. On each side, place some ginger cubes.
Place some muscovado sugar at the position of 8 o'clock.
Put 1 drop of vinegar reduction at the position of 10 o'clock and in between 5 and 6 o'clock.
Spoon a small mountain of cooked cauliflower couscous in the centre of each plate.
Drizzle the lamb sauce around the cauliflower couscous to serve.

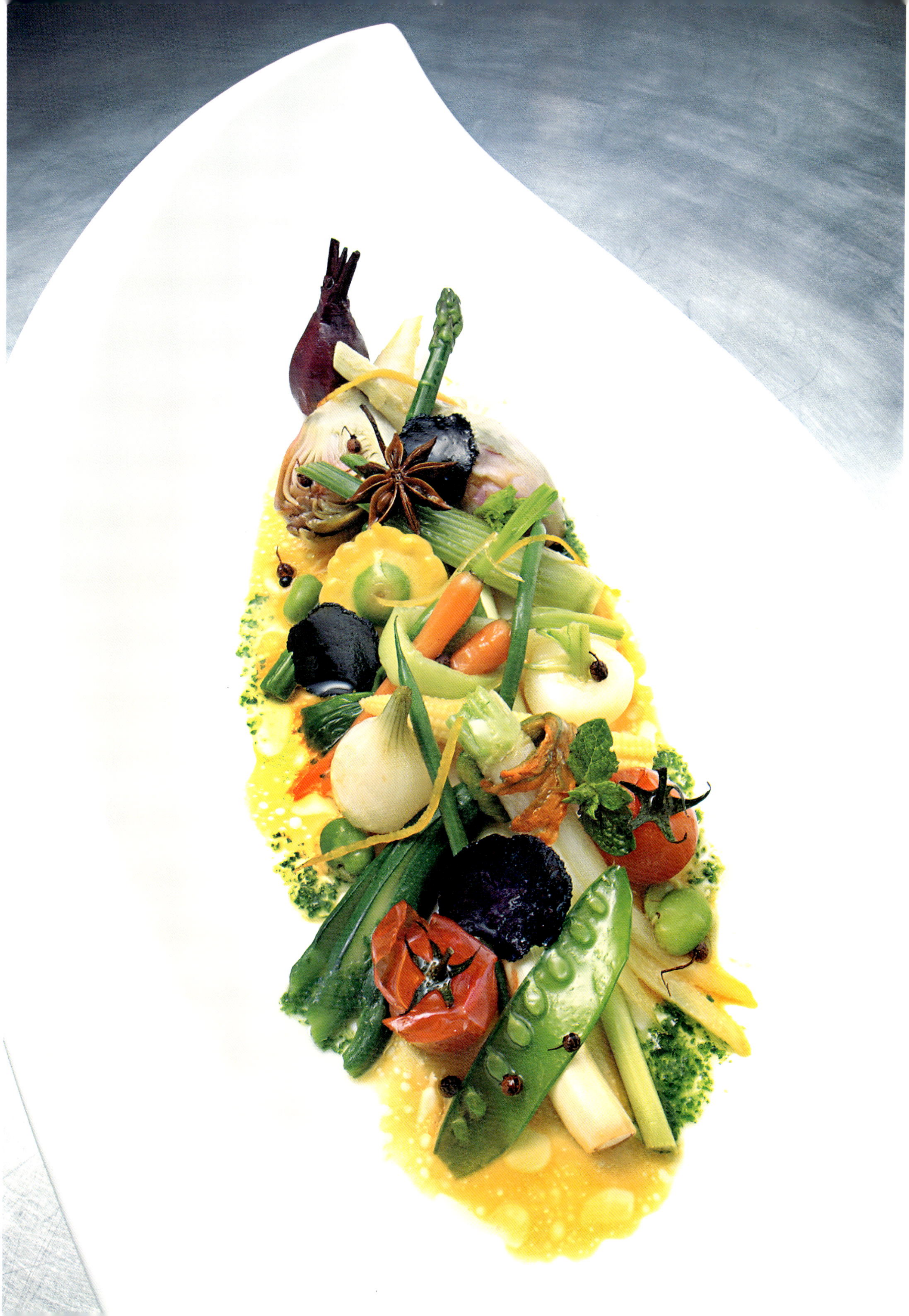

Freddy Schmidt

Freddy Schmidt is an entire chef's dream team rolled into one. He can orchestrate more than a dozen restaurants simultaneously, making them run like clockwork, while demonstrating his culinary ability in all their kitchens, which range widely in style. Although an export of Alsace, home to many French gastro-greats such as Jean-Georges Vongerichten, Schmidt is also fluent in English, German and Japanese and equally eloquent in these cuisines. The best witness to his multiple talents is Raffles Hotel in Singapore, where he has managed all 18 food-and-beverage outlets from 1996, for five years running.

When he was the youngest Chef de Cuisine ever on the ocean liner Queen Elizabeth II, he visited almost every exotic speck on the planet and embraced a wide range of ingredients and cuisines. He quickly incorporated this diversity into his versatile cooking style. And over the years, he's made quite a reputation for first mastering the classics, then doctoring them. Always on the hunt for new tastes and textures, he flavours his Brittany lobster nage with green apple juice and hazelnut oil emulsion, serves his pan-fried foie gras with wasabi potatoes and beetroot vinaigrette, and garnishes his olive oil ice cream with strawberries marinated in balsamic vinegar, wild thyme syrup and a tapenade tuile.

Schmidt has cooked for kings and queens, presidents and pop stars, and has a Japanese language cookbook published while he was working in Japan. He's shared stoves with Kiyomi Mikuni, Michel Troisgros, Joël Robuchon and most of Michelin's top guns. Currently he's injecting new sparkle into The Oriental Hotel's dining rooms. What challenges remain? Always forward-looking, this culinary adventurer desires nothing less than to be 'the first chef to cook on the moon'.

RIGHT AND EXTREME RIGHT: 'Art of the Orient' is The Oriental, Singapore's dominant design theme.
BELOW: Guests of the hotel can enjoy the spectacular creations of Executive Chef Freddy Schmidt.

The Oriental

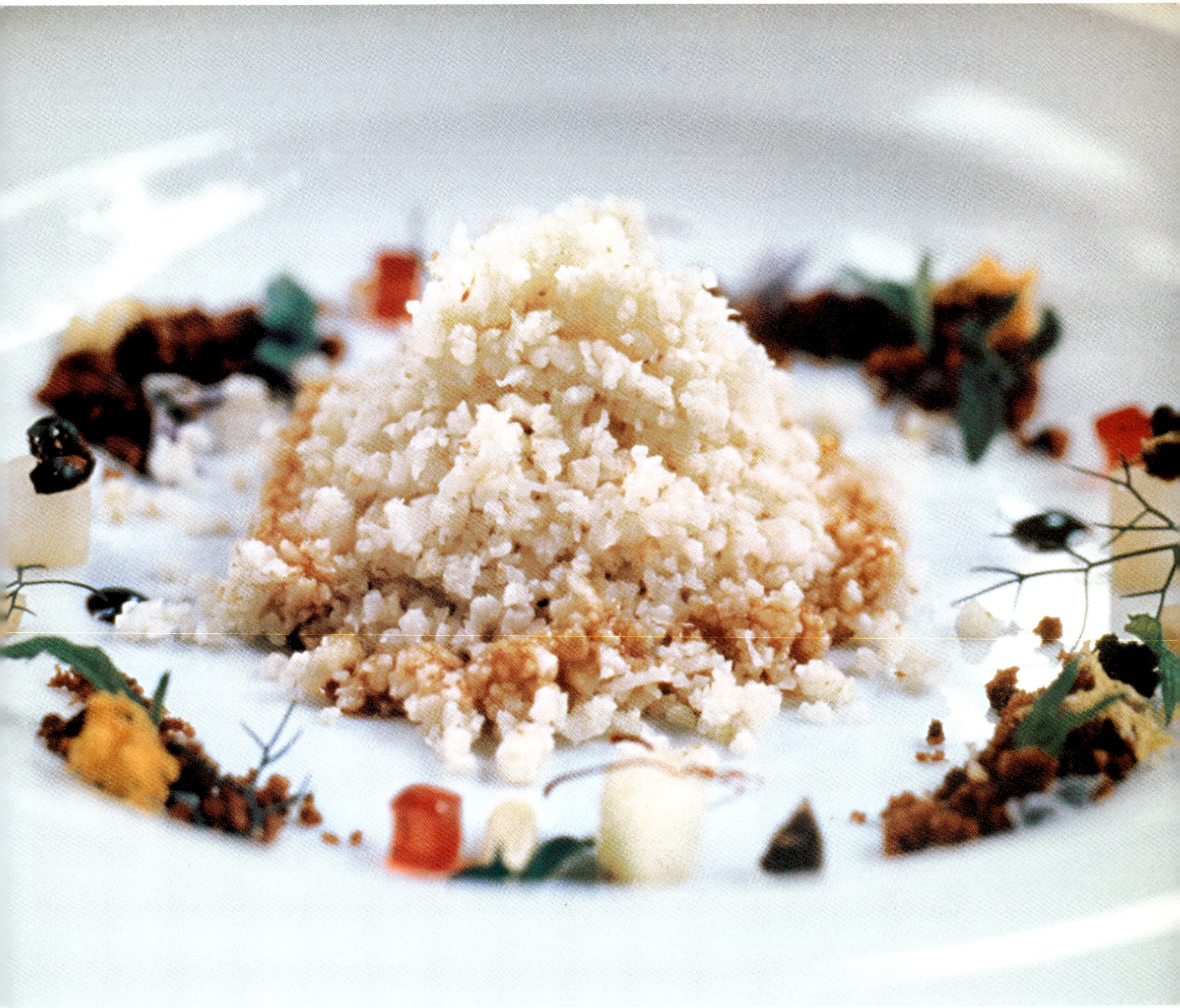

▶ YELLOW FIN TUNA WITH CAVIAR DRESSING AND CUCUMBER LEMON SALSA   Serves 4

INGREDIENTS

Cucumber Lemon Salsa
120 g/4¼ oz cucumber, diced; 6 tsp chopped shallots;
20 g/¾ oz/¼ cup chopped hardboiled egg;
20 g/¾ oz/⅛ cup diced lemon flesh (zest removed);
1 tsp grated lemon zest; 2 tbsp lemon juice;
1 tbsp chopped tarragon; 1 tbsp chopped coriander;
2 tbsp virgin olive oil;
salt; freshly ground black pepper

Caviar Dressing
60 g/2⅛ oz/¼ cup Royal Oscietra caviar;
3 tbsp extra virgin olive oil; 1 tbsp lemon juice;
salt; freshly ground white pepper

Yellow Fin Tuna
320 g/11¼ oz yellow fin tuna

Balsamic Reduction
100 ml/3⅜ fl oz/⅜ cup balsamic vinegar

Garnish
10 g/⅜ oz/½ cup daikon cress

PREPARATION

About 10 minutes before serving, combine all the ingredients in a bowl and toss well. Season to taste with salt and freshly ground black pepper. Keep refrigerated until required.

Combine the Royal Oscietra caviar, extra virgin olive oil and lemon juice in a bowl and mix well. Season to taste with salt and freshly ground white pepper.

Just before serving, cut the yellow fin tuna into even slices.

Reduce the balsamic vinegar in a small pot over low heat until about 1 tbsp remains.

PRESENTATION

Divide the cucumber lemon salsa among 4 plates. Arrange a few slices of yellow fin tuna on top and spoon the caviar dressing over. Garnish with daikon cress and some balsamic vinegar reduction on the side to serve.

◀ YOUNG VEGETABLE CASSEROLE WITH ORANGE AND SICHUAN PEPPER EMULSION   Serves 4

INGREDIENTS

Young Vegetable Casserole
8 young carrots; 4 young turnips;
4 young beetroots; 4 green asparagus;
4 pearl onions; 4 young artichokes;
juice from ½ lemon; salt; 4 young zucchinis;
4 young leeks; 4 young fennels; 8 French beans;
8 fava beans; 4 young yellow squashes;
4 young corn; 4 snow peas; 8 cherry tomatoes

Orange and Sichuan Pepper Emulsion
2 shallots, sliced; olive oil;
100 ml/3⅜ fl oz/⅜ cup dry white wine;
300 ml/10⅛ fl oz/1¼ cups orange juice;
a few threads of saffron; 1 bouquet garni;
2 star anise; ½ tsp crushed coriander seeds;
2 tsp Sichuan peppercorns; sea salt

Orange and Lemon Zest Confit
5 g/⅛ oz orange zest, cut into thin strips;
5 g/⅛ oz lemon zest, cut into thin strips;
50 ml/1¾ fl oz/¼ cup water; 5 tsp sugar

Parsley Oil
100 g/3½ oz Italian parsley leaves;
100 ml/3⅜ fl oz/⅜ cup grapeseed oil

Garnish
A few pistachios, shells removed;
100 ml/3⅜ fl oz/⅜ cup extra virgin olive oil;
salt; 2 stalks lemon grass;
12 slices black truffles;
1 sprig mint leaves

PREPARATION

Peel the carrots, turnips, beetroots, asparagus and pearl onions.
Wash them under running water with the other vegetables.
Trim the artichokes, remove the first layer of leaves and use only the hearts.
Bring a pot of water to the boil and add the lemon juice and some salt.
Cook the artichokes in the water and refresh them with iced water once they are cooked.
Cook all the remaining vegetables, except the cherry tomatoes, in a separate pot of salted boiling water.
Refresh with iced water immediately.
Blanch the cherry tomatoes for a few seconds in the boiling water. Refresh with iced water immediately.
Peel the tomatoes and set everything aside until required.

Sauté the sliced shallots in some olive oil without colouring them.
Add the white wine and reduce the mixture to a glaze.
Add the orange juice, saffron, bouquet garni, star anise, crushed coriander seeds and half the Sichuan peppercorns. Mix well and season to taste with sea salt.
Simmer the mixture for 15 minutes with the lid on, then remove from the heat and allow the mixture to infuse for another 15 minutes.
Skim and strain the emulsion. Discard the solid ingredients.

Blanch the orange and lemon zest strips for a few seconds, then refresh in iced water immediately.
Bring the water and sugar to the boil, lower the heat, add the zest and simmer for 10 to 15 minutes.
Remove from the heat and let the mixture cool to room temperature.
Keep refrigerated until required.

Rinse the parsley leaves under running water.
Blanch the parsley leaves in the salted boiling water for a few seconds, then refresh them immediately with iced water. Pat the leaves dry with kitchen tissue.
Process the leaves and grapeseed oil in a blender to obtain a smooth purée.
Keep refrigerated until required.

PRESENTATION

Warm the orange and Sichuan pepper emulsion. Add the remaining Sichuan peppercorns and all the vegetables, except the cherry tomatoes, to the emulsion and simmer for 2 to 3 minutes.
Add the cherry tomatoes, orange and lemon zest confit and pistachios.
Remove from the heat, add the extra virgin olive oil, then season to taste with salt.
Place the lemon grass in a big serving dish and arrange the vegetables over.
Coat the vegetables generously with the emulsion.
Garnish with the black truffle slices and sprig of mint leaves. Drizzle some parsley oil around to serve.

Le Pré Catelan
Paris

RIGHT: Le Pré Catelan's luxurious interior is testimony to the flamboyant lifestyle of the belle époque era.
ABOVE: The restaurant is situated in a stunning Napoleon III edifice in the centre of the Bois de Boulogne.
ABOVE RIGHT: Outdoor dining in Le Pré Catelan's beautiful garden is not to be missed during summer.

Frédéric Anton

Joël Robuchon is a perfectionist and during his reign, his Paris restaurants, Jamin and Joël Robuchon, were shrines to classical French cuisine. Frédéric Anton was Robuchon's trusted right hand for several years before the master announced his retirement plans. He learned well. When he stepped into the historic Le Pré Catelan restaurant in the Bois de Boulogne, it had a single Michelin star. Two years under Anton's supervision and it was awarded another. Despite his newfound fame, Anton acknowledges his background with great pride, attributing his success to his mentor Robuchon, and to his teachers Gérard Boyer, Robert Bardot and Gérard Veissiere.

A good dish, to Anton, begins with perfect seasonal ingredients. Then the challenge lies in finding a balance of flavours by injecting an appropriate level of acidity. Like Robuchon, he will not allow less-than-ideal produce in his kitchen. His cooking is based on treating the ingredients simply in order to enhance their natural flavours. He refuses to be known as a chef who specialises in a particular area of cooking, insisting that he is just a cook—a modest claim for someone with a gift for giving French classics a contemporary edge and who gets to wear France's national colours around his starched collars. This privilege is reserved for an elite group of French chefs, including the venerable Paul Bocuse, who have passed the gruelling Meilleur Ouvrier de France exams.

▲ YOUNG CARROT CONFIT CARAMELISED WITH GINGERBREAD SAUCE Serves 4

INGREDIENTS

Young Carrot Confit
40 ml/1¾ fl oz/⅛ cup olive oil;
20 young carrots, peeled; scant 1 tsp salt;
150 ml/5 fl oz/⅝ cup white stock (recipe on page 148);
10 g/⅜ oz butter; 30 ml/1 fl oz/⅛ cup acacia honey;
4 tsp sherry vinegar

Gingerbread Sauce
2 slices gingerbread, diced;
70 ml/2¾ fl oz/⅓ cup dry white wine;
70 ml/2¾ fl oz/⅓ cup white stock
(recipe on page 148); 1 tsp sugar;
2 tsp white vinegar

Chicken Cream Sauce
150 ml/5 fl oz/⅝ cup white stock (recipe on page 148);
50 ml/1¾ fl oz/¼ cup cream;
60 g/2⅛ oz butter; salt; pepper

Garnish
1 slice dried gingerbread; 4 young carrots;
200 ml/6¾ fl oz/⅞ cup groundnut oil;
juice from 1 orange, reduced by half;
1 tsp chopped chervil

PREPARATION

Warm the olive oil in a pot over low heat.
Season the carrots with salt, then add the carrots to the heated olive oil and stir carefully.
Add the white stock and butter, mix well, then cover the pot and simmer for 20 minutes.
Add the acacia honey and deglaze with the sherry vinegar. Mix well.
Keep warm until required.

Put the gingerbread cubes in a bowl and add the white wine. Toss well.
Let the mixture marinate for 2 hours. Keep refrigerated during this time.
Bring the white stock to the boil, add the marinated gingerbread and cook for 15 minutes.
In a separate pot, heat the sugar and vinegar until the sugar caramelises.
Add the gingerbread mixture and simmer for another 15 minutes. Strain the mixture.

Reduce the white stock by half, then add the cream and butter to give the sauce a smooth and glossy texture.
Season to taste with salt and pepper.

PRESENTATION

Process the dried gingerbread in a blender to obtain breadcrumbs.
Deep-fry the young carrots in groundnut oil for garnishing. Divide the carrot confit among 4 plates.
Coat the carrots with gingerbread sauce, then spoon the orange juice reduction over.
Garnish with deep-fried carrots, gingerbread crumbs and chopped chervil.
Drizzle some chicken cream sauce around to serve.

OVEN-ROASTED PARTRIDGE WITH GRATINATED MACARONI AND STUFFING ON TOAST
Serves 4

INGREDIENTS

Oven-Roasted Partridge
2 partridges; 40 g/1¾ oz butter;
salt; pepper;
1 clove garlic, crushed;
40 ml/1¾ fl oz/⅜ cup Cognac

Stuffing on Toast
20 g/¾ oz fat bacon, diced finely;
80 g/2⅞ oz chicken liver; fresh thyme;
scant ½ tsp sugar; salt; pepper;
50 g/1¾ oz foie gras, cooked;
3 tsp mustard; 1 tsp vinegar; 2 tsp Cognac;
butter; 4 slices baguette; ½ clove garlic

Gratinated Macaroni
4 pieces big macaroni;
500 ml/1 pt 1 fl oz/2⅛ cups water;
500 ml/1 pt 1 fl oz/2⅛ cups milk;
butter; 30 g/1 oz Comté cheese, grated;
¼ bunch chives, chopped

Garnish
Butter; 4 cèpes; salt; pepper;
½ tsp chopped garlic;
3 tsp shallot confit (recipe on page 149);
1 tsp chopped Italian parsley

PREPARATION

Preheat the oven at 180°C (356°F). Rub the partridges with butter, then season them with salt and pepper. Roast the partridges for about 10 minutes in the oven (or preferably on a revolving skewer over a spit) until they are brown on all sides, then remove them from the heat and set aside to cool for 10 minutes.
Remove the partridges' innards. Discard the gizzards, pass the remaining giblet through a fine-mesh sieve and set aside. Detach the breasts and legs from the body and set aside.
Chop the carcasses into small pieces and sauté them with butter and garlic.
Deglaze with Cognac and add enough cold water to cover the bones, then simmer for 1 hour to obtain a rich sauce. Strain and set aside.

Heat the fat bacon in a saucepan. When most of the fat has melted, add the chicken liver, thyme, sugar, salt and pepper, and sauté for a few minutes.
Remove the chicken liver from the pan and set aside to cool.
Pass the cooked chicken liver and foie gras through a fine-mesh sieve.
Add the giblet mousse, mustard, vinegar and Cognac and mix well. Season to taste with salt and pepper.
Spread some butter on the baguette slices, rub some garlic over and toast the bread.
Spread the stuffing on the toasted baguette and toast in the oven for another 5 minutes.

Cook the macaroni in water and milk for 7 minutes until the macaroni is al dente.
Refresh it in cold water and strain.
Melt some butter in a saucepan and toss the macaroni for 2 minutes.
Sprinkle the Comtè cheese and chives over.
Toss well, then set aside until required.

PRESENTATION

Pan-fry the partridge breasts and legs (only on the sides with skin) in some butter.
Sauté the cèpes separately in butter and season to taste with salt and pepper.
When the cèpes are almost cooked, add the chopped garlic and toss well.
Arrange a piece of macaroni in the centre of a plate. Place a partridge breast and leg on it.
Place a portion of toast beside the partridge and garnish with the sautéed cèpes and shallot confit.
Sprinkle the chopped Italian parsley over and spoon the partridge's cooking juice around to serve.

Gordon Ramsay
London

LEFT: Gordon Ramsay played professional football for the Glasgow Rangers before scoring a scintillating career in the kitchen.

BELOW: Ramsay's elegant restaurant occupies the former grounds of the legendary La Tante Claire, owned by his mentor, Pierre Koffman.

Gordon Ramsay

Football was once his career of choice, he looks and talks like a longshoreman, and his temper is legendary. He has blithely tossed Joan Colllins and food critic A.A. Gill out of his restaurant, dealt out stern punishment—a process now christened 'getting Ramsayed' to careless cooks, and reduced negligent staff to tears. But to the delight of all who have had a taste of his food, Gordon Ramsay cooks like an angel. And he remains a great chef and role model to his team, who showed their undying loyalty on the fateful day he stomped out of Aubergine restaurant—they too, threw aside their torchons, and followed suit. Good move, because his eponymous restaurant, Gordon Ramsay's, is now London's only three-Michelin-star restaurant.

Having braised and sautéed alongside the best in the business, honing his craft and picking up knowledge from French-cooking greats such as Joël Robuchon, Albert Roux, Pierre Koffman and Guy Savoy, Ramsay has developed a cooking style that is simple, focused and refined. 'The essence of my cooking is that it should prepare you to get up and go. Not feel like going to bed for three days afterwards,' he says. Robuchon's obsession with precision and Koffman's mastery of foie gras have obviously rubbed off on him because Ramsay's signature Mosaic of Foie Gras, highlighting three preparation styles—roasted, terrine and parfait—has attained culinary perfection.

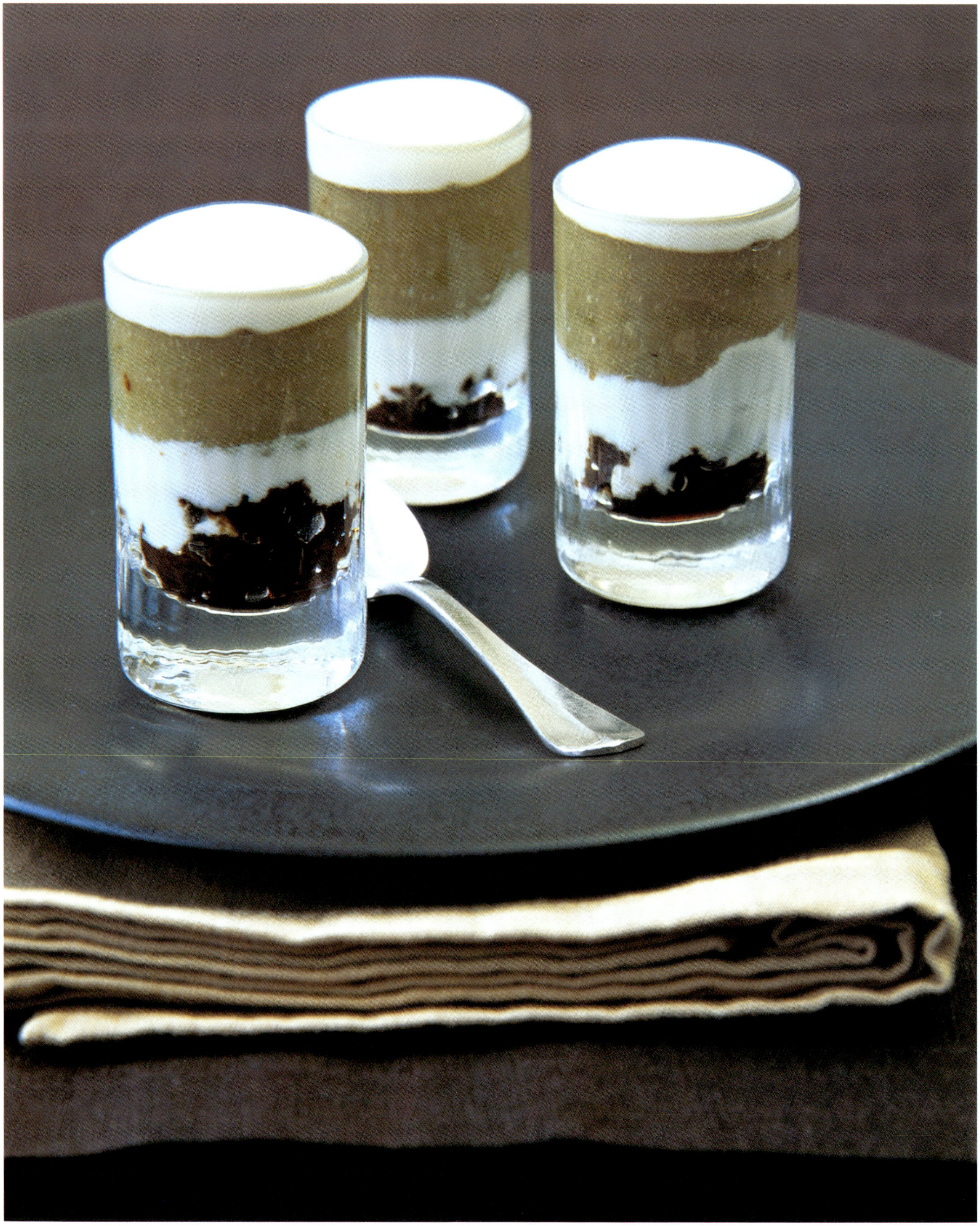

◀ **APPLE, PRUNE, BUTTERSCOTCH AND YOGHURT COMPOTE** Serves 4 to 8

INGREDIENTS

Brandied Prunes
100 ml/3⅜ fl oz/⅜ cup Armagnac, Calvados or other brandy;
8 to 10 plump semi-dried Agen prunes

Apple Pureé
1 large Granny Smith apple, peeled, cored and chopped;
2 tbsp water; 1 vanilla pod; 2 tbsp castor sugar

Butterscotch
100 g/3½ oz/½ cup castor sugar;
100 g/3½ oz unsalted butter;
100 ml/3⅜ fl oz/⅜ cup double cream

Yoghurt
300 ml/10⅛ fl oz/1¼ cups whole-milk yoghurt (Greek-style yoghurt preferred)

PREPARATION

Prepare the brandied prunes 1 day ahead.
Warm the brandy of your choice in a small saucepan without letting it boil.
Remove from the heat and stir in the prunes. Macerate overnight.
The next day, drain the prunes, remove the stones and chop the flesh roughly. Set aside.

Combine the chopped apple and water in a small pan. Slit the vanilla pod and scrape out the seeds.
Mix the vanilla seeds with the castor sugar and add to the pan. Mix well.
When the mixture is sizzling, cover the pan and cook for 5 to 7 minutes, stirring occasionally, until it is soft and pulpy. Remove from the heat and set aside to cool. Using a fork, mash the mixture into a chunky purée.

In another saucepan, gently warm the castor sugar with a splash of water until the sugar completely dissolves.
During this time, stir occasionally.
Turn up the heat and stir in the butter. Cook until the mixture turns a light caramel in colour.
Do not stir or it will become a fudge.
Remove from the heat and set aside to cool for 5 minutes, then add the cream. Mix well.
Set aside to cool to room temperature, then mix in the apple. Keep refrigerated until required.

Stir the whole-milk yoghurt until it is smooth.

PRESENTATION

Divide the brandied prunes among 4 to 8 glasses.
Divide half the yoghurt among the glasses, spooning it on top of the prunes.
Cover the yoghurt with apple pureé, then top the apple purée with the remaining yoghurt to serve.

▼ **SUMMERY QUAILS WITH TOMATO TARRAGON DRESSING** Serves 4

INGREDIENTS

Tomato Tarragon Dressing
½ small tomato, seeds removed and chopped finely;
½ shallot, chopped finely; ½ tsp tomato ketchup;
½ tsp coarse grain mustard; ½ tsp lemon juice;
1 tsp chopped fresh tarragon; 3 tbsp olive oil;
sea salt; freshly ground black pepper

Summery Quails
4 quails; olive oil; sea salt; freshly ground black pepper

Sautéed Celery and Girolles
2½ tbsp olive oil;
4 small sticks celery, cut into small pieces;
100 ml/3⅜ fl oz/⅜ cup chicken stock or vegetable nage (recipes on pages 148 and 149);
sea salt; freshly ground black pepper;
70 g/2½ oz/⅓ cup girolles, ends trimmed, then halved if large

Garnish
A few celery leaves (may be deep-fried if desired)

PREPARATION

Combine the chopped tomato, shallot, tomato ketchup, coarse grain mustard, lemon juice, tarragon and olive oil in a bowl and mix well.
Season to taste with sea salt and freshly ground black pepper.

Preheat the oven at 190°C (374°F).
Brush the quails lightly with olive oil and season to taste with sea salt and pepper.
Roast the quails for 12 minutes. Remove from the heat and set aside for 10 minutes.
Using a sharp boning knife, remove the lightly cooked breasts from the bones, keeping them whole.
Mix the breasts with the tomato tarragon dressing and set aside to cool.

Heat 1 tbsp of olive oil in a pan and sauté the celery pieces until they turn brown in colour.
Add the chicken stock or vegetable nage and season to taste with sea salt and freshly ground black pepper.
Cover the pan and simmer for 10 minutes until the celery softens and the liquid evaporates.
In the meantime, sauté the girolles in the remaining olive oil for 5 minutes, stirring once or twice, then season to taste with sea salt and freshly ground black pepper.

PRESENTATION

Divide the celery among 4 plates and top them with the girolles.
Arrange the quail breasts on top of the girolles and drizzle the remaining tomato tarragon dressing over.
Garnish with the celery leaves to serve.

BELOW: Le Grand Véfour's opulent interior is the ultimate setting for the enjoyment of haute French cuisine.

Le Grand Véfour Paris

Guy Martin

The building that houses Le Grand Véfour dates from before the French Revolution; the restaurant itself is from the 1820s. Tucked into a neo-classical colonnade, part of the Palais-Royal, this multi-mirrored, ornately gilded confection is a living piece of history and a monument to haute cuisine and the extravagance of the 1800s. It is a spectacular space imbued with style and nostalgia and haunted by the gourmet-ghosts of former regulars Napoleon Bonaparte and Victor Hugo—and here you can find Guy Martin, who runs the restaurant's kitchen.

Despite the restaurant's classical façade, Martin's headline-grabbing back-of-house activities have provoked critics to label his domain 'the upside-down kitchen'. His dishes involve unexpected combinations such as chestnuts and truffles in an iced parfait, tomato sorbet with black olives, and garden pea ice cream, and they force diners to reconsider their own stereotyped expectations of the sweet and savoury kitchens. In fact, such an unorthodox marriage of flavours has been practised by anonymous home cooks across France for centuries. Some French chefs even claim that the movement was founded with the birth of Grande Cuisine Francaise some 300 years ago. Its popularity soared in the 1970s when pioneers of Nouvelle Cuisine, such as Michel Guérard and Alain Senderens, started mixing glazed chestnuts with truffles and lobster with vanilla. Perhaps its transience can be attributed to those who combined mackerel with raspberries and caramel with sweet potato soup. Regardless, Martin proclaims this to be the cuisine of the third millennium.

▶ PARMENTIER OF OXTAIL AND BLACK TRUFFLES   Serves 4

INGREDIENTS

Oxtails
2 oxtails; 2 carrots, cut into pieces;
2 onions, halved and scorched with an open flame;
1 stick celery, cut into pieces; 1 leek, cut into pieces;
1 bouquet garni; 1 juniper berry; 2 cloves;
salt; freshly ground black pepper

Mashed Potatoes
500 g/1 lb 1⅝ oz Ratte potatoes;
2 tsp milk; 50 g/1¾ oz butter;
1 tsp truffle juice;
20 g/¾ oz black truffles, chopped;
salt; freshly ground black pepper

Oxtail and Black Truffle Sauce
2 tsp truffle juice;
60 g/2⅛ oz black truffles, chopped;
100 g/3½ oz butter;
salt; freshly ground black pepper

Garnish
32 slices black truffles

PREPARATION

Prepare the oxtails 1 day ahead. Put the oxtails in a stockpot and fill two-thirds of the pot with water. Bring to the boil, skim off the material that floats to the surface. Add the carrots, onions, celery, leek, bouquet garni, juniper berry and cloves, and season to taste with salt and freshly ground black pepper. Lower the heat and simmer the oxtails for 6 to 7 hours.
Remove the oxtails from the stock and separate the meat from the tail bones.
Discard the tail bones and set the meat aside. Strain the stock and set aside.

Cook the Ratte potatoes in salted boiling water for 20 to 25 minutes.
Remove from the heat and peel the cooked potatoes while they are still warm.
Mash them with a fork and pass the mash through a fine-mesh sieve.
Add the milk, butter, truffle juice and chopped truffles and mix well.
Season to taste with salt and freshly ground black pepper. Keep warm until required.

Reheat the oxtail meat in some of the oxtail stock and reduce the remaining stock by half.
Add the truffle juice, chopped truffles and butter to the reduced stock and mix well.
Season to taste with salt and freshly ground black pepper.

PRESENTATION

Brush the insides of 4 ring moulds, each measuring 4.5 cm (1.8 inches) in depth and 8 cm (3.2 inches) in diameter, with some butter. Place each ring in the centre of a plate. Remove the reheated oxtail meat from the stock and fill the rings with meat. When the rings are half full, top the meat with the mashed potatoes. Smoothen the surface with a spatula and arrange 8 slices of truffles on each portion to form a rosette. Carefully remove the rings, spoon the sauce around and sprinkle some sea salt over to serve.

▼ GREEN PEA ICE CREAM   Serves 10

INGREDIENTS

Green Pea Ice Cream
700 g/1 lb 8⅝ oz/8¾ cups green peas, shelled;
200 ml/6¾ fl oz/⅞ cup milk;
300 ml/10⅛ fl oz/1¼ cups cream;
3 eggs; 100 g/3½ oz/½ cup sugar;
½ bunch mint

Ice Cream Cone
300 g/10½ oz/2¼ cups plain flour, sifted;
300 g/10 ½ oz/1½ cups sugar;
120 ml/4 fl oz/½ cup clarified butter;
1 egg; 50 ml/1¾ fl oz/¼ cup water

PREPARATION

Poach the shelled green peas in salted boiling water for 8 minutes until they are cooked.
Strain and refresh them in iced water immediately. Process the peas in a blender to obtain a smooth purée, then pass the purée through a fine-mesh sieve to remove any lumps. Keep refrigerated until required.
Combine the milk and cream in a pan and bring to the boil. Whisk the eggs and sugar until the mixture becomes light and fluffy. Transfer this into a pot and pour in the boiling milk and cream.
Stir the mixture slowly with a wooden spatula over low heat until it reaches about 83°C (182°F), then remove the pot from the heat and set it on a bed of ice to cool. Strain the mixture and add it to the pea purée.
Mix well. Pour the mixture into an ice cream maker and process according to the specifications.
Slice the mint leaves thinly and when the ice cream is almost ready, add the mint leaves and continue processing until the ice cream is ready. Keep frozen until required.

Combine the sifted plain flour and sugar in a bowl and mix well. Add the clarified butter and egg and mix well. Add the water slowly and mix into a rich batter.
Spoon this batter into a ice-cream-cone or wafer maker and cook for 1 to 2 minutes until the batter turns golden brown in colour. Remove immediately and quickly roll each portion into a cone.
Once it cools, it will harden into an ice cream cone. Repeat this process with the remaining batter.

PRESENTATION

Fill each cone with a scoop of green pea ice cream and serve immediately.

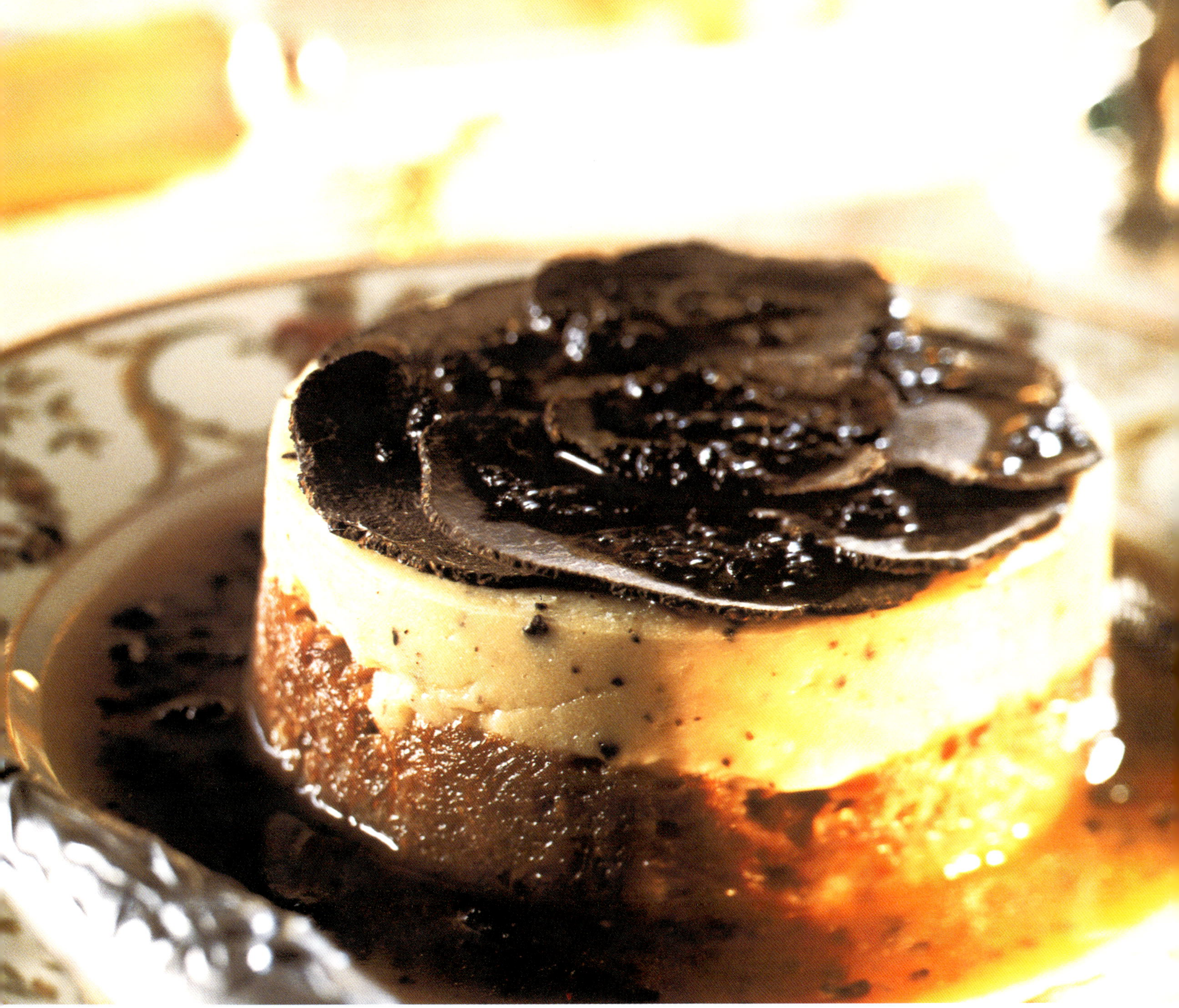

Restaurant Guy Savoy
Paris

ABOVE: Guy Savoy basks in the limelight thrown on the hugely successful restaurant that carries his name.
RIGHT: The newly renovated Restaurant Guy Savoy recently scooped its third Michelin star.
BELOW: A fully committed crew is one of the main pillars of Savoy's empire.

Guy Savoy

By the time a chef opens a restaurant in his name, he has arrived—both in his own mind and in those of the diners who dote on his repertoire. To chef and owner Guy Savoy, Restaurant Guy Savoy is a dream fulfilled, the crowning achievement of a life as kitchen trainee, cook, chef and restaurateur. Now, his parents are truly proud of the son who disappointed them at the age of 16, when an overriding passion for cooking drove him to leave school for an apprenticeship with the local confectioner. But he knew what he wanted and persevered.

Working in the kitchens of Troigros in Roanne, in Paris' famed Lasserre, and as sous chef at the prestigious Le Lion d'Or in Geneva, and while cooking for thousands of hungry soldiers during his national service, Savoy accumulated a vast and valuable storehouse of knowledge on every facet of restaurant procedure. He was unstinting in energy and had his eye on a place of his own one day. These days, Savoy's popular restaurant in Paris caters to a parade of company heads, politicians and leading lights in show business, along with many who have saved up for the opportunity to sample specialities of the house such as his seared bluefin tuna blanketed with dried cherries, served on a bed of fresh snap peas and washed over with a fennel ginger sauce. In early 2002, when the *Red Guide* finally bestowed a third Michelin star upon his restaurant, this tenacious, jovial, 'epicurean of the heart' broke down and cried.

▲ VEGETABLE POTÉE AND BEETROOT AND BLACK TRUFFLE MILLE FEUILLE WITH FOIE GRAS SAUCE Serves 4

INGREDIENTS

Vegetable Potée
12 young carrots, peeled; 12 young turnips, peeled;
4 Savoy cabbage leaves;
½ head broccoli, cut into florets; 4 young leeks;
200 g/7 oz celeriac, cut into diamond-shaped pieces;
100 g/3½ oz/1 cup snow peas;
100 g/3½ oz/½ cup haricot beans

Foie Gras Sauce
50 g/1¾ oz foie gras; 50 g/1¾ oz butter;
100 ml/3⅜ fl oz/⅜ cup chicken stock
(recipe on page 148); 4 tsp truffle juice;
salt; freshly ground black pepper

Beetroot and Black Truffle Mille Feuille
1 litre/2 pts 1⅞ fl oz/4¼ cups groundnut oil;
1 beetroot;
100 g/3½ oz/⅔ cup plain flour;
salt; 200 g/7 oz black truffles;
12 sea salt crystals

Finishing
30 g/1 oz butter; salt; freshly ground black pepper

PREPARATION

Cook all the vegetables and pulses separately in salted boiling water.
Refresh them in iced water immediately.
Drain off excess water and set aside.

Mix the foie gras and butter.
Combine the chicken stock and truffle juice in a small pot and reduce over medium heat for 5 minutes.
Add the foie gras mixture and mix well. Season to taste with salt and freshly ground black pepper.
Pass the mixture through a fine-mesh sieve to remove any lumps. Set aside.

Preheat the groundnut oil in a deep-fryer until it reaches 180°C (356°F).
Peel the beetroot and cut it into paper-thin slices. Dust both sides of the beetroot with plain flour and deep-fry in the groundnut oil for 30 seconds until crispy. Remove them from the hot oil with a strainer and place on a plate lined with kitchen tissue to absorb the excess oil. Season the crispy beetroot to taste with salt.
Slice the black truffles thinly and set 12 slices aside.
Cut the remaining slices into 0.5-by-0.5-cm (0.2-by-0.2-inch) diamond-shaped pieces for garnishing.
To prepare a mille feuille, sandwich 1 slice of black truffle and 1 sea salt crystal between 2 beetroot crisps.

PRESENTATION

Warm the vegetable potée and mix in some butter. Season to taste with salt and freshly ground black pepper.
Divide the mille feuille among 4 plates and arrange the vegetables around.
Spoon the foie gras sauce over the vegetables and garnish with the diamond-shaped black truffles to serve.

▼ MILK-FED LAMB LEG, VEGETABLE CASSEROLE, SPINACH AND SAUTÉED LAMB NECK *Serves 4*

INGREDIENTS

Sautéed Lamb Neck
Butter; 1 milk-fed lamb neck, sliced;
600 g/1 lb 5⅛ oz spinach, stems removed;
1 clove garlic, minced;
salt; freshly ground black pepper

Vegetable Casserole
1 Swiss chard, peeled; juice from ½ lemon;
1 carrot, peeled; ½ stick celery, peeled;
400 g/14⅛ oz Ratte potatoes, peeled;
butter; 1 shallot, peeled and sliced;
salt; freshly ground black pepper

Milk-fed Lamb Leg
2 (700 to 800 g/1 lb 8⅝ to 1 lb 12¼ oz each) milk-fed lamb legs (those from Pyrénées preferred);
salt; freshly ground black pepper; butter

Garnish
1 sprig fresh thyme

PREPARATION

Heat the butter in a pan until it is golden brown in colour and gives off a nutty smell. Pan-fry the lamb neck slices on both sides until they turn brown in colour. Add enough water to cover the meat and cook over low heat until the meat softens.
Wash the spinach under cold running water, then blanch it in salted boiling water for a few seconds. Refresh it in iced water immediately and drain off the excess water.
Shred the cooked lamb neck, then heat some butter in a pan until it is golden brown in colour and gives off a nutty smell. Sauté the shredded lamb neck until crispy, then add the blanched spinach and minced garlic and toss well. Season to taste with salt and freshly ground black pepper.

Cut the peeled Swiss chard into 4-by-1-cm (1.6-by-0.4-inch) sticks.
Soak them in cold water spritzed with the lemon juice. Dice the peeled carrot and celery finely.
Wash the Ratte potatoes, then cut them into 0.5-cm- (0.2-inch-) thick slices.
Melt some butter in a pot until it is golden brown in colour and gives off a nutty smell.
Add the Swiss chard sticks, carrot and celery cubes, and Ratte potato and shallot slices, and sauté until the vegetables soften. Season to taste with salt and freshly ground black pepper. Add the lamb neck's cooking juices, lower the heat and cover the pot. Simmer for 15 to 20 minutes until the potato is tender but still firm.

Preheat the oven at 180°C (356°F). Season the lamb legs with salt and freshly ground black pepper.
Melt some butter in a pan until it is golden brown in colour and gives off a nutty smell, then sear all sides of the lamb legs. Place the seared lamb legs on a roasting pan and roast them in the oven for 14 to 15 minutes. Remove the lamb legs from the heat and keep warm until required. Discard the fat on the pan and pour the remaining lamb neck's cooking juices onto the pan. Return it to the oven to simmer for a few minutes, then season the sauce to taste with salt and freshly ground black pepper.
Pass the liquid through a fine-mesh sieve and keep warm until required.

PRESENTATION

Place the lamb legs on a wooden cutting board.
Serve the sautéed lamb neck and spinach, and vegetable casserole on separate platters.
Garnish the vegetable casserole with the thyme leaves. Serve the lamb sauce separately on the side.

BELOW: Besides a three-Michelin-star restaurant, Residenz Heinz Winkler, located near the Chiemsee, also offers luxurious accommodation for tourists visiting Aschau.
LEFT: Heinz Winkler and his crew of 20 in their spacious, state-of-the-art kitchen.

Residenz Heinz Winkler
Aschau

Heinz Winkler

Heinz Winkler was voted Germany's 'Chef of the Year' for two consecutive years while running the kitchen at the highly regarded Tantris restaurant in Munich. At the age of 31, he became the youngest three-Michelin-star chef in the world. Quite a feather in his toque, and it only gets better. He has also compiled a powerful portfolio of guests. John D. Rockefeller, Queen Sofia and King Juan Carlos of Spain, Gianni Agnelli, Helmut Kohl, Riccardo Muti, Lorin Maazel and Jean Paul Belmondo are but some names on the list of luminaries he's fed. And he's found the time to write eight successful cookbooks.

Winkler is a chef whose stature has risen steadily over the years; he has gained considerable recognition for his contributions to gastronomy. Yet he thanks Paul Bocuse for being his muse and inspiring him to do great things. Although he has cooked in kitchens in Switzerland, Spain, Italy and France, these days he prefers to pamper his guests at his own Residenz Heinz Winkler. Nestling in idyllic Aschau, less than an hour's drive from Munich, Kitzbühel and Salzburg, his charming establishment, a member of Relais & Châteaux which has under its umbrella Europe's most exclusive hotels and restaurants, was once again, presented with three stars by Michelin's *Red Guide* in 1999.

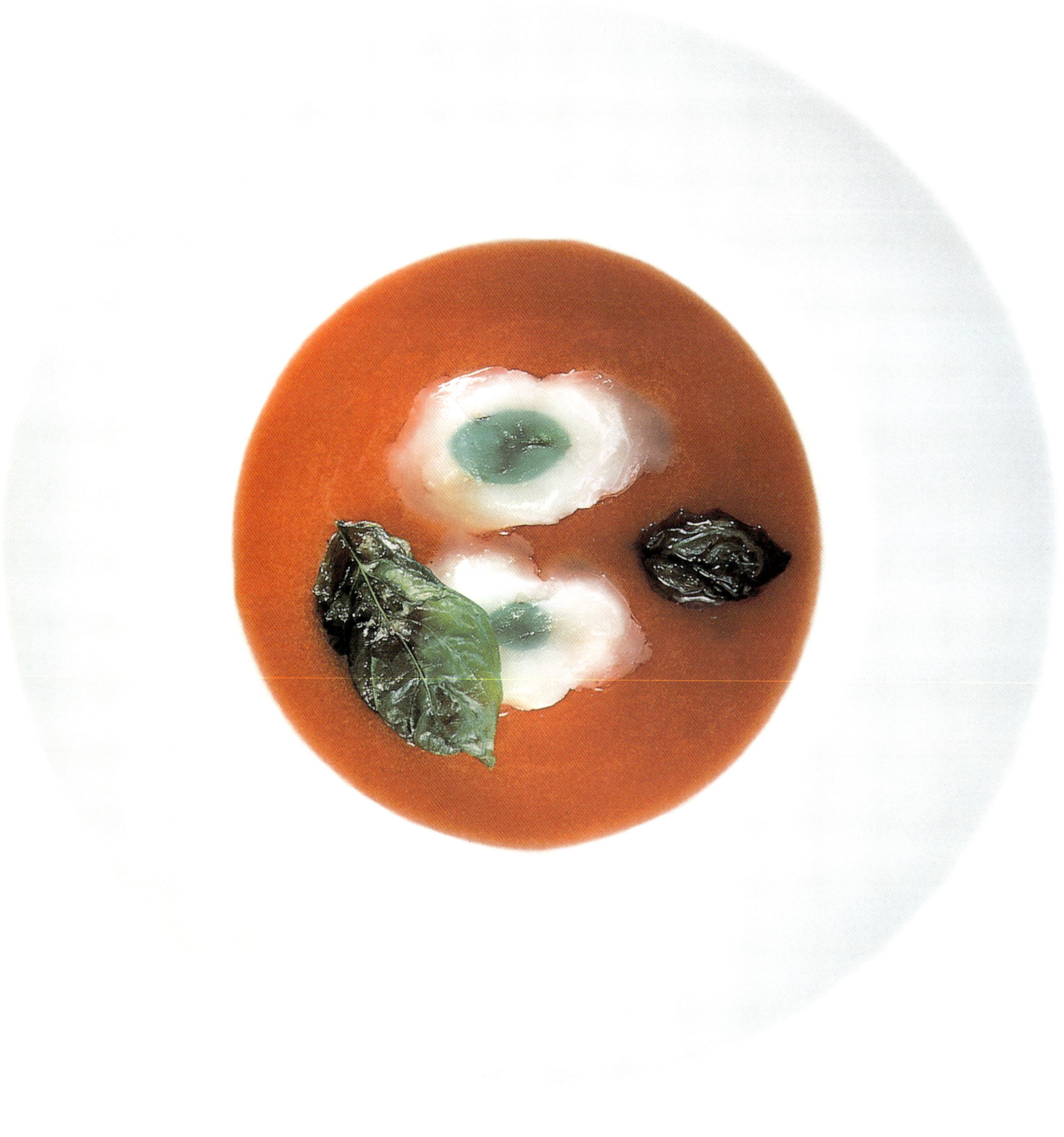

PARFAIT OF SMOKED SALMON AND TOMATO JELLY WITH CUCUMBER SAUCE Serves 4

INGREDIENTS

Tomato Jelly
- 600 g/1 lb 5⅛ oz ripe tomatoes;
- 200 ml/6¾ fl oz/⅞ cup fish stock (recipe on page 148); 3 egg whites;
- 1 small piece leek, finely chopped;
- ½ tbsp Pernod; 1 tbsp tarragon vinegar;
- 5 sheets gelatine, soaked in water and squeezed dry

Parfait of Smoked Salmon
- 300 g/10½ oz smoked salmon, diced;
- 50 g/1¾ oz carrots, diced;
- 50 g/1¾ oz leek, diced;
- 50 g/1¾ oz zucchini, diced;
- 50 g/1¾ oz butter;
- 300 ml/10⅛ fl oz/1¼ cups fish stock (recipe on page 148);
- 1 tbsp reduced Noilly Prat;
- 1 tbsp dry white wine; 1 egg yolk;
- 4 sheets gelatine, soaked in water and squeezed dry;
- salt; freshly ground black pepper;
- 20 g/¾ oz dill, chopped finely

Cucumber Sauce
- 1 cucumber; a pinch of cornflour;
- 1 tbsp olive oil;
- salt; freshly ground black pepper; sugar

Garnish
- 100 ml/3⅜ fl oz/⅜ cup whipped cream;
- Keta caviar; chervil leaves

PREPARATION

Cut the tomatoes into small pieces and process in a blender to obtain a smooth purée. Pass this through a fine-mesh sieve. Mix the purée with the fish stock and egg whites. Bring the chopped leek, Pernod and tarragon vinegar to the boil in a saucepan. After 5 minutes, pass the mixture through a muslin strainer and add the soaked gelatine. Mix well.

Keep 100 g/3½ oz of the smoked salmon cubes and all the carrots, leek and zucchini cubes refrigerated. When they are cool, blanch each ingredient separately in boiling water and strain. Warm the butter in a saucepan until it starts to foam, then sauté the remaining smoked salmon cubes until they turn light brown in colour. Remove from the heat and use a strainer to remove the salmon to a plate lined with kitchen tissue to absorb the excess butter. Add the fish stock to the butter in the saucepan and bring to the boil. Add the Noilly Prat and white wine, followed by the sautéed salmon. Mix well and process this mixture in a blender to obtain a smooth purée. Pass this through a fine-mesh sieve. Add the egg yolk and slowly whisk the mixture in a bain-marie (place the mixing bowl over a bigger basin of hot water so that indirect heat is applied on the mixture while you whisk). Add the soaked gelatine and more Noilly Prat, white wine, salt and freshly ground black pepper if necessary. When the gelatine has dissolved completely, remove the mixing bowl from the bain-marie and keep stirring the mixture until it is cool. Add the blanched salmon and vegetable cubes, and chopped dill and mix well. Pour the mixture into a large, flat-based dish and refrigerate.

Peel the cucumber, cut into 3 pieces, length-wise, and remove the pips. Process 2 pieces of cucumber in a blender to obtain a smooth purée, then bring it to the boil. Mix in the cornflour and allow to cool. Dice the remaining piece of cucumber and sauté it in the olive oil until it turns light brown in colour. Add the sautéed cucumber to the purée and stir the mixture, placing the mixing bowl on a basin of ice cubes, until it is smooth and cool. Season to taste with salt, pepper and sugar.

PRESENTATION

Divide the cucumber purée among 4 plates. Use a ring cutter to cut the salmon parfait into 4 circles and place each circle on a portion of cucumber purée. Glaze the parfait with some tomato jelly. Garnish with whipped cream, Keta caviar and chervil leaves as shown.

CHILLED TOMATO SOUP WITH DEVILFISH MEDALLIONS Serves 4

INGREDIENTS

Cold-stirred Tomato Soup
- 1 kg/2 lb 3¼ oz Roma tomatoes, quartered;
- a dash of red wine vinegar; 2 tbsp olive oil;
- 10 basil leaves; a dash of Noilly Prat; salt;
- freshly ground white pepper; a pinch of sugar

Medallions of Devilfish
- 40 g/1⅜ oz devilfish; 4 basil leaves

Garnish
- 8 deep-fried basil leaves

PREPARATION

Process the tomatoes in a blender to obtain a smooth purée. Pass the purée through a fine-mesh sieve. Add the red wine vinegar (taking care not to add too much because the tomatoes are already acidic), olive oil, basil leaves and Noilly Prat to the tomato purée. Mix well and season to taste with salt, freshly ground white pepper and sugar.
Chill the tomato soup for at least 1 hour before serving.

Slice the devilfish into 4 medallions and place a basil leaf on top of each slice.
Steam for 10 minutes until the fish is cooked.

PRESENTATION

Pour the chilled tomato soup into 4 cold plates and place a devilfish medallion on each plate.
Garnish with the deep-fried basil leaves to serve.

La Bastide Saint-Antoine
Grasse

RIGHT: The two-Michelin-star La Bastide Saint-Antoine is also a member of Relais & Châteaux, a prestigious association made up of Europe's most acclaimed restaurants and luxurious boutique hotels.

BELOW: La Bastide Saint-Antoine is in Grasse, the 'perfume capital of the world'. Here the precious May Rose is grown exclusively for Chanel's signature No. 5 perfume.

Jacques Chibois

Jacques Chibois enrolled for agricultural studies when he was a young man, but was persuaded by his family to take up an apprenticeship in a restaurant in Limoges, his native city. This decisive experience inspired a countrywide tour in the early seventies that brought him into contact with many famous French chefs. After spending a year each in the kitchens of Jean Delaveyne, Roger Vergé and Louis Outhier, Chibois was noticed by Michel Guérard, and began a five-year apprenticeship at Les Prés d'Eugénie—a period which shaped his professional career significantly. In 1996, Chibois took over an old manor house in the Grasse countryside and launched La Bastide Saint-Antoine.

Chibois' menu can be described as soft and sensitive, in harmony with the colours, flavours and lifestyle of the area. His signature dishes include bass with lemon and verbena, which combines fish, eggplant, olive oil, verbena, basil and zucchini to create rich, tangy flavours; and langoustines served with crunchy spears of purple asparagus. Drawing inspiration from the traditions of Provence, Chibois composes poetry in his spare time and also co-authored *Olive Oil*, a cookbook detailing the benefits and versatility of this staple ingredient, with connoisseur and olive oil producer Olivier Baussan. Madame Chibois helps run an adjoining luxury hotel for diners wishing to spend the night and perhaps take in more of Chibois' cuisine the next day.

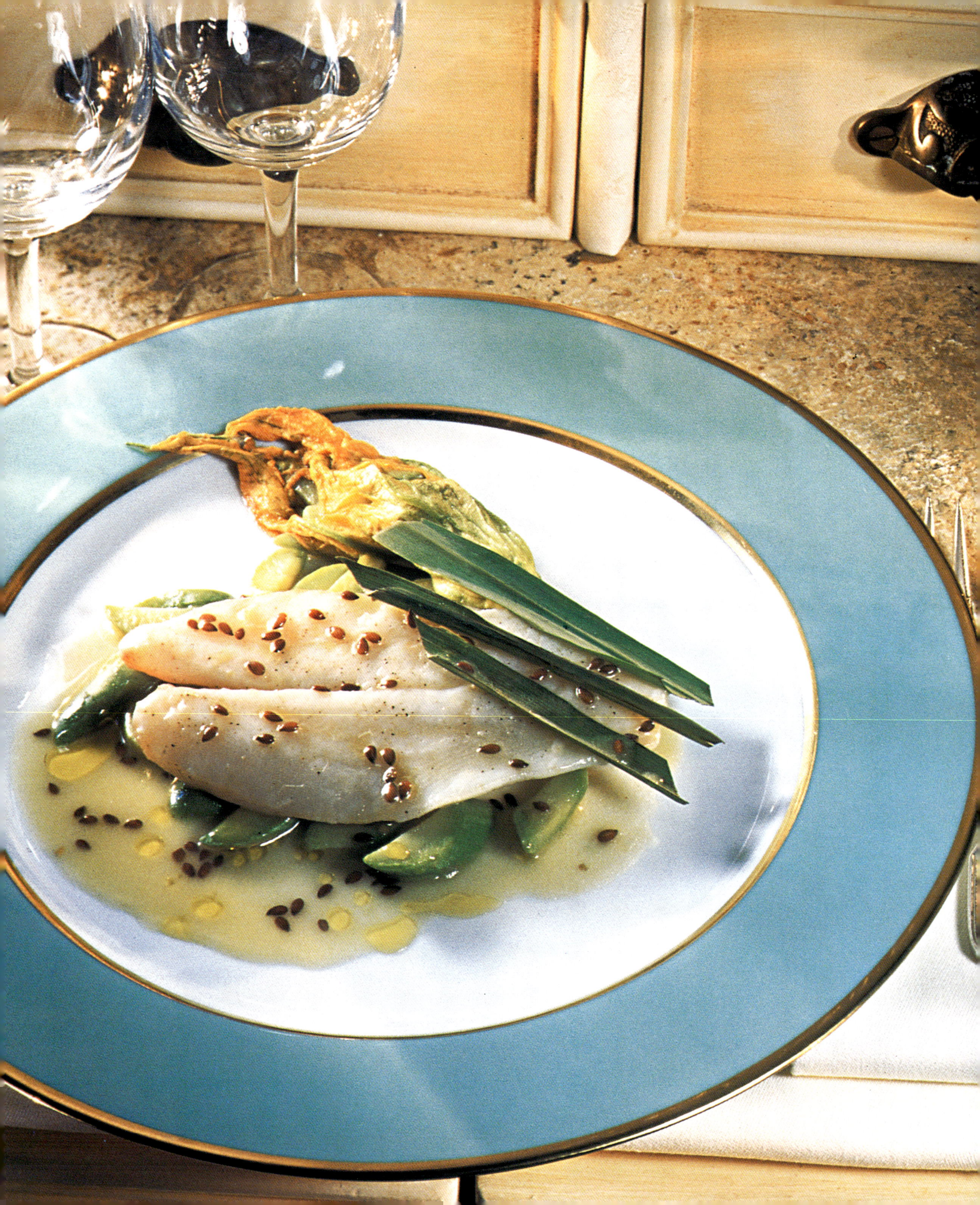

◄ JOHN DORY AND NIÇOISE ZUCCHINI WITH CITRONELLE AND LINSEED SAUCE — Serves 4

INGREDIENTS

Niçoise Zucchini
1 tsp linseeds; 200 ml/6¾ fl oz/⅞ cup water;
250 g/8⅞ oz zucchini; 10 g/⅜ oz butter;
1 tbsp olive oil; zest from 1 lemon, grated;
1 tbsp chopped dill;
salt; freshly ground black pepper

Citronelle Sauce
3 tbsp vermouth (Noilly Prat);
1 tbsp dry white wine; 1 tbsp chopped shallots;
15 g/½ oz citronelle with stalk, chopped
(use kaffir lime leaves if unavailable);
200 ml/6¾ fl oz/⅞ cup whipping cream;
100 ml/3⅜ fl oz/⅜ cup olive oil;
lemon juice; salt; freshly ground black pepper;
50 g/1¾ oz butter, cut into cubes

John Dory
25 g/⅞ oz citronelle with stalk,
cut into 8- to 10-cm (3.2- to 4-inch) pieces;
4 zucchini flowers, halved;
4 John Dory fillets, skin removed;
salt; freshly ground black pepper

Garnish
A few citronelle leaves;
lemon juice;
extra virgin olive oil

PREPARATION

Soak the linseeds in the water for 1 hour, then rinse them and set aside.
Cut the zucchini lengthwise into 4, then cut into diamond-shaped pieces.
Sauté the zucchini pieces in the butter and olive oil until they are slightly soft.
Add the grated lemon zest and chopped dill, and season to taste with salt and freshly ground black pepper.
Keep cooking for another 4 to 5 minutes, then add the soaked linseeds and toss well. Set aside.

Pour the vermouth and white wine in a small pot and add the chopped shallots and citronelle.
Bring to the boil, lower the heat to a simmer and reduce the mixture to a quarter of its original amount.
Add the whipping cream and olive oil, and mix well.
Season to taste with lemon juice, salt and freshly ground black pepper.
Whisk in the cold butter cubes gently, then pass the mixture through a muslin strainer.
Keep warm until required.

Pour some water into a non-stick pan and add the citronelle and zucchini flowers.
Season the John Dory fillets to taste with salt and freshly ground black pepper.
Arrange them on top of the citronelle, then put the lid on.
Cook the John Dory over low heat for a few minutes on each side.
Keep warm until required.

PRESENTATION

Divide the Niçoise zucchini among 4 plates. Reserve the liquid for the sauce.
Place the John Dory fillets on top of the zucchini and spritz a little lemon juice on the fish. Arrange 2 halves of a zucchini flower on the side.
Add the liquid from the Niçoise zucchini to the citronelle sauce, mix well, then spoon the sauce over the John Dory fillets. Garnish with citronelle leaves and a few drops of extra virgin olive oil to serve.

▼ MELON AND TOMATOES WITH LEMON AND OLIVE OIL EMULSION AND POPPY SEEDS — Serves 4

INGREDIENTS

Melon and Tomatoes
3 small sweet melons;
6 ripe tomatoes;
salt; freshly ground black pepper;
olive oil

Lemon and Olive Oil Emulsion
200 ml/6¾ fl oz/⅞ cup olive oil; juice from ½ lemon;
salt; freshly ground black pepper

Garnish
1 tsp poppy seeds;
8 basil leaves, cut into thin strips

PREPARATION

Remove the melon skin and cut each melon into half. Remove the seeds and cut the melon lengthwise into 16 slices, each about 0.4-cm (0.16-inch) thick. Cut the remaining melon into 1-cm (0.4-inch) cubes.
Keep refrigerated until required.
Blanch the tomatoes for a few seconds in boiling water, then refresh in iced water immediately.
Peel off the skin and cut each tomato into half, lengthwise. Remove the seeds and cut into 12 'petals', each about 4 cm (1.6 inches) wide. Dice the remaining tomatoes. Keep refrigerated until required.
Season the melon slices and tomato petals with salt and freshly ground black pepper. Sauté the melon slices in some olive oil for 30 seconds. Remove from the heat and transfer the melon slices onto a plate to cool.
Sauté the tomato petals in some olive oil for 30 seconds. Remove from the heat and set aside to cool.
When cool, keep both refrigerated until required.

Mix the olive oil and lemon juice, then season to taste with salt and freshly ground black pepper.

PRESENTATION

Divide half the melon and tomato cubes among 4 plates. Cover each portion with 3 tomato petals, arranged to resemble a flower. Place 4 slices of melon around each flower and spoon the remaining melon and tomato over. Sprinkle the poppy seeds and sliced basil leaves over, then drizzle the lemon and olive oil emulsion around to serve.

Le Jardin Des Sens
Montpellier

ABOVE: Le Jardin Des Sens (garden of the senses), Montpellier's three-Michelin-star restaurant, is an environment created to stimulate the senses.
ABOVE RIGHT: The brothers Pourcel, adept at blending the rustic and refined, highlight the flavours of Provence and the Mediterranean in their cuisine.
RIGHT: Designed by architect Bruno Borrione, the main dining room overlooks five Japanese gardens, each representing a different sense.

Jacques and Laurent Pourcel

Jacques and Laurent Pourcel are more like two halves of the same person than two individuals. Although they were identical at birth, by divine intervention one has a penchant for working with fish and making pastries, while the other has found his métier in meats and appetisers. When the twins met sommelier Olivier Chateau, both food and wine were to receive the respect they deserved at Le Jardin des Sens, the brothers' restaurant in Montpellier. Even the fussiest diners were addicted to the brothers' gift for blending rustic and refined tastes, returning again and again to Montpellier. The year the twins turned 30, Michelin's inspectors rewarded their efforts with three stars in the *Red Guide*.

These days, Parisians seeking a taste of the Pourcels' genius can head for the Théâtre des Champs-Elysées and the blazingly white, rooftop restaurant Maison Blanche. The brothers haven't forsaken Montpellier, but happily travel between the two establishments. Maison Blanche offers a stunning city view along with your plate of tiny penne, fresh clams and al dente fava beans, topped with aged Parmesan and a sublime pistou sauce. The setting of Le Jardin des Sens in Montpellier is more homely, with soothing moat and charming outdoor garden terrace to accompany Pourcel signatures such as white-truffle bouillon sprinkled with fresh truffles and nuts, and pineapple ravioli with raspberries.

PINEAPPLE RAVIOLI WITH RASPBERRIES Serves 4

INGREDIENTS

Verbena Sorbet

Juice from 6 lemons; 400 g/14$\frac{1}{8}$ oz/ 2 cups sugar; 400 ml/13$\frac{1}{2}$ fl oz/1$\frac{2}{3}$ cups water; 60 g/2 oz verbena; 2 egg whites; 300 ml/10$\frac{1}{8}$ fl oz/1$\frac{1}{4}$ cups Perrier

Crystallised Pineapple

1 ripe pineapple; 300 g/10$\frac{1}{2}$ oz/1$\frac{1}{2}$ cups sugar; 1 litre/2 pts 1$\frac{7}{8}$ fl oz/4$\frac{1}{4}$ cups water

Vanilla Syrup

1 vanilla pod; 300 ml/10$\frac{1}{8}$ fl oz/1$\frac{1}{4}$ cups pineapple syrup (from macerating the pineapples); 20 g/$\frac{3}{4}$ oz/scant $\frac{1}{8}$ cup potato flour

Raviolis

1 ripe pineapple; 600 g/1 lb 5$\frac{1}{8}$ oz/3 cups sugar; 1 litre/2 pts 1$\frac{7}{8}$ fl oz/4$\frac{1}{4}$ cups water; 400 g/14$\frac{1}{8}$ oz/scant 3 cups raspberries; 100 ml/3$\frac{3}{8}$ fl oz/$\frac{1}{3}$ cup strawberry coulis

Garnish

Mint leaves

PREPARATION

Bring the lemon juice, sugar and water to the boil.
Add the verbena and infuse until the mixture cools to room temperature. Strain.
Add the egg whites and Perrier to the liquid. Mix well and strain again.
Process the liquid in an ice cream maker set to sorbet specifications.
When ready, keep the sorbet frozen until required.

Preheat the oven at 70°C (158°F).
Peel the pineapple and remove the 'eyes'. Slice it thinly (using a slicing machine if available).
Bring the sugar and water to the boil. Remove from the heat and set aside to cool.
Macerate the pineapple slices in the syrup for 3 hours. Arrange the pineapple slices on a non-stick baking tray and let them dry slowly in the oven for 3 hours. Reserve the pineapple syrup for preparing the vanilla syrup.

Cut the vanilla pod into half lengthwise and scrape out the seeds.
Add the seeds to the pineapple syrup and bring to the boil.
Add a little cold water to the potato flour and mix well. Pour this into the hot syrup and stir gently until it reaches a smooth consistency. Set aside to cool and keep refrigerated until required.

Peel the pineapple and remove the 'eyes'. Slice it thinly, allocating 6 slices to 1 guest.
Bring the sugar and water to the boil, then set it aside to cool to room temperature before refrigerating.
Macerate the pineapple slices in the syrup for 2 hours. Mix the raspberries and strawberry coulis.
Place some raspberries in the centre of a pineapple slice, then top it with another.
Press a round cookie cutter down into the pineapple 'sandwich' to make a ravioli.
Prepare 11 more raviolis with the remaining ingredients. Keep refrigerated until required.

PRESENTATION

Prepare 4 plates and arrange 3 raviolis on each plate. Top each portion with a scoop of verbena sorbet.
Garnish the sorbet with a few crystallised pineapples as shown.
Drizzle the vanilla syrup on the raviolis and garnish with the mint leaves to serve.

PAN-FRIED FILLET OF SOLE WITH SAFFRON-SHELLFISH FRICASSEE Serves 4

INGREDIENTS

Snow Peas and Fava Beans

150 g/5$\frac{1}{4}$ oz/1$\frac{1}{2}$ cups snow peas; 300 g/10$\frac{1}{2}$ oz/2$\frac{1}{2}$ cups fava beans

Pan-fried Fillet of Sole

3 (600 g/1 lb 5$\frac{1}{8}$ oz each) Dover soles; butter; 50 ml/1$\frac{3}{4}$ fl oz/$\frac{1}{4}$ cup olive oil

Saffron-Shellfish Fricassee

3 big shallots; 100 ml/3$\frac{3}{8}$ fl oz/$\frac{3}{8}$ cups dry white wine; 15 strands of saffron; salt; 8 oysters; 32 clams; 32 mussels; 80 g/2$\frac{7}{8}$ cold butter; 1 tbsp olive oil; 2 tomatoes, peeled, seeds removed and diced; 1 tbsp chopped chives; juice from $\frac{1}{2}$ lemon; freshly ground black pepper

PREPARATION

Remove the stalks and veins from the snow peas and fava beans.
Cook them separately in salted boiling water and refresh both with iced water immediately.
Strain and keep refrigerated until required.

Debone the Dover soles and remove the skin. Cut into 12 fillets and keep refrigerated until required.
Just before serving, pan-fry the fillets in some butter and olive oil for about 1 minute (or more if the fillet is thick) on each side until the fish is cooked.

Preheat the oven at 140°C (284°F).
Peel the shallots and slice 2 of them into rings. Combine them in a pot with white wine, 4 strands of saffron, and some water and salt. Reduce over medium heat until dry, then set aside to cool.
Scrub the oysters, clams and mussels under running water, making sure that all the filaments and parasites attached to the mussels are removed.
Arrange the oysters on a baking tray and bake them for 7 to 8 minutes until they are cooked.
In the meantime, slice the last shallot and add it, together with the remaining saffron strands, to another pot.
Add the clams and mussels and cover them with water and bring the mixture to the boil for 1 minute.
Remove from the heat. At this stage, the clams and mussels should not be cooked.
Set 8 clams and 8 mussels (with shells intact) aside for garnishing.
Discard the remaining shells and set the flesh aside.
Remove the oysters from the oven. Remove the top shell of 4 oysters and set these oysters, still in their bottom shell, aside for garnishing. Remove the remaining oyster flesh from their shells and set aside.
Strain the oyster juices into a bowl.
Mix the oyster juice into the wine-and-saffron mixture. Add the cold butter, olive oil, diced tomatoes, chopped chives and lemon juice and mix well. Season to taste with salt and freshly ground black pepper.

PRESENTATION

Divide all the shellfish (those with shells and without), snow peas and fava beans among 4 plates.
Spoon the saffron-shellfish fricassee and shallot rings over and arrange the sole fillets carefully in the centre.
Drizzle some olive oil over to serve.

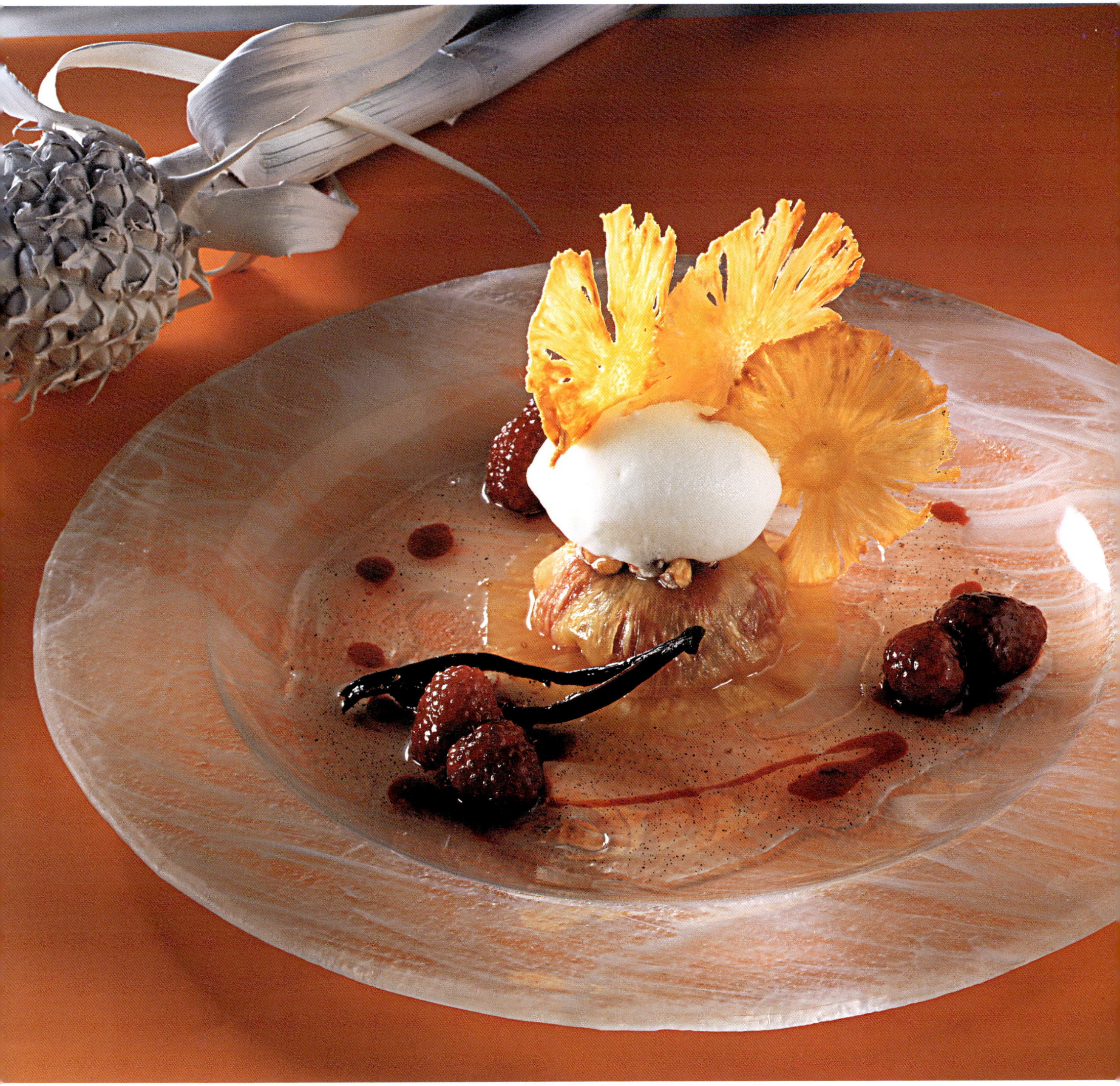

LEFT: The sleek reception area at Jean Georges, with a soothing taupe, ecru and silver colour scheme.
EXTREME LEFT: Modern art aficionados will find pleasure on the walls as well as on their plates.
ABOVE: Jean Georges' main dining room is decorated from floor to ceiling with etched glass and geometric motifs.

Jean Georges
New York

Jean-Georges Vongerichten

Awards paper his walls, his scrapbooks bulge with gushing reviews from every respected food critic on the planet, and his outstanding restaurants dot the globe. Yet, he once mused, 'Nothing would make me happier than working behind the counter of a cosy little joint where I would personally cook every dish for a small but loyal clientele.' They couldn't believe that when he was making a name for himself in someone else's kitchen; and they certainly can't believe it now. His restaurants have become legends for their eloquent gastronomy, impeccable service and stylish surroundings.

Jean Georges, his eponymous temple to haute cuisine across from Central Park, is in a hushed, sanctified class all by itself. His successful trio of Vongs is a sleek testament to his French-Thai fusion philosophy which set the culinary community afire years ago. The plush Prime Steakhouse packs in Vegas high rollers nightly. The brick, brash Mercer Kitchen in lower Manhattan feeds the city's young and savvy. Paradise Island's Dune is another kettle of fish altogether. The common thread? Exquisite mouthfuls from start to finish.

His fused oils and vinegars sell well at Williams-Sonoma. His cookbooks fly off the shelves. Following a sucessful new bistro in Paris are plans for a spice shop in Manhattan and a cosy hotel in Greenwich Village. All this from a modest, soft-spoken, forty-something chef from Alsace who simply took a brainwave—substituting healthy vegetables and fruit juices for oil and butter—and ran with it.

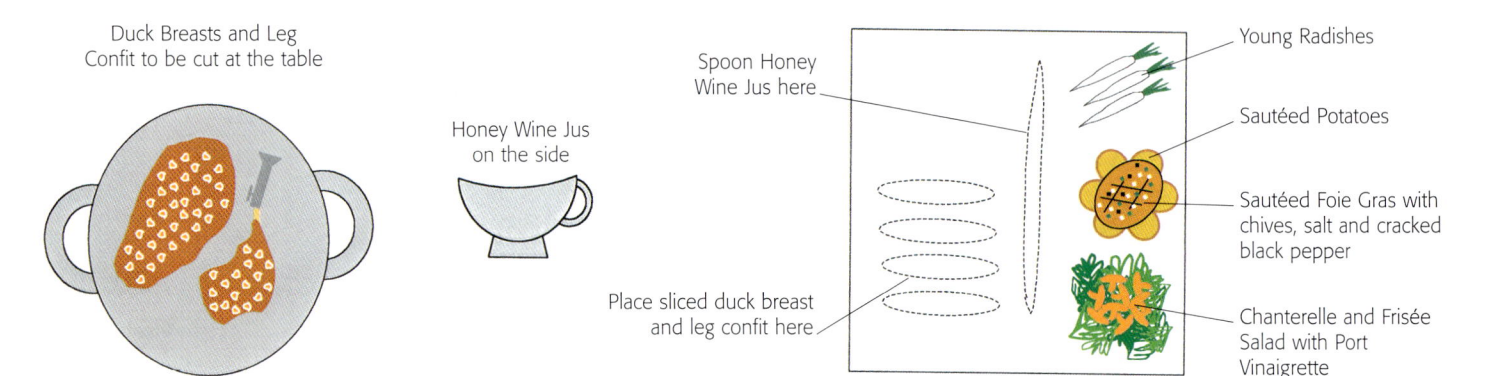

▲ DUCK BREAST AND LEG CONFIT TOPPED WITH CRACKED JORDAN ALMONDS, YOUNG RADISHES, SAUTÉED FOIE GRAS AND HONEY WINE JUS   Serves 4

INGREDIENTS

Duck Jus
Necks, wings, backs and gizzards from 2 ducks; oil; 1 carrot, chopped; 1 onion, chopped; 240 ml/8⅛ fl oz/1 cup water; 240 ml/8⅛ fl oz/1 cup chicken stock (recipe on page 148)

Leg Confit
4 duck legs; 2 tbsp salt; ½ tbsp black peppercorns; 4 sprigs thyme; 1 sprig rosemary; 2 cloves garlic, crushed; duck fat

Duck Breast
4 duck breasts; salt; pepper; 8 tbsp cracked Jordan almonds

Honey Wine Jus
50 ml/1¾ fl oz/¼ cup white port; 100 ml/3⅜ fl oz/⅜ cup honey wine; ½ tsp chestnut honey; juice from 1 lemon; 1 tbsp butter; salt; pepper

Port Vinaigrette
2 tbsp sherry vinegar; 2 tbsp white port; 1 tbsp hazelnut oil; 3 tbsp walnut oil; 2 tbsp grapeseed oil; salt; pepper

Chanterelle and Frisée Salad
420 g/14⅞ g/2 cups young chanterelles; 1 shallot, chopped; butter; 2 tbsp parsley chifonnade; 50 g/1¾ oz/2 cups white frisée

Sautéed Foie Gras
4 slices (30 g/1 oz each) foie gras; oil; salt; pepper

Sautéed Potatoes
2 sprigs fresh thyme; 2 cloves garlic, peeled and crushed; salt; 455 g/1 lb Ratte potatoes, unpeeled; butter

Garnish
12 young radishes (or turnips) with tops, blanched; butter; salt; pepper; cracked black pepper; chives

PREPARATION

Chop the duck parts and brown them in a roasting pan with some oil.
Add the chopped carrot and onion and roast until they are lightly caramelised.
Add the water and chicken stock and bring to the boil.
Lower the heat and simmer for 1 hour 30 minutes, then strain the stock.
Discard the solid ingredients and reduce the stock to a light jus consistency.

Marinate the duck legs in salt, black peppercorns, thyme, rosemary and crushed garlic for 24 hours.
Place the legs in a pot and cover them with duck fat. Simmer over low heat for 2 hours until the meat is tender. Remove from the heat and set aside to cool. When cool, remove the thigh bones, but keep the leg bones intact. Trim the meat and keep them in the duck fat until required.

Season the duck breasts with salt and pepper. Sauté them, skin side facing downwards, until the skin turns crispy and golden brown in colour. Flip the breasts over and cook to just below desired temperature because they will cook more when the almonds are caramelised. Coat the duck breasts with the cracked almonds and caramelise them under high heat (under the salamander or in an oven), taking care not to burn them.

Combine the white port, honey wine, chestnut honey and lemon juice in a saucepan and mix well.
Reduce the mixture over low heat until about 50 ml/1¾ fl oz/¼ cup remains.
Add 100 ml/3⅜ fl oz/⅜ cup of duck jus and the butter and mix well.
Season to taste with salt and pepper.
Add lemon juice to taste.

Combine the sherry vinegar, white port and oils in a bowl and mix well.
Season to taste with salt and pepper.

Sauté the young chanterelles and chopped shallots in some butter.
When the chanterelles are cooked, add the shredded parsley and toss well.
Just before serving, toss the white frisée in the port vinaigrette.

Pan-fry the foie gras in some oil until they are crispy and golden brown in colour on both sides.
Season to taste with salt and pepper.

Add the thyme, crushed garlic and some salt to a pot of water and bring to the boil.
Cook the Ratte potatoes in the boiling water until they are almost done. Remove and set aside.
Just before serving, peel and cut them into 0.5-cm- (0.2-inch-) thick slices.
Quickly sauté them in some butter.

PRESENTATION

Reheat the young radishes (or turnips) in boiling water containing some butter, salt and pepper.
Arrange the duck breasts and leg confit on a carving dish. Pour the honey wine jus into a sauceboat.
Arrange the young radishes (or turnips) in the top right corners of 4 square plates and the sautéed potatoes just below. Place the sautéed foie gras on the potatoes and garnish with chives, salt and cracked black pepper. Arrange the tossed white frisée in the bottom corners and top with the sautéed chanterelles.
Carve the duck breasts and leg confit in front of your guests and place the slices on the empty half of each plate. Spoon the honey wine jus on the side as shown.

▼ SPICE ISLAND LOBSTER, SALSIFY PURÉE AND FIG-DATE CHUTNEY Serves 4

INGREDIENTS

Spice Island Lobster
455 g/1 lb fresh or dried seaweed such as konbu;
6 (680 g/1 lb 8 oz each) lobsters;
salt; cayenne pepper; butter

Spice Mix
1 tsp allspice powder; 2 nutmegs;
seeds from 1 vanilla pod

Spice Oil
500 ml/1 pt 1 fl oz/2⅛ cups grapeseed oil;
2 tbsp annatto seeds

Lobster Broth
50 g/1¾ oz ginger, chopped;
20 g/⅝ oz galangal, chopped; butter;
200 ml/6¾ fl oz/⅞ cup chicken stock (recipe on page 148);
200 ml/6¾ fl oz/⅞ cup lobster stock (recipe on page 148);
1 lemongrass, sliced; 1 tbsp tamarind paste;
seeds from 2.5-cm (1-inch) vanilla pod;
120 g/4 oz basil leaves; 2 tbsp butter;
2 tbsp lobster roe; 4 tbsp salted butter;
salt; cayenne pepper; lime juice

Salsify Purée
260 g/9⅛ oz salsify;
lemon water (for every 500 ml/1 pt 1 fl oz/2⅛ cups of water, add the juice from ½ lemon);
2 cloves garlic; 1 sprig rosemary; 2 sprigs thyme

Fig-Date Chutney
1 lime, peeled; 4 dried dates, finely diced;
3 dried figs, finely diced;
a pinch of five-spice powder

Garnish
Young lettuce salad

PREPARATION

Add the seaweed to a pot of water and bring to the boil. Cook the lobsters whole in the boiling water for 2 minutes, then refresh them with cold water. Remove the tails and claws, then cook the lobster bodies in the boiling water for another 5 minutes. Refresh them with cold water again. Cut the lobsters' belly shells with a pair of scissors and remove the shells as shown. Cut each lobster body into 3 medallions. Set aside. Reserve the lobster roe for preparing the lobster broth. Just before serving, season the lobster medallions and claws to taste with salt and cayenne pepper and sauté in some butter.

Grind the spices to a powdered mix.

Combine the grapeseed oil and annatto seeds in a pot and simmer for 2 hours.
Pass the mixture through a muslin strainer and set aside.

Sauté the chopped ginger and galangal in some butter.
Add the spice mix, 1 tbsp of the spice oil, chicken and lobster stock, sliced lemongrass, tamarind paste and vanilla seeds, and mix well. Simmer for 1 hour 30 minutes.
Add the basil leaves and infuse for 20 minutes. Strain.
Process the butter and lobster roe in a blender to mix well.
Whisk this mixture and the salted butter into the broth and mix well, taking care not to boil the mixture.
Season to taste with salt, cayenne pepper and lime juice. Set aside.
Warm up the broth without boiling just before serving.

Peel the salsify and soak in lemon water immediately to prevent discolouring.
Chop the salsify roughly and add to a pot filled with fresh lemon water and a muslin sachet filled with the garlic, rosemary and thyme, and cook for about 20 minutes until tender.
Process the salsify and some of the lemon water in a blender to obtain a smooth purée.

Cut 3 segments from the lime and set them aside. Squeeze the juice from the leftover lime and set aside.
Heat the diced dried fruit with the lime segments in a pan.
Add the lime juice and sprinkle the five-spice powder over. Mix well.
Remove from the heat and keep at room temperature until required.

PRESENTATION

Pour the lobster broth into 4 sauceboats. Place a spoonful of fig-date chutney on the rim of each plate. Place a mound of young lettuce salad on the left side of the chutney. Spoon 3 streaks of salsify purée in the centre of each plate and top with the lobster medallions and claws. Serve with sauceboat on the side.

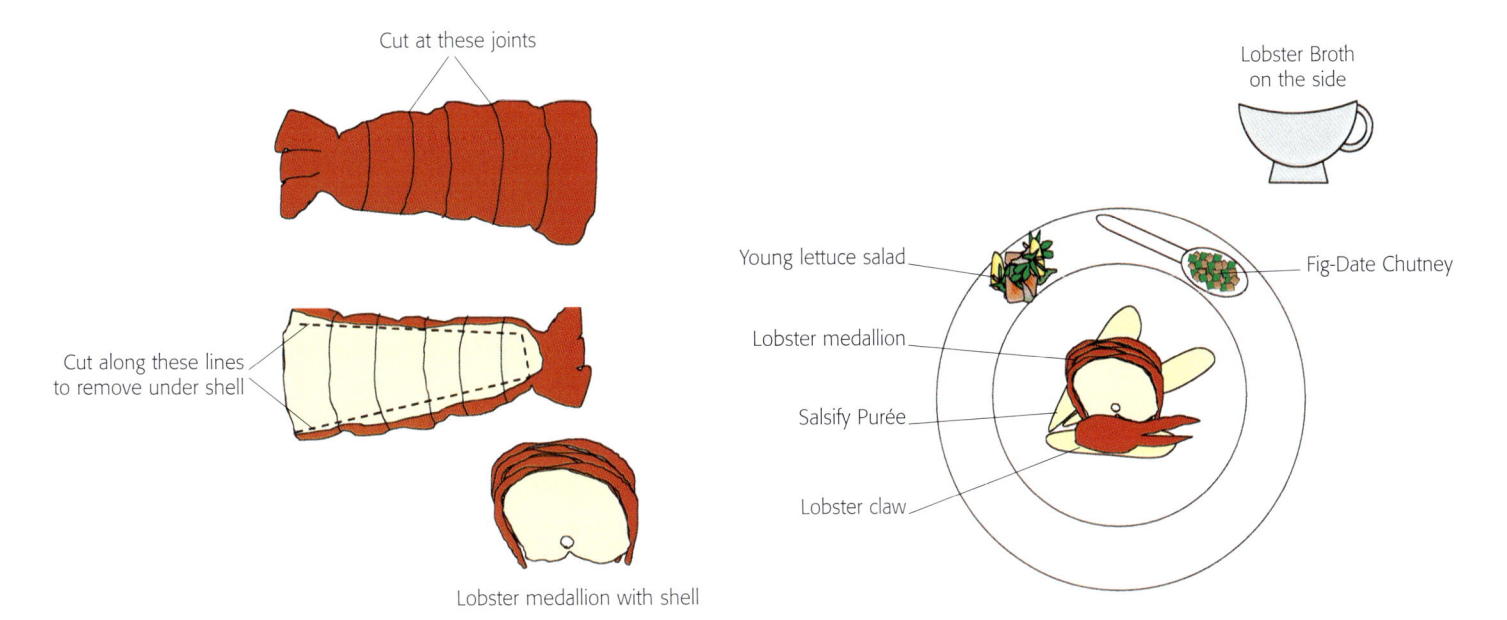

Joël Atlanta

RIGHT: The Cellar Room, a 16-seat private dining room, has a glass-enclosed wall where 5,000 bottles of wine are stored.
ABOVE: An 18.9-metre (62-foot) stove in Joël's kitchen produces creative French cuisine spiked with flavours from Asia and the Mediterranean, which is then served in the 128-seat brasserie.
BELOW: Terrace seats allow guests at Joël to enjoy the Italian-style architecture of The Forum building in which the restaurant is located.

Joël Antunes

Not too long ago, if Americans longed for more complex fare than fried chicken and pepperoni pizza, they had to fly to New York City or Los Angeles. Then came the revolution. And before we could say 'Julia Child-uses-store-bought-bouillon', Americans were feasting on lobster ravioli in Minneapolis and gorgonzola-stuffed figs in Albuquerque. So, while Joël Antunes, a Frenchman raised in the Auvergne, did not bring sophisticated fare to the people of Atlanta single-handedly, he is intent on keeping it going. After poaching, roasting and caramelising at the Negresco in Nice, for Paul Bocuse in Lyon, Duquesnois in Paris, Antunes worked with Michel Troisgros as his sous chef and as head chef of Le Normandie at The Oriental Hotel in Bangkok, before taking his expertise to London's critically acclaimed Les Saveurs. As chef-partner, he saw it earn a Michelin star and 'Restaurant of the Year' title from *Decanter* magazine. When he took over the kitchen at the Ritz-Carlton Buckhead in Atlanta, Georgia, The Dining Room became the only restaurant in the Southeast of the United States to hold both an AAA Five-Diamond Award and a Mobil Five-Star rating simultaneously.

John Mariani, food critic for *Esquire* magazine once said, 'If I was mayor of Atlanta, I would put a roadblock on the highway the day Joël attempted to leave Atlanta.' Now that Antunes has opened the restaurant nearby which carries his name, and with such dishes as pineapple confit with coconut sorbet and lemon grass sauce to perk up palates, his fan club will keep growing.

▸ TUNA TARTARE WITH TOMATO PULP, TOMATO DRESSING AND MICRO BASIL Serves 4

INGREDIENTS

Lemon Confit

5 lemons; 450 ml/15$\frac{1}{4}$ fl oz/1$\frac{7}{8}$ cups water (enough to cover the lemons); 5 g/$\frac{1}{8}$ oz fresh tumeric, minced; 2 tsp coriander seeds; 110 g/3$\frac{3}{4}$ oz/$\frac{1}{4}$ cup salt; 110 g/3$\frac{3}{4}$ oz/scant $\frac{2}{3}$ cup sugar; 1 clove

Tuna Tartare

250 g/8$\frac{7}{8}$ sashimi-grade tuna, diced; 10 g/$\frac{3}{8}$ oz chives, chopped; 10 g/$\frac{3}{8}$ oz shallots, chopped; 5 g/$\frac{1}{8}$ oz lemon confit; 6 drops of Tabasco sauce; 6 drops of Worcestershire sauce; 35 ml/1$\frac{1}{8}$ fl oz/$\frac{1}{8}$ cup olive oil; salt; pepper

Tomato Pulp

500 g/1 lb 1$\frac{5}{8}$ oz red Roma tomatoes; 65 g/2$\frac{1}{4}$ oz/$\frac{1}{3}$ cup sugar; 10 basil leaves; salt; pepper

Tomato Dressing

100 ml/3$\frac{3}{8}$ fl oz/$\frac{3}{8}$ cup olive oil; 150 ml/5 fl oz/$\frac{5}{8}$ cups tomato water (from preparing the tomato pulp); salt

Garnish

Micro basil; extra virgin olive oil; sea salt

PREPARATION

Cut off the ends of the lemons and make 4 incisions in the middle.
Boil them in the water for 20 minutes.
Remove from the heat and separate the lemons from the water used to cook them.
Insert the minced tumeric in the incisions on the lemons.
Combine the lemons, coriander seeds, salt, sugar and clove in a jar.
Cover the ingredients with the cooking water. Refrigerate for three weeks before using.

Toss the diced tuna in all the remaining ingredients.
Season to taste with salt and pepper.

Cut the tomatoes into half. Combine them with the sugar and basil in a large bowl. Season to taste with salt and pepper. Mix well. Cover the bowl with plastic film and cook over a bain-marie for 1 hour 30 minutes. Let the mixture sit for 24 hours, then pass it through a muslin strainer. Reserve the liquid for the tomato dressing. Remove the basil from the pulp and pass the pulp through a fine-mesh sieve.

Add the olive oil to the tomato water and mix well.
Season to taste with salt.

PRESENTATION

Prepare 4 plates. Place a ring mould in the centre of each plate and fill it with the tuna tartare.
Cover the tuna with a thin smooth layer of tomato pulp. Remove the ring, spoon the dressing around and garnish with some micro basil. Pour some olive oil and sprinkle some sea salt over to serve.

▾ ROASTED CHILEAN SEA BASS, TOMATO AND LEMON GRASS BROTH Serves 4

INGREDIENTS

Roasted Chilean Sea Bass

4 (200 g/7 oz each) Chilean sea bass fillets; 120 ml/4 fl oz/$\frac{1}{2}$ cup sake; 120 ml/4 fl oz/$\frac{1}{2}$ cup mirin; 100 ml/3$\frac{3}{8}$ fl oz/$\frac{3}{8}$ cup rice wine vinegar; 50 g/1$\frac{3}{4}$ oz/$\frac{1}{4}$ cup sugar; 40 g/1$\frac{3}{8}$ fl oz/scant $\frac{1}{4}$ cup miso paste

Eggplant Caviar

500 g/1 lb 1$\frac{5}{8}$ oz eggplants; 80 g/2$\frac{7}{8}$ oz/$\frac{3}{8}$ cup sugar; 30 ml/1 fl oz/$\frac{1}{8}$ cup lemon juice; $\frac{1}{2}$ clove garlic, peeled and crushed; salt; pepper; 10 g/$\frac{3}{8}$ oz thyme; 60 ml/2 fl oz/$\frac{1}{4}$ cup hazelnut oil

Tomato and Lemon Grass Broth

250 g/8$\frac{7}{8}$ oz vine tomatoes; $\frac{1}{2}$ onion, peeled and roughly chopped; 40 ml/1$\frac{3}{8}$ fl oz/scant $\frac{1}{8}$ cup honey; 40 ml/1$\frac{3}{8}$ fl oz/$\frac{1}{8}$ cup soya sauce; 1 lemon grass; 5 coriander leaves; $\frac{1}{2}$ black cardamom seed; 1.5 litres/3 pts 2$\frac{3}{4}$ fl oz/6$\frac{1}{3}$ cups water; butter; salt; pepper

Garnish

Micro coriander; sea salt

PREPARATION

Marinate the sea bass fillets in the remaining ingredients for 6 hours.
Preheat the oven at 220°C (428°F).
Place the fish fillets in a skillet with 2 tbsp of marinade and roast them in oven for 10 minutes.
Remove from the heat and grill the fillets or place them under the salamander for a few seconds just before serving.

Preheat the oven at 190°C (374°F).
Peel the eggplants and cut them into bite-sized pieces.
Toss them in the sugar, lemon juice and garlic, then wrap them up in aluminium foil.
Bake in the oven for 45 minutes.
Remove from the heat and season the eggplants to taste with salt, pepper, thyme and hazelnut oil.

Roast the tomatoes and onion over medium heat in a roasting pan for a few minutes, then add the honey, soya sauce, lemon grass, coriander leaves and black cardamom.
Toss well and cook for 10 minutes, then add the water and simmer for 2 hours.
Remove from the heat and pass the mixture through a muslin strainer.
Whisk in some butter and season to taste with salt and pepper just before serving.

PRESENTATION

Place each fish fillet in the middle of a soup bowl and top with a quenelle of eggplant caviar.
Garnish with some micro coriander and spoon some tomato and lemon grass broth around the fish.
Sprinkle some sea salt over the fish to serve.

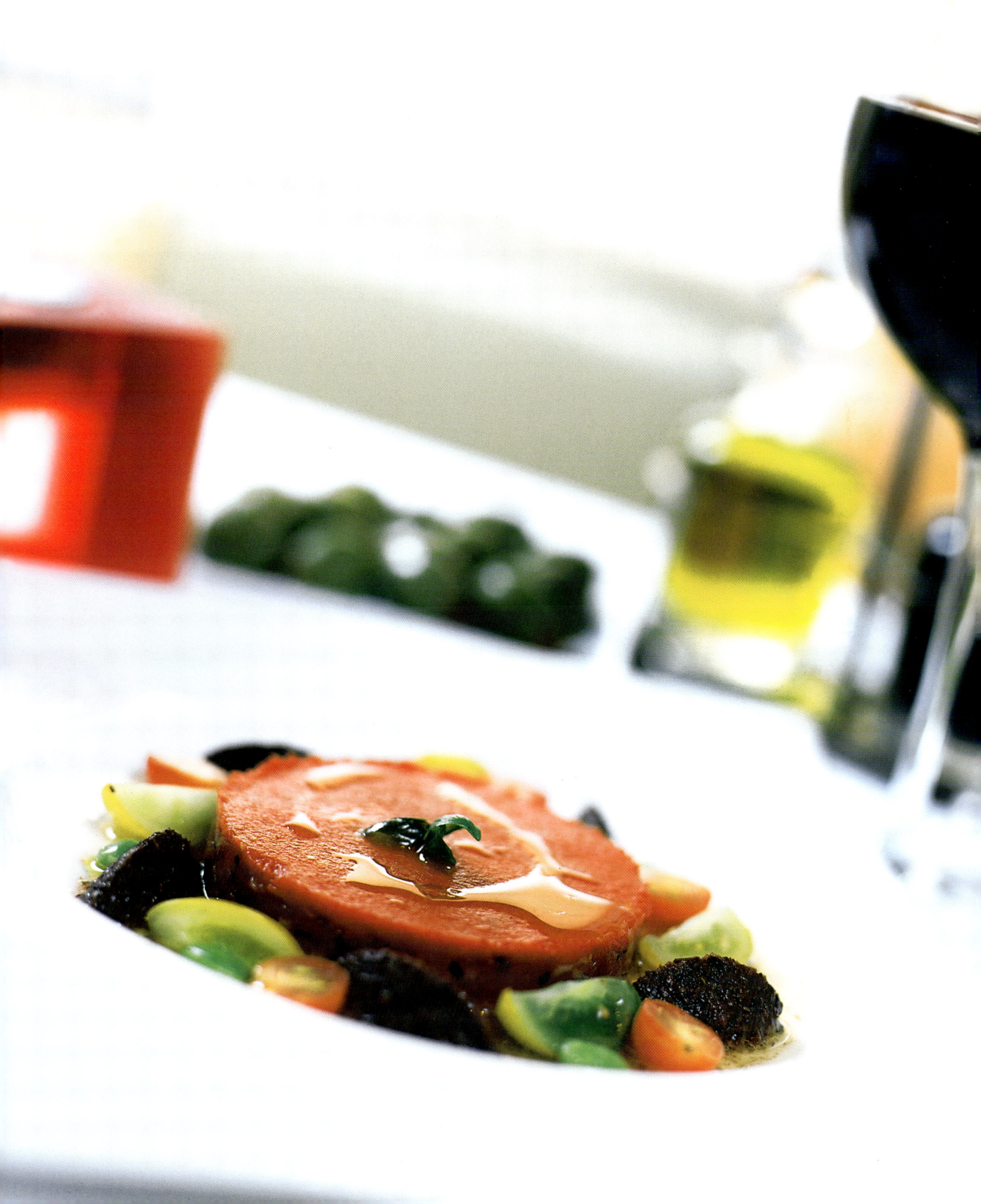

Hotel De Mikuni

Tokyo

LEFT: The sophisticated and highly efficient kitchen design at Hotel de Mikuni is inspired by the famous kitchen of Troisgros in Roanne, France.
EXTREME LEFT: The name Hotel de Mikuni is a bow to Kiyomi Mikuni's French training and inspiration.
BELOW: The intimate dining room accommodates nine or 10 tables for admirers of Mikuni's 'French kaiseki'.

Kiyomi Mikuni

Soon after learning from his father in a fishing village near Hokkaido how to clean fish, Kiyomi Mikuni set his mind on becoming a chef. As a teenager, this gutsy Japanese travelled to France and Switzerland to work with and learn from his idols, Fredy Girardet, Alain Chapel and Louis Outhier among others, and even named his daughter after friend and mentor Jean Troisgros.

Audaciously he calls himself a genius. Yet being a strict taskmaster, he has been known to kick his cooks in the shins if they err in the kitchen; or indeed smash stacks of bowls in a fit of temper. Yet, he is an energetic dynamo whose passion for food is obviously transferred to the plate. His restaurant in Tokyo, Hotel de Mikuni, offers a set menu that amazingly changes daily.

A typical meal might begin with champagne and crab and vegetable terrine on watercress coulis. Then followed by three fish of wildly different textures, colours and tastes bathed in a saffron sauce dotted with a crunchy carrot and celery confetti, all on a vivid blue dish. Next, a tribute to Troisgros—thinly sliced duck breast capping a mound of apple and Calvados purée alongside a heady mélange of mushrooms, followed by soft, white, herbed cheese floating in a pool of liquid pink pomegranate. Chestnut ice cream on a cinnamon crisp, doused in rum-infused hot chocolate sauce, completes the experience.

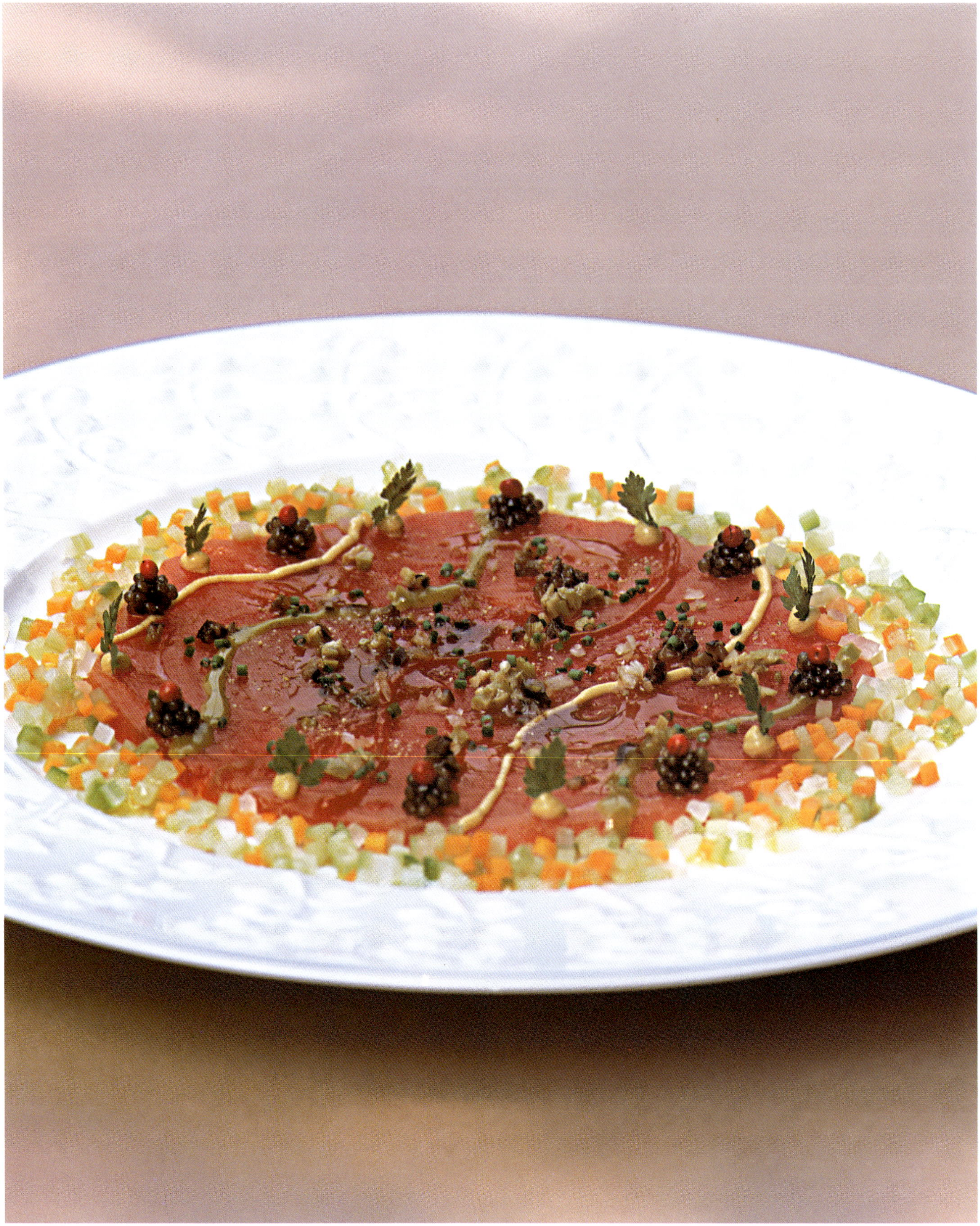

▲ PLATINUM OF FRESH MINT – KIYOMI MIKUNI Serves 4

INGREDIENTS

Custard Cream

1 vanilla pod; 2 litres/4 pts $3\frac{5}{8}$ fl oz/$8\frac{1}{2}$ cups milk; 2 egg yolks; 50 g/$1\frac{3}{4}$ oz/$\frac{1}{4}$ cup sugar; scant 5 tsp cornflour

PREPARATION

Cut the vanilla pod into half, lengthwise.
Scrape out the seeds, then combine the seeds with the milk in a pot, and bring to the boil.
Combine the egg yolks and sugar in a mixing bowl and whisk until the mixture is firm and creamy.
Fold in the cornflour and warmed milk, then transfer the mixture into a pot and cook it slowly over low heat, stirring constantly with a wooden spatula until the mixture thickens.
Pour the mixture into a bowl and set aside to cool.

Mint Sorbet

1 litre/2 pts $1\frac{7}{8}$ fl oz/$4\frac{1}{4}$ cups water; 200 g/7 oz/1 cup sugar; 30 g/1 oz mint leaves; 30 ml/1 fl oz/$\frac{1}{8}$ cup lemon juice; 500 ml/1 pt 1 fl oz/$2\frac{1}{8}$ cups mint liqueur

Combine the water, sugar and mint leaves in a pot and bring to the boil.
Let the mint infuse for 5 minutes, then strain the mixture and set aside to cool.
Add the lemon juice and mint liqueur and mix well.
Process the mixture in an ice cream maker set to sorbet specifications.
When ready, keep frozen until required.

Garnish

100 small mint leaves; 4 silver leaves; 4 chocolate squares; 2 tsp chocolate glaze

PRESENTATION

Pour the custard cream on 4 plates. Arrange the small mint leaves around the custard cream, allocating about 25 leaves per portion. Top each portion of custard cream with a scoop of mint sorbet.
Place a silver leaf on a chocolate square, then gently place the chocolate square on top of the sorbet.
Drizzle the chocolate glaze across the silver-coated chocolate to serve.

◀ CARPACCIO OF YELLOW FIN TUNA WITH THREE MUSTARDS Serves 4

INGREDIENTS

Carpaccio of Yellow Fin Tuna

300 g/$10\frac{1}{2}$ oz yellow fin tuna; 40 g/$1\frac{3}{8}$ oz/$\frac{1}{4}$ cup onion brunoise; 60 g/$2\frac{1}{8}$ oz/$\frac{1}{3}$ cup carrot brunoise; 80 g/$2\frac{7}{8}$ oz/$\frac{1}{2}$ cup cucumber brunoise; salt; freshly ground black pepper; 20 ml/$\frac{5}{8}$ fl oz/$\frac{1}{8}$ cup Dijon mustard; 20 ml/$\frac{5}{8}$ fl oz/$\frac{1}{8}$ cup red mustard (mix Dijon mustard with a little ketchup); 20 ml/$\frac{5}{8}$ fl oz/$\frac{1}{8}$ cup green mustard; 10 g/$\frac{3}{8}$ oz/$\frac{1}{8}$ cup black olive brunoise; 10 g/$\frac{3}{8}$ oz/$\frac{1}{8}$ cup green olive brunoise

PREPARATION

Trim the excess fat and gristle off the tuna and slice it thinly.
Divide the slices into 4 portions and overlap each portion on a plate to form a circle.
Sprinkle the onion, carrot and cucumber brunoise around the tuna and season to taste with salt and freshly ground black pepper.
Spoon the 3 types of mustard on the tuna and sprinkle the black and green olive brunoise over.

Balsamic Vinaigrette

200 ml/$6\frac{3}{4}$ fl oz/$\frac{7}{8}$ cup virgin olive oil; 35 ml/$1\frac{1}{8}$ fl oz/$\frac{1}{8}$ cup balsamic vinegar; 35 ml/$1\frac{1}{8}$ fl oz/$\frac{1}{8}$ cup light soya sauce; a spritz of lemon juice; salt; freshly ground white pepper

Combine all the ingredients in a bowl and mix well.

Garnish

10 g/$\frac{3}{8}$ oz/$\frac{1}{4}$ cup chopped chives; 4 sprigs chervil; caviar (optional)

PRESENTATION

Spoon the balsamic vinaigrette over the tuna and garnish with chopped chives, chervil sprigs and caviar (optional) to serve.

Aquavit New York

ABOVE: At the ground-floor bar, guests are served tasting-portions of traditional Swedish appetisers while they sip on flavoured aquavit.
RIGHT: Aquavit's contemporary interior complements the edible sculptures to be found on the tables.
BELOW: Aquavit's atrium dining room, designed with a sleek waterfall against one burnished copper wall, used to be the courtyard of John D. Rockefeller's town house.

Marcus Samuelsson

An Ethiopian chef preparing gourmet Scandinavian food in a fine New York City restaurant is a rarity indeed. Orphaned at three after a tuberculosis epidemic in Ethiopia, Marcus Samuelsson and his sister were adopted by a Swedish couple and brought up and educated in Sweden. Their Swedish foster-grandmother, a professional cook, whetted the young boy's appetite, and serious culinary studies were followed by an apprenticeship at the three-Michelin-star Georges Blanc in Vonnas. Eventually he met Håkan Swahn, the owner of Aquavit, and was asked to run New York's grandest Scandinavian restaurant. Under Samuelsson's aegis, Aquavit received a three-star rating from *The New York Times* and constant praise in culinary publications and television programmes across the globe.

The future of cooking, Samuelsson says, is 'personal'. The food will convey the chef's personal experiences rather than his nationality. This phenomenon is already apparent in the way he skilfully adds new zip and flair to traditional Swedish cuisine. He does gravlax but with pickled fennel and avocado. His lobster roll is a tantalising combination of chunky seafood, seaweed and caviar. Manipulating flavour, texture and the aesthetic, he performs memorable gastronomic feats such as a white cylinder of frozen goat cheese and lemon grass alongside a scoop of blueberry sorbet. And those who have experienced his silken foie gras ganache with porcini, washed down with an icy cold Aquavit, are fans for life.

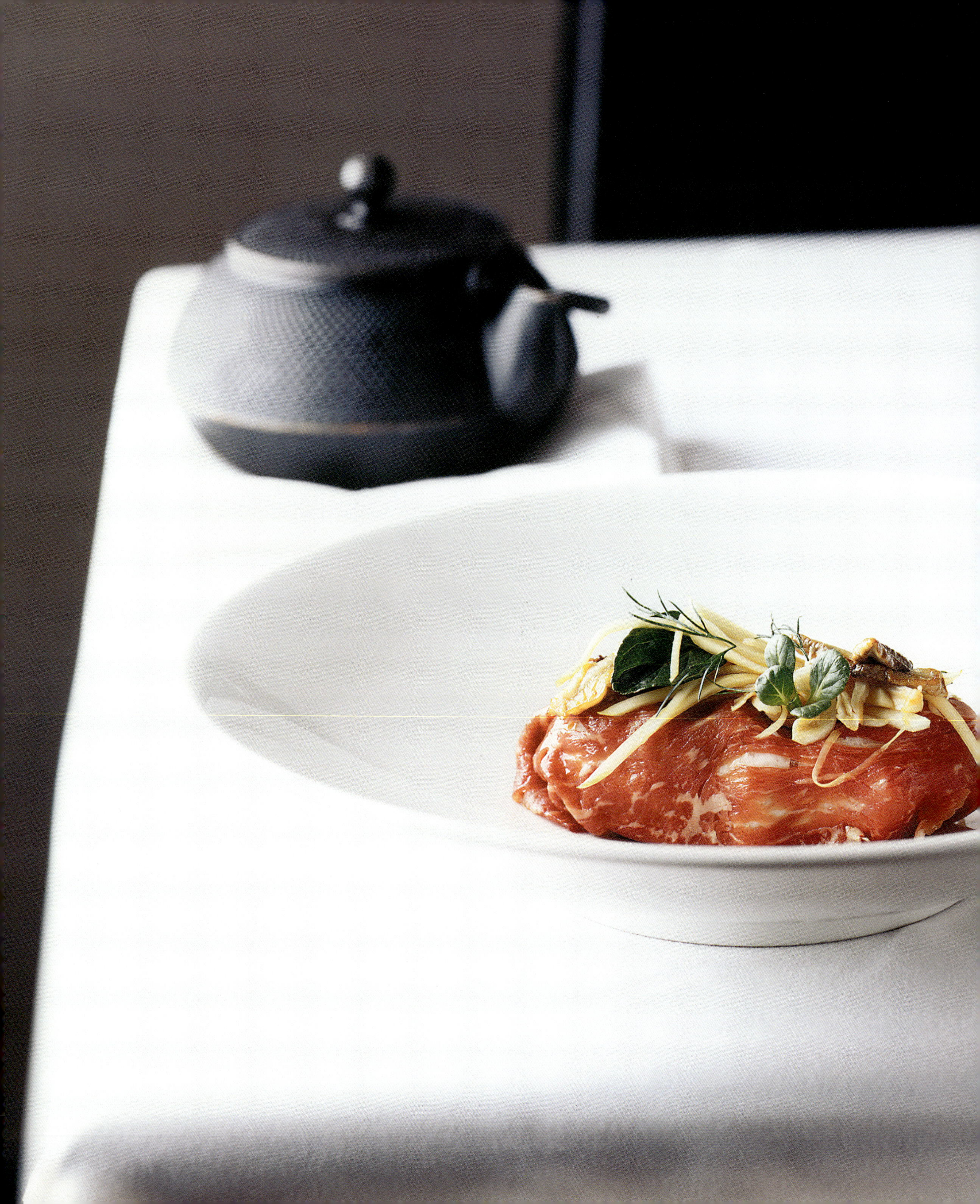

LOBSTER ROLL WITH HOT AND SOUR BROTH Serves 4

INGREDIENTS

1-2-3 Vinegar

240 ml/8$\frac{1}{8}$ fl oz/1 cup white wine vinegar; 400 g/14$\frac{1}{8}$ oz/2 cups sugar; 700 ml/1 pt 7$\frac{5}{8}$ fl oz/3 cups water

PREPARATION

Combine all the ingredients in a bowl and mix well.

Lobster Roll

2 handfuls of salt; 2 (470 g/1$\frac{1}{2}$ lb each) lobsters (lobster meat may be substituted with cooked crabmeat, shrimp or salmon); 2 Asian pears, unpeeled; 2 tsp miso paste; 1 tbsp mayonnaise; 50 ml/1$\frac{3}{4}$ fl oz/$\frac{1}{4}$ cup freshly squeezed lime juice; $\frac{1}{4}$ tsp sambal oelek (or 6 drops of Tabasco sauce); 1 tbsp finely chopped coriander; 2 medium tomatoes, peeled, seeds removed and diced

Bring a large pot of water to the boil, then add the salt, followed by the lobsters. Cover the pot and boil the lobsters for 15 minutes until they are cooked and turn bright red in colour. Remove the lobsters from the water and set them aside to cool. Remove the lobster meat from the shell and cut them into bite-sized pieces. Set aside. Cut the Asian pears into paper-thin slices with a mandoline. Place the sliced pears in a small bowl and pour 240 ml/8$\frac{1}{8}$ fl oz/1 cup of the 1-2-3 Vinegar over. Set aside to marinate for 20 minutes. Combine the miso paste, mayonnaise, lime juice, sambal oelek (or Tabasco sauce), chopped coriander, cooked lobster meat and diced tomatoes in a bowl and toss well. Lay out a sheet of plastic film measuring 10 by 15 cm (4 by 6 inches) on a clean and smooth surface. Arrange 10 slices of pears on the plastic film in 2 overlapping rows. Spread about 2 tbsp of the lobster mixture along 1 end of the sliced pears, then roll up as tightly as possible, peeling off the plastic film along the way. Repeat this step with the remaining pear slices and lobster mixture to form 3 more rolls. These may be prepared 6 to 7 hours in advanced, but keep refrigerated until required.

Hot and Sour Broth

3 bird's eye chilli; 1 tbsp olive oil; 480 ml/1 pt $\frac{1}{4}$ fl oz/2 cups lobster stock (recipe on page 148); juice from 5 limes; 1 tbsp double cream, whipped; 3 tbsp butter

Sauté the bird's eye chilli in the olive oil in a pot for 2 minutes, then add the lobster stock. Bring to the boil and remove from the heat. Set aside. Just before serving, add the lime juice, followed by the heavy cream and butter. Whisk well.

Mint Oil

50 g/1$\frac{3}{4}$ oz basil leaves; 200 g/7 oz mint leaves; 240 ml/8$\frac{1}{8}$ fl oz/1 cup grapeseed oil

Blanch the basil and mint leaves in boiling water for 20 seconds, then set them aside to cool. Process the herbs and grapeseed oil in blender to obtain a smooth purée. Pour the mixture into an airtight container and cover. Shake the container 5 times, once every 30 minutes.

Garnish

2 tsp Sevruga caviar (optional)

PRESENTATION

Place each roll on a plate and garnish with a thin line of black caviar (optional) along the top of each roll. Serve the hot and sour broth on the side with a dash of mint oil. Serve chilled or at room temperature.

KOBE BEEF RAVIOLI WITH TRUFFLE TEA Serves 4

INGREDIENTS

Kobe Beef Ravioli

225 g/8 oz ribeye Kobe beef

PREPARATION

Trim the fat from the beef, pat it dry with kitchen tissue and wrap it in plastic film. Freeze for 2 hours. Cut the frozen beef into 8 thin slices and place each slice between 2 sheets of plastic film. Pound each wrapped slice with the blunt edge of a cleaver, then keep refrigerated until required.

Taro Mash Filling

4 shallots, peeled; 1.8 kg/4 lbs taro, peeled and diced; 910 g/2 lbs new potatoes, peeled and diced; 2 cloves garlic, peeled; 1 tsp olive oil; 480 ml/1 pt $\frac{1}{4}$ fl oz/2 cups chicken stock (recipe on page 148); 960 ml/2 pts/4 cups milk; 480 ml/1 pt $\frac{1}{4}$ fl oz/2 cups whipping cream; salt; pepper; 225 g/8 oz cold butter; 1 tbsp truffle oil; 2 tsp truffle trimmings; leaves from 2 sprigs thyme; 450 g/15$\frac{7}{8}$ oz/2 cups cooked and diced beef brisket

Sauté the peeled shallots, taro and potato cubes, and garlic in the olive oil. Add the chicken stock, milk and whipping cream, and bring to the boil. Boil the mixture for 25 minutes, remove from the heat and mash it with a fork. Season to taste with salt and pepper. Add the butter, truffle oil and trimmings, thyme leaves and cooked beef brisket cubes. Mix well and set aside.

Truffle Tea

60 g/2 oz/2 cups dried shiitake mushrooms; 140 g/5 oz/1 cup citrus infusion powder; 960 ml/2 pts/4 cups water; 1 shallot, peeled; 1 [7.5-cm- (3-inch-)] pc ginger, peeled; 1 lemon grass; 10 g/$\frac{3}{8}$ oz/1 cup bonito flakes; 2 tbsp soya sauce; 1 sheet dried kelp

Process half the dried shiitake mushrooms in a blender to obtain a fine powder. Mix the powder with the citrus infusion powder and set aside. Bring the water to the boil. Add the peeled shallot and ginger, lemon grass, bonito flakes, soya sauce, dried kelp and the remaining dried shiitake mushrooms. Lower the heat and simmer the mixture for 5 minutes. Remove from the heat and add half the mushroom and citrus infusion powder. Let the mixture sit for 5 minutes, then pass it through a muslin strainer. Set aside. Divide the remaining mushroom and citrus infusion powder into 4 portions and fill each filter of 4 teapots with the powder. Set aside.

Garnish

2 hearts of palm, thinly sliced; fresh wasabi, grated; 1 tsp truffle oil; 120 ml/4 fl oz/$\frac{1}{2}$ cup sherry

PRESENTATION

Overlap 2 slices of beef and place 1 tbsp of the taro mash filling in the centre. Wrap it up as shown and prepare 3 more raviolis with the remaining ingredients. Place each ravioli in the centre of a soup plate. Garnish with the hearts of palm and some wasabi. Add a little truffle oil into each teapot. Add the sherry to the truffle tea and mix well. Pour the truffle tea into the teapots and serve each plate of ravioli with a pot of truffle tea on the side. Pour the truffle tea over the ravioli before eating.

Auberge De L'Éridan
Veyrier Du Lac

LEFT: Auberge De L'Eridan, Marc Veyrat's flagship three-Michelin-star restaurant.
ABOVE: Veyrat's rustic cooking highlights the herbs which grow on the mountains of Annecy.
BELOW: In place of the chef's toque, the crew at Auberge De L'Eridan puts on Veyrat's trademark black felt hat.

Marc Veyrat

He's been called the 'enfant terrible of French gastronomy' and the 'Mozart of cuisine'. Marc Veyrat is a man of great passion who devotes his life to the culinary arts and does an exemplary job of it. He believes that cooking 'is an expression of one's emotions and the act of eating is an emotional experience'. Veyrat was voted 'Best Chef in France' in 1996 for his innovative cooking at Auberge De L'Éridan, his three-Michelin-star restaurant in Annecy; the *Red Guide* gave him another three stars for La Ferme de Mon Père, his new restaurant and chalet at a ski resort in Megève, only a year after it was opened in 2000.

Veyrat concentrates on clarity of flavours in his cooking. His dishes, such as pistachio cheese accentuated with liquorice leaves, are marked by the flavours of plants and wild herbs, which he personally picks from mountains near his restaurants in the small hours every morning. According to Veyrat, a chef must keep abreast of what other chefs are cooking in order to improve. Hence, he established the Group of Eight together with Michel Troisgros, Jean-Michel Lorain, Pierre Gagnaire, Oliver Roellinger, Michel Bras, Alain Passard and Jacques Chibois to find alternatives to the strictly traditional side of French cuisine. The group's activities stress a spontaneous, innovative method of cooking that 'accepts diversity, combines virtuoso technique and free improvisation, and respects the integrity of the product'. For him, 'there are not two types of kitchen, only the best'. Similarly, 'no two types of chef, only the truly passionate kind!'

▶ SAVOYARD-STYLE CHICKEN NUGGETS WITH PEANUT AND REINE DES PRÉS SAUCES Serves 4

INGREDIENTS

Vegetable Stock
3 carrots, peeled and diced; 1 leek (white part only);
1 clove garlic, peeled; ½ onion, peeled;
1 shallot, peeled; 1 bouquet garni;
200 ml/6¾ fl oz/⅞ cup dry white wine;
2 litres/4 pts 3⅝ fl oz/8½ cups water

Peanut Sauce
250 ml/8½ fl oz/1 cup vegetable stock;
150 ml/5 fl oz/⅝ cup cream; scant 1¼ tsp salt;
¼ tsp pepper; scant 1¼ tsp sugar;
50 g/1¾ oz/⅓ cup skinless, toasted peanuts

Reine des Prés Sauce
250 ml/8½ fl oz/1 cup vegetable stock;
150 ml/5 fl oz/⅝ cup cream; salt; pepper;
30 g/1 oz Reine des Prés

Savoyard-style Chicken Nuggets
1 liquorice stick; 100 g/3½ oz chicken breast;
100 g/3½ oz duckling breast;
50 ml/1¾ fl oz/¼ cup groundnut oil;
salt; pepper

PREPARATION

Combine all the ingredients in a stockpot and bring to the boil.
Reduce the heat and simmer the mixture for 35 minutes.
Strain the stock and set aside to cool.

Reduce the vegetable stock by half, add the cream, salt, pepper and sugar, then bring to the boil.
Add the toasted peanuts and mix well. Bring the mixture to the boil again, then remove from the heat.
Set aside to rest for 10 minutes.
Strain the sauce and season it to taste with more salt and pepper if necessary.
Keep warm until required.

Reduce the vegetable stock by half, add the cream and bring to the boil.
Season to taste with salt and pepper, then add the Reine des Prés and leave it to infuse for 10 minutes.
Strain the sauce and season to taste with more salt and pepper if necessary.
Keep warm until required.

Cut the liquorice stick into half, then cut each half into 8 small skewers.
Cut the chicken and duckling breasts into 5-by-1-cm (2-by-0.4-inch) strips.
Place a duckling strip on top of a chicken strip, roll them up and pierce them with a liquorice skewer.
Repeat this step with the remaining ingredients. Season the nuggets to taste with salt and pepper.
Pan-fry the nuggets on all sides with the groundnut oil over high heat, then reduce the heat and allow them to cook completely. The whole process should take about 3 minutes.

PRESENTATION
Arrange the nuggets on a platter and serve with both sauces on the side.

▼ LIQUORICE FLAVOURED FROGS' LEGS WITH SPRING SALAD AND FIELD FLOWERS Serves 4

INGREDIENTS

Orange Vinaigrette
2 oranges; 1 (5 g/⅛ oz) sugar cube;
1 tbsp hazelnut oil;
4 tbsp groundnut oil;
juice from ½ lemon;
salt; pepper; a few drops of vinegar (optional)

Frogs' Legs with Liquorice
40 frogs' legs; 50 g/1¾ oz butter; salt;
80 g/2⅞ oz/¾ cup liquorice powder

Spring Salad
100 g/3½ oz rocket; 100 g/3½ oz mizuna;
100 g/3½ oz Chénopode Bon Henri;
100 g/3½ oz sedum
(use other salad leaves if unavailable)

Garnish
Edible field flowers
(rimevères, bourrache and aspérule from the
mountains of Haute Savoie preferred)
(use other edible flowers if unavailable)

PREPARATION
Peel 1 orange, grate the zest and reduce its pulp and juice in a pot over low heat until the liquid reaches the consistency of a glaze (slightly thick and sticky). Add some of the grated orange zest and sugar cube to the mixture and mix well. Let the mixture cook for 5 minutes, then remove from the heat and pour it into a blender. Process the mixture in a blender to obtain a smooth purée.
Add the oils, lemon juice, juice from half of the remaining orange and season to taste with salt and pepper.
Add the vinegar (optional) if more acidity is desired. Mix well and set aside.

Pan-fry the frogs' legs with the butter in a non-stick pan for 1½ minutes on both sides.
Season to taste with salt and set aside to cool. Dust the frogs' legs evenly with liquorice powder.
Keep refrigerated until required.

Mix the salad leaves and divide them into 4 portions.

PRESENTATION
Arrange each portion of spring salad in the corner of a square plate and spoon the orange vinaigrette over.
Garnish each mound of salad with the edible field flowers.
Deep-fry the frog legs at 180°C (356°F) for 1 minute. Place the fried frogs' legs on kitchen tissue to absorb the excess oil. Arrange 10 frogs' legs in the centre of each plate to serve.

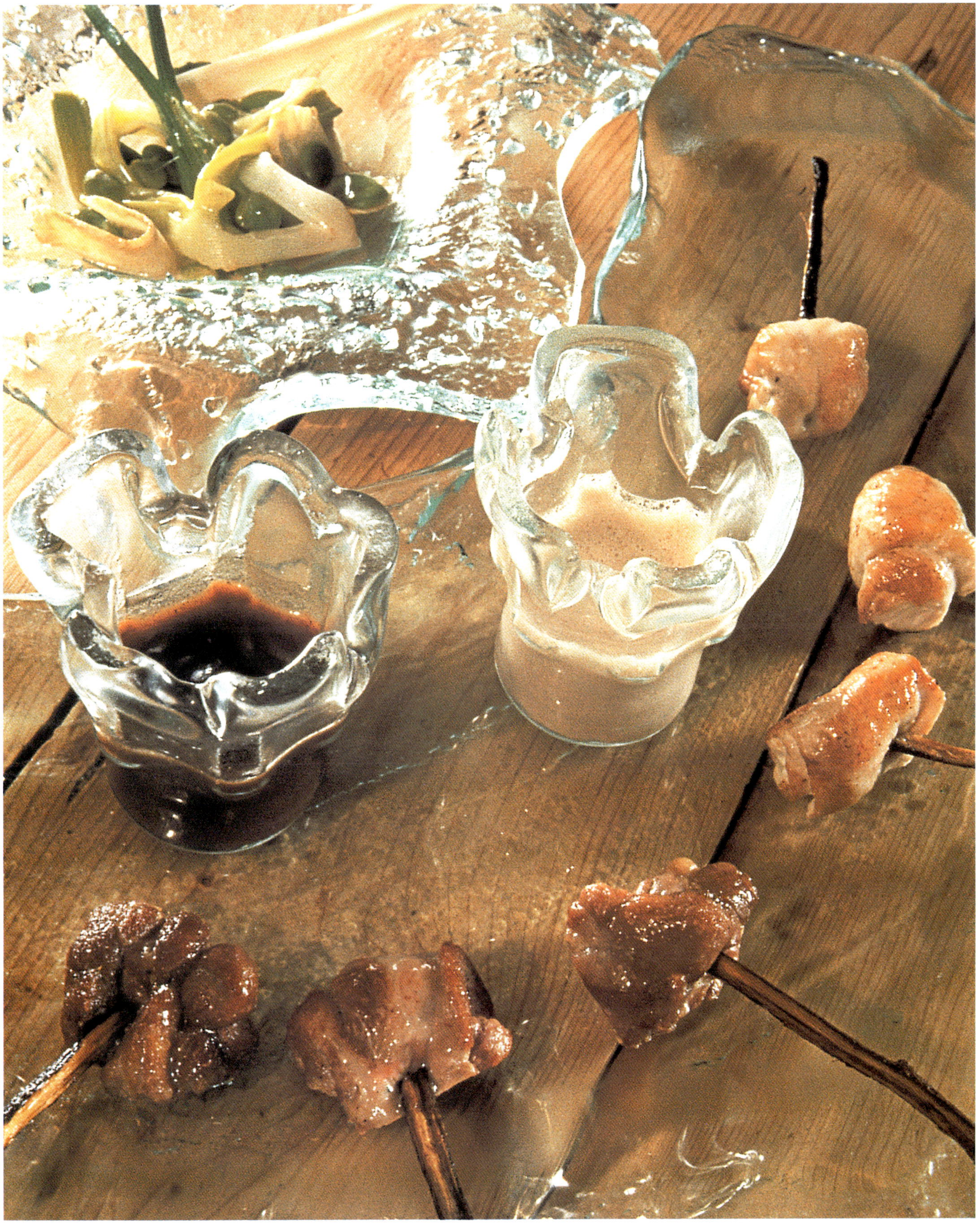

Martin Berasategui
Lasarte Guipuzcoa

RIGHT: Restaurant Martin Berasategui has joined the ranks of Spain's three-Michelin-star restaurants.
ABOVE: New Basque Cuisine was first served at Martin Berasategui's table.

Martin Berasategui

Having ridden the crest of a culinary wave for 30 years, Martin Berasategui continues to make headlines at his restaurant in San Sebastián. Back in the seventies, this seaside resort, formerly a favourite retreat of Spanish nobility, saw a kitchen revolution which turned it into Spain's gastronomic Mecca. As word of Nueva Cucina Vasca spread, some of the inventors of this New Basque Cuisine were lured across the country to cook for appreciative diners from Barcelona to Marbella.

Berasategui, one of the original innovators, stayed on. He cooked and shared his experience with young Basque cooks. Many of his disciples, including Andoni Luis Aduriz at Mugaritz and Bixente Arrieta at Berasategui's Guggenheim restaurant, are now famous in their own right. 'My goal has always been to transmit my philosophy of food and cooking through my methods and techniques. But we cannot move forward without keeping the past in mind,' he says. 'And respect for tradition must come before you can try to improve on the time-honoured recipes.'

He recently earned his third Michelin star by creating dishes such as Napoleon of smoked eel, foie gras and caramelised apple, and the simple but eloquent pairing of anchovies with a velvety marmalade of wood-roasted red peppers. 'Estupendo!' cry the critics, as food-lovers from all over the world still journey to San Sebastián.

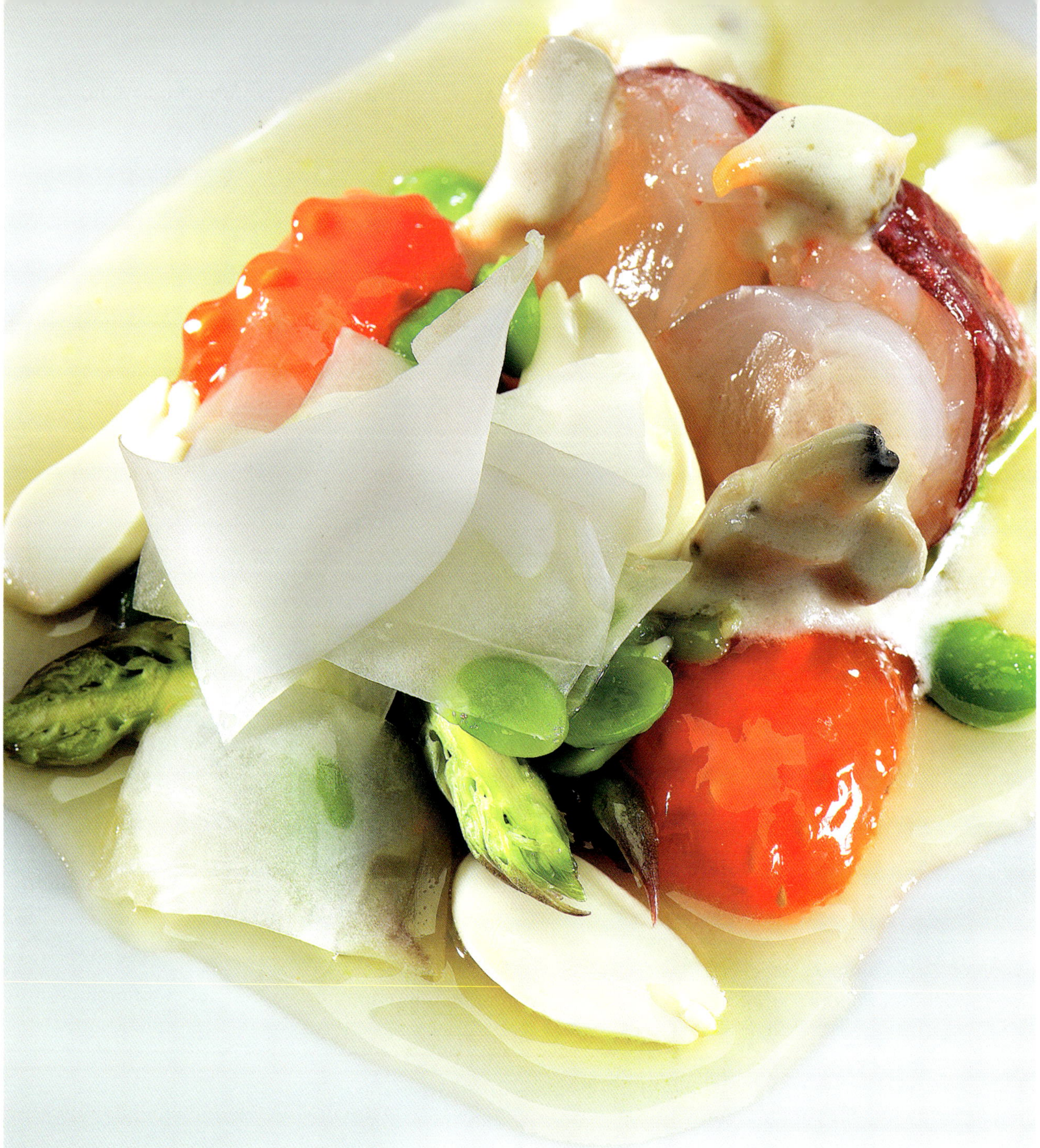

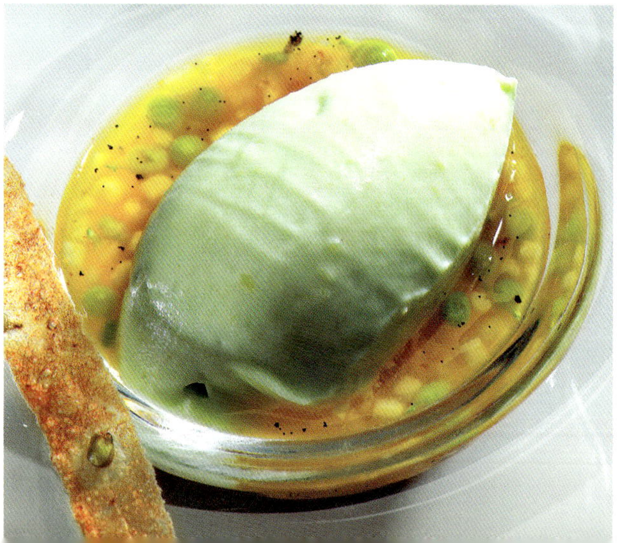

LOBSTER AND TOMATO JUICE GELATINE WITH WARM SALAD OF ASPARAGUS, CAULIFLOWER STEMS AND VEGETABLES Serves 6

INGREDIENTS

Tomato Juice Gelatine

3 kg/6 lb 9⅞ oz very ripe tomatoes (bruised), cored; 55 g/1⅞ oz/⅛ cup salt; 40 g/1⅜ oz/scant ¼ cup sugar; ¼ tsp gelatine powder for every 1 litre/2 pts 1⅞ fl oz/4¼ cups of clear tomato juice

PREPARATION

Cut each tomato into 6 pieces. Combine the tomatoes with the salt and sugar and blend with a hand mixer for 5 minutes until the mixture reaches a soupy consistency. Use a muslin strainer to extract the juice.
Refrigerate for 12 hours to obtain a clear tomato juice. Heat about 10 per cent of the clear tomato juice, add the gelatine powder and bring to the boil, stirring continuously until the gelatine powder dissolves completely. Remove from the heat and set aside to cool. When the mixture reaches 40°C (104°F), stir in the remaining tomato juice. Pour the mixture into 6 soup plates. Allow the gelatine to set in a cool place.

Fried Asparagus

6 green asparagus, trimmed; olive oil; salt

Cut each asparagus into 4, lengthwise, and fry them in the olive oil. Season to taste with salt. Set aside.

Cauliflower Stems

1 tbsp cider vinegar; 3 tbsp olive oil; 2 or 3 cauliflower stems, peeled and sliced thinly

Mix the cider vinegar and olive oil. Plunge the sliced cauliflower stems into iced water, pat dry with kitchen tissue and mix them with the cider vinaigrette. Set aside.

Lettuce Cream

15 g/½ oz butter; 150 g/5¼ oz spring onion, cut into thin strips; 200 ml/6¾ fl oz/⅞ cup chicken stock (recipe on page 148); 200 g/7 oz lettuce; salt

Heat the butter and spring onion strips in a saucepan, add the chicken stock and bring to the boil for 15 minutes. In the meantime, blanch the lettuce, then refresh them in iced water immediately.
Add the lettuce to the saucepan and toss well. Remove from the heat and process the mixture in a blender to obtain a smooth purée. Season to taste with salt. Pass the mixture through a fine-mesh sieve and set aside in a cool place until required.

Hearts of Tomato

12 medium ripe tomatoes

Cut off the tops and bottoms of the tomatoes and trim off the flesh without smashing the 'heart'.
Prepare at least 12 whole 'hearts'. Set aside.

Sautéed Broad Beans

100 g/3½ oz/1 cup small onions, chopped; olive oil; 280 g/9¾ oz/2¼ cups small broad beans; salt

Sauté the chopped onion in some olive oil until translucent, then remove from the heat. Add the broad beans and sauté until cooked. Season to taste with salt and transfer to a plate lined with kitchen tissue to absorb the excess oil. Set aside.

Lobster

1 (1.15 kg/2 lb ½ oz) lobster, cleaned

Grill the lobster and remove the flesh. Cut into 12 thick medallions.

Garnish

Olive oil; Idiazábal or Parmesan shavings

PRESENTATION

Place the plates of tomato juice gelatine under intense heat (under a salamander or in a heated oven) until the gelatine is slightly melted and coloured. Spoon some lettuce cream in the centre of each plate and top with the fried asparagus. Arrange 2 medallions of lobster and 2 hearts of tomato around the fried asparagus on each plate and drizzle some olive oil over. Place the cauliflower stems in the centre, and arrange the broad beans around.
Garnish with Idiazábal or Parmesan shavings. Do this quickly so that the tomato gelatine may be served warm.

PEA AND BANANA SOUP WITH GREEN APPLE SORBET AND VINEGAR AND PEA TUILE Serves 6

INGREDIENTS

Pea and Banana Soup

100 g/3½ oz/1¼ cups small green peas; 150 ml/5 fl oz/⅝ cup water; 200 g/7 oz/1 cup sugar; 2 vanilla pods, cut into half lengthwise and seeds scraped out; a pinch of grated orange zest; 700 g/1 lb 8⅝ oz bananas; 30 ml/1 fl oz/⅛ cup orange juice, strained; juice from 1 lemon, strained

PREPARATION

Blanch the green peas and refresh with iced water immediately.
Combine the water, sugar, vanilla seeds and grated orange zest in a saucepan and bring to the boil, without caramelising. Remove from the heat and set aside.
Dice the bananas into 0.3-by-0.3-by-0.3-cm (0.1-by-0.1-by-0.1-inch) cubes.
When the water, sugar and vanilla mixture has cooled to 65°C (149°F), add the orange and lemon juices and the diced banana. Mix well and leave it to cool. When cool, add the green peas and toss well.
Set 30 peas aside for the vinegar and pea tuile.
Mash the rest of the peas and the diced banana with a fork and pass the mixture through a fine-mesh sieve.

Green Apple Sorbet

475 g/1 lb ⅞ oz/2⅜ cups sugar; 50 g/1¾ oz/¼ cup dextrose (grape sugar); 59 ml/2 fl oz/¼ cup water; 125 g/4⅜ oz/½ cup glucose; 1.25 litres/2 pts 10¼ fl oz/5¼ cups green apple juice (from peeled and cored green apples); juice from 1 lemon, strained; 4 gelatine leaves, soaked in cold water

Combine all the ingredients, except the fruit juices and gelatine leaves, in a saucepan. Warm over low heat.
Add the soaked gelatine leaves to the mixture and stir until they dissolve completely.
Add the juices, mix well, then strain.
Transfer the mixture into an ice cream maker set to sorbet specifications.
When ready, keep frozen until required.

Vinegar and Pea Tuile

250 g/8⅞ oz/2 cup plain flour, sieved; 250 ml/8½ fl oz/1 cup sherry vinegar; 125 g/4⅜ oz/⅔ cup icing sugar; 30 peas (from preparing the pea and banana soup)

Preheat the oven at 180°C (356°F). Mix all the ingredients, except the peas, and pass the mixture through a fine-mesh sieve to smoothen it. Spread a thin layer, measuring 1-by-15 cm (0.4-by-6 inches), on a baking sheet. Repeat this step with the remaining mixture to make 6 or 7 tuiles. Decorate each tuile with 5 peas, then bake for 4 minutes, until the tuiles are cooked and crispy.

PRESENTATION

Pour the pea and banana soup into soup plates, top each portion with a scoop of green apple sorbet, and garnish with a vinegar and pea tuile to serve.

LEFT: The kitchen in Troisgros is acknowledged by chefs and design professionals to be one of the world's most sophisticated and well-planned spaces.
BELOW: Troisgros' tasteful and understated interior is designed by Parisian architect François Champsaur.
BOTTOM LEFT: The lounge, to which guests head for coffee, tea and petits fours after a meal in the restaurant.

Troisgros
Roanne

Michel Troisgros

Michel Troisgros is destined for culinary greatness. In *Asterix*, the comic series by Goscinny and Uderzo, Obelix gained his special powers when he fell into the magic cauldron. 'Likewise,' Michel explains, 'when I was young, I "fell" into my family's signature dish, the Escalope of Salmon with Sorrel, which gave me the power to upkeep my family's legacy.' With a family name like Troisgros (three greats), undeniable talent, and training by his father Pierre and his late uncle Jean—legendary chefs and pioneers of Nouvelle Cuisine—Troisgros is under tremendous pressure to maintain the family's three Michelin stars. But he is not about to sacrifice his individuality in the process.

Inspired by Apple Computer's slogan, he insists that one has to 'think different' to survive the restaurant business. Troisgros and its cuisine have evolved dramatically. The interior has been renovated from 'what's considered modern by my father's generation' to a more timeless style. 'The food is simpler and emphasises taste rather than the aesthetics,' he explains. 'While my father and uncle's cuisine is more French, I am influenced by my Italian grandmother's cooking. I also pick up new ideas when travelling.' Some conservative chefs want to stop the evolution of French cuisine by sticking closely to tradition. Troisgros champions the opposite approach through the Group of Eight, an association he established with chef friends who share his goals to advocate diversity in French cooking, improvisation based on skilful technique, and respect for the ingredients.

▼ POACHED EGGPLANT AND LIME GELATINE WITH A TOUCH OF CUMIN Serves 4

INGREDIENTS

Consommé
4 duck carcasses; oil;
3 litres/6 pts 5½ fl oz/12⅔ cups water;
2 onions, halved;
2 carrots, peeled and cut into pieces;
1 leek, cut into pieces;
1 stick celery, cut into pieces;
1 bouquet garni; salt

Poached Eggplant
2 eggplants,
washed and halved lengthwise

Gelatine
Salt; 3 sheets gelatine, soaked in water;

Garnish
12 slices lemon; 1 tsp sea salt;
¼ tsp crushed cumin; red chilli slices;
diced lime flesh (zest removed);
grated lime zest; coriander leaves

PREPARATION

Chop the duck carcasses into pieces.
In a deep pan or stockpot, sauté them in some oil until they turn light brown in colour.
Add the water and bring to the boil. Skim the fat and grease off the surface carefully.
Scorch the onion halves on all sides in a hot pan.
Add the onions, carrots, leek, celery and bouquet garni to the stock and lower the heat.
Simmer for 1 hour, then pass the stock through a muslin strainer.
Discard the solid ingredients and bring the liquid to the boil.
Reduce until about 1 litre/2 pts 1⅞ fl oz/4¼ cups of consommé remain. Season to taste with salt.

Poach the eggplants in the consommé using very low heat for about 3 hours until they are cooked.
Test by piercing the eggplants with the tip of a small knife. The flesh should be soft when cooked.
If there isn't enough consommé to cover the eggplants while they are cooking, add water.
When cooked, remove the eggplants from the consommé and set aside to cool.
When cool, wrap in plastic film and keep refrigerated until required.

Strain the consommé and season to taste with salt.
Dissolve the soaked gelatine sheets in 1 litre/2 pts 1⅞ fl oz/4¼ cups of consommé.
Divide the mixture among 4 soup plates. Refrigerate overnight to set.

PRESENTATION

Gently place half a poached eggplant on each plate of gelatine.
Top each eggplant with 3 slices of lemon as shown.
Sprinkle sea salt, crushed cumin, red chilli slices, diced lime flesh and grated lime zest around.
Garnish with coriander leaves to serve.

▲ THE APPLE FOR SWEET DREAMS AT NIGHT Serves 4

INGREDIENTS

Apples
4 small Elstar or Royal Gala apples, peeled and cored;
4 strips orange zest; 4 strips lemon zest;
2 vanilla pods, halved; 50 g/1¾ oz butter;
500 ml/1 pt 1 fl oz/1¾ cups syrup

Walnut Ice Cream
1 litre/2 pts 1⅞ fl oz/4¼ cups milk;
8 egg yolks; 250 g/8¾ oz/1¼ cups sugar;
15 g/½ oz walnut paste;
5 tsp glucose

Caramel Sauce
200 g/7 oz/1 cup sugar;
150 ml/5 fl oz/⅝ cup water; 30 g/1 oz salted butter

Almond Brioche
100 ml/3¾ oz/⅜ cup almond cream;
4 pcs [10 by 3 by 0.7 cm (4 by 1.2 by 0.3 inch) each] almond brioche;
almond flakes; icing sugar

Garnish
20 pistachios

PREPARATION

Preheat the oven at 85°C (185°F).
Stuff the hollow core of each apple with a strip each of orange and lemon zest, and half a vanilla pod.
Coat the apples in butter and syrup and bake for 12 hours.

Bring the milk to the boil. Whisk the egg yolks and 100 g/3½ oz/½ cup of sugar with some warm milk, then add the mixture to the rest of the milk. Slowly bring the mixture to the boil, stirring constantly with a wooden spatula for a smooth texture. Strain the mixture into a mixing bowl and set the bowl on a basin filled with ice to cool. When cool, add the walnut paste, glucose and the remaining sugar and mix well.
Pour the mixture into an ice cream maker and process according to the specifications.
When ready, keep frozen until required.

Combine the sugar and 60 ml/2 fl oz/¼ cup of water in a saucepan and caramelise over low heat.
Deglaze with the remaining water and mix until the caramel dissolves completely.
Add the butter and mix well for a smooth texture.

Preheat the oven at 200°C (392°F). Apply almond cream on each piece of almond brioche.
Arrange the almond flakes on the cream to resemble fish scales as shown.
Sprinkle some icing sugar over and place them on a non-stick baking tray.
Toast them in the oven until crispy and golden brown in colour, then place them under intense heat under a salamander to glaze the icing sugar.

PRESENTATION

Remove the apples from the baking juices and place each apple on a plate. Arrange 5 pistachios on top of each apple to form a star. Place 1 scoop of walnut ice cream beside each apple. Drizzle the caramel sauce over the apples and serve with the almond brioche on the side.

LEFT: Belfry Garden, set in a restored building which was formerly a cathedral, is one of Hiroshima's prime locations for French dining.
BELOW: The elegant dining room has hosted countless glamorous parties attended by Japan's elite.

Belfry Garden
Hiroshima

Mitsuhiro Oda

Getting three Michelin stars or the equivalent rating may be prestigious and extremely good for business, but after you get there, what's next? A career in the kitchen makes a cook a chef and if he or she tops the popularity polls, a consultant's job could be next. Although airline food is a long way from the gourmet variety, a consultancy contract with a national carrier is probably one of the biggest compliments that can be paid to a chef for his ability to draw an international clientele.

Detail Mitsuhiro Oda's job as an Inflight Services Consultant with Singapore Airlines and observe the envy among chefs. He zips from Tokyo to Los Angeles to Taipei and destinations across the globe to inspect the elaborate first- and business-class menus. These are designed by the airline's International Culinary Panel, made up of eminent chefs such as Georges Blanc, Gordon Ramsay and Yoshihiro Murata. Oda's nod of approval is required before any food gets served. And he is not easily impressed, having gained his own expertise in classic French cooking from some of Europe's best before returning to Japan.

When he isn't travelling, Oda consults for several restaurants in Kyoto and Tokyo as well as for the luxurious Belfry Garden in Hiroshima. A French restaurant showcasing Oda's creative cuisine, shaped as it is by his Japanese heritage, French training and travels, Belfry Garden also specialises in catering for private parties that can afford the exclusive attention of a top-notch chef.

▲ FOIE GRAS TORCHON ON BRIOCHE WITH TRUFFLE ICE CREAM AND SAUTERNES-CONSOMMÉ GELATINE

Serves 4

INGREDIENTS

Foie Gras Torchon

800 g/1 lb $1\frac{1}{4}$ oz foie gras, veins removed; a pinch of salt; a dash of pepper; a pinch of sugar; 50 ml/$1\frac{3}{4}$ fl oz/$\frac{1}{4}$ cup white port wine; 4 tsp Armagnac

Brioche dough

40 g/$1\frac{3}{8}$ oz/$\frac{1}{4}$ cup yeast; 210 ml/$7\frac{1}{8}$ fl oz/$\frac{7}{8}$ cup lukewarm milk; 450 g/$15\frac{7}{8}$ oz butter; 450 ml/$15\frac{1}{4}$ fl oz/$1\frac{7}{8}$ cups eggs; scant $2\frac{3}{4}$ tsp salt; 120 g/$4\frac{1}{4}$ oz/$\frac{2}{3}$ cup sugar; 1 kg/2 lb $3\frac{1}{4}$ oz/$7\frac{2}{3}$ cups extra-strength flour, sieved; 2 egg yolks, beaten

Truffle Ice Cream

180 ml/6 fl oz/$\frac{3}{4}$ cup egg yolks; 250 ml/$8\frac{1}{2}$ fl oz/1 cup milk; 100 g/$3\frac{1}{2}$ oz/$\frac{1}{2}$ cup sugar; 80 ml/$2\frac{3}{4}$ fl oz/$\frac{1}{3}$ cup white port wine; 50 g/$1\frac{3}{4}$ oz truffles, chopped; 20 ml/$\frac{5}{8}$ fl oz/4 tsp truffle juice; 250 ml/$8\frac{1}{2}$ fl oz/1 cup fresh cream;

Sauternes-Consommé Gelatine

50 g/$1\frac{3}{4}$ oz meat from duck legs, minced; 80 g/$2\frac{7}{8}$ oz meat from beef shin, minced; 180 g/$6\frac{3}{8}$ oz/$2\frac{1}{4}$ cups mirepoix; 2 egg whites; salt; pepper; 350 ml/$11\frac{7}{8}$ fl oz/$1\frac{1}{2}$ cups beef stock (recipe on page 148); 350 ml/$11\frac{7}{8}$ fl oz/$1\frac{1}{2}$ cups chicken stock (recipe on page 148); 2 ripe tomatoes, cut into small chunks; 300 ml/$10\frac{1}{8}$ fl oz/$1\frac{1}{4}$ cups Sauternes; 4 g/scant $\frac{1}{8}$ oz gelatine leaves, soaked in water

Candied Orange

500 g/1 lb $1\frac{5}{8}$ oz/$2\frac{1}{2}$ cups sugar; 600 ml/1 pt $4\frac{1}{4}$ fl oz/$2\frac{1}{2}$ cups warm water; 1 orange, cut into wedges

Blood Orange Sauce

20 g/$\frac{3}{4}$ oz/$\frac{1}{8}$ cup marmalade; 50 ml/$1\frac{3}{4}$ fl oz/$\frac{1}{4}$ cup blood orange juice; 4 tsp syrup from candied orange; 20 g/$\frac{3}{4}$ oz candied orange

Garnish

4 herb bouquets of Italian parsley, chervil and basil

PREPARATION

Season the foie gras with salt, pepper and sugar, then marinate it in white port wine and Armagnac overnight.
The next day, wrap the foie gras with plastic film, followed by a cloth, and poach it in warm water [60 to 70°C (140 to 158°F)] for 30 to 40 minutes until it is cooked.
Remove from the water and strain.

Stir the yeast into the lukewarm milk until it dissolves completely. Set aside.
Melt the butter and stir in the eggs, salt and sugar. Add the milk and butter mixtures to the flour and work the mixture into a smooth dough. If the dough is too firm, add more milk. Leave the dough to rise at room temperature for 30 minutes, then place the dough in a lightly floured brioche mould and leave it to rise at room temperature for another 30 to 45 minutes. Preheat the oven at 220°C (428°F).
Lightly brush the top of the dough with the beaten egg yolks and bake for 40 to 45 minutes until the brioche is light and spongy.

Whisk the egg yolks, milk, sugar and white port wine until the ingredients are well mixed.
Add the chopped truffles and truffle juice and mix well.
Process the mixture in an ice cream maker until it thickens slightly, then add the fresh cream and continue processing until the ice cream is ready.
Freeze the mixture until it sets and keep frozen until required.

Mix the meat, mirepoix and egg whites, then season to taste with salt and pepper.
Work the ingredients by hand until they are well mixed, then add the beef and chicken stocks and mix well.
Bring the mixture to the boil, then add the tomato chunks. Reduce the heat and allow the mixture to simmer for 45 to 50 minutes until the egg whites separate.
Stir in the Sauternes slowly, then remove the mixture from the heat and pass it through a muslin strainer.
Add the soaked gelatine leaves and stir until they dissolve completely.
Pour the mixture into a mould and set aside to cool.
Refrigerate when cool and keep chilled until required.

Mix the sugar and warm water until the sugar dissolves completely.
Cook the orange wedges in the syrup over low heat until they are cooked and tender.
Remove from the heat and leave the orange wedges in the syrup until required.

Combine all the ingredients in a blender and process until you obtain a smooth sauce.

PRESENTATION

Serve the foie gras torchon on toasted brioche with truffle ice cream, Sauternes-consommé gelatine, candied oranges, herb bouquet and blood orange sauce on the side.

ROASTED LOBSTER AND VODKA SORBET WITH CRABMEAT AND CORAL Serves 4

INGREDIENTS

Vodka Sorbet with Crabmeat and Coral
100 g/3½ oz/⅓ cup crab coral;
80 ml/2¾ fl oz/⅓ cup fresh cream; a pinch of sugar;
50 ml/1¾ fl oz/¼ cup vodka;
80 g/2⅞ oz/½ cup crabmeat; a dash of balsamic vinegar;
250 ml/8½ fl oz/1 cup clear, fresh tomato juice;
salt; pepper

Consommé Jelly
120 ml/4 fl oz/½ cup consommé (recipe on page 149);
2 to 3 g/scant ⅛ oz gelatine leaves, soaked

Grapefruit Chips
500 ml/17 fl oz/2 cups water;
600 g/1 lb 8⅝ oz/3 cups sugar; 1 grapefruit

Garden Vegetables
30 green soya beans; 20 broad beans;
8 white asparagus spears; 8 green asparagus spears;
a handful of broccoli, trimmed into florets;
3 to 4 tbsp olive oil; a few drops of sherry vinegar;
salt; pepper

Roasted Lobster
4 lobsters; 10 g/⅜ oz fennel, roughly chopped;
20 g/¾ oz carrots, roughly chopped;
50 g/1¾ oz onion, roughly chopped;
15 g/½ oz celery, roughly chopped; 3 cloves garlic;
1 sprig thyme; 1 sprig rosemary;
3 sprigs tarragon; olive oil

Garnish
4 hearts of tomato; 1 bunch fresh sansho pepper;
4 herb bouquets of chervil, dill, sage and tarragon

PREPARATION

Combine the crab coral, fresh cream, sugar and vodka in a pot, mix well and bring to the boil.
Remove from the heat and set aside to cool.
Process the mixture in a blender until it is smooth, then add the crabmeat, balsamic vinegar and tomato juice. Mix well and season to taste with salt and pepper.
Transfer the mixture into an ice cream maker set to sorbet specifications and process until it thickens slightly.
Add a dash of vodka and continue to process until the sorbet is ready.
Keep frozen until required.

Combine the consommé and soaked gelatine leaves in a pot and bring to the boil.
Remove from the heat and pass the mixture through a muslin strainer. Pour into a rectangular mould and set aside to cool. Refrigerate overnight for the jelly to set. Keep chilled until required.

Combine the water and sugar in a pot and bring to the boil. Mix well until the sugar is completely dissolved.
Remove from the heat and set aside to cool. Cut the grapefuit with a mandolin into paper-thin slices.
Soak the grapefruit slices in the syrup for 2 to 3 hours.
Preheat the oven at 80°C (176°F). Remove the grapefruit slices from the syrup and arrange them on a baking tray. Bake them in the oven for 6 to 7 hours until they are crispy.

Blanch all the pulses and vegetables, then toss them in the olive oil and the sherry vinegar.
Season to taste with salt and pepper.

Preheat the oven at 180°C (356°F).
Arrange the lobsters, chopped fennel, carrots, onion and celery, as well as garlic, thyme, rosemary and tarragon on a baking tray, and drizzle olive oil over.
Roast in the oven for 8 to 10 minutes until the lobsters are cooked.
Remove from the oven and and keep warm until required.

PRESENTATION

Remove the lobster shells and cut each lobster body into 2. Place each portion in the centre of a plate and arrange the garden vegetables around. Spoon about 30 g/1 oz of consommé jelly on each plate, and place a scoop of vodka sorbet on each portion of lobster. Garnish with the hearts of tomato, fresh sansho pepper, herb bouquets and grapefruit chips to serve.

Dal Pescatore
Mantova

RIGHT: The three-Michelin-star Dal Pescatore in Mantova.
ABOVE: Service staff waiting for the first guests to arrive.
ABOVE RIGHT: Crystal, silver and freshly picked flowers adorn the tables at Dal Pescatore.

Nadia Santini

Paul Bocuse once remarked that he would gladly give up his 40 years in the kitchen, his great successes and awards, to be the Santinis of Mantova. They make people feel more welcome than any other three-Michelin-star establishment, and have 'the very best restaurant in the world'. Higher praise is simply not possible.

In 1920, when Antonio Santini's grandfather bought a little fisherman's shack, he little dreamed that it would blossom into the internationally acclaimed Dal Pescatore. In keeping with the traditions of a family-run restaurant, today grandson Antonio manages the restaurant; Antonio's wife Nadia cooks and Antonio's daughter-in-law Bruna makes the pasta. Credit for Bocuse's compliment must be shared among all the Santinis, and their philosophy of using traditional recipes and local ingredients.

As Nadia's skill and creativity flowered, she adapted and fine-tuned her family's recipes, leaning towards lighter, healthier preparations which are more suited to current lifestyles, but always maintaining a delicate balance between tradition and innovation. Attention to local produce is certainly paid, and with delicious results, but the kitchen is not tied to the territory. For while Nadia never forgets her local roots, she manages to rejuvenate regional dishes and each memorable bite displays the confidence of a cook who knows when no additional embellishment is necessary. This is evidenced in such aromatic specialities as pan-fried porcini with velvety calf liver simmered in butter and rosemary, home-made tortelli with goat's cheese and white truffles, and smooth and ribbed penne with crispy eel and candied lime.

▲ COMPOSITION OF TOMATO, EGGPLANT, BASIL FLOWERS AND OLIVE OIL Serves 4

INGREDIENTS
Tomato and Eggplant Terrine
20 ml/⅔ fl oz/4 tsp extra virgin olive oil (Tuscan variety preferred);
8 [0.1-cm (0.04-inch) thick] eggplant slices (peeled and sliced lengthwise);
250 g/8⅞ oz ripe tomatoes, peeled and top stems removed

Vegetable Gelatine
50 ml/1¾ fl oz/¼ cup vegetable stock (recipe on page 148);
5 g/⅛ oz/½ tsp gelatine powder;
30 g/1 oz ice cubes

Garnish
Basil flowers or leaves; rock salt;
50 ml/1¾ fl oz/¼ cup extra virgin olive oil (Tuscan variety preferred)

PREPARATION
Warm the extra virgin olive oil in an aluminium pan and lightly fry the eggplant slices until they are crispy and golden brown in colour. Do not overcook the eggplants or they will be excessively oily and change colour.
Line a small terrine with plastic film, then line the sides with the fried eggplants, leaving enough eggplants on the top to cover the filling completely. Squeeze the tomatoes with your hands to fill the base of the terrine with some juices, then press the flesh into the terrine to fill it evenly.
Fold the excess eggplant over the tomatoes to cover the filling completely

Pour the vegetable stock into a pan and bring it to the boil.
Add the gelatine powder and stir continuously until the gelatine powder dissolves completely.
Remove from the heat and add the ice cubes to the mixture to cool it quickly.
Spoon the mixture over the terrine and spread evenly.
Refrigerate the terrine for at least 2 hours before serving.

PRESENTATION
Remove the terrine from the mould. Cut the terrine into 2-cm- (0.8-inch-) thick slabs and use a spatula to transfer each portion onto the centre of a plate.
Garnish with basil flowers or leaves and rock salt. Drizzle the extra virgin olive oil around to serve.

▶ LETTUCE OF CARNEVALE Serves 8 to 10

INGREDIENTS
Lettuce of Carnevale
½ kg/1 lb 1⅝ oz/4 cups plain flour, sifted;
1 egg; 4 egg yolks;
1 vanilla pod;
grated orange zest;
2 tsp extra virgin olive oil;
a pinch of salt;
50 ml/1¾ fl oz/¼ cup milk;
30 ml/1 fl oz/⅛ cup Strega liquor;
50 g/1¾ oz butter;
1 litre/1 pt 1⅞ fl oz/4¼ cups oil

PREPARATION
Mound the flour on a clean board (or other smooth surfaces) and create a well in the centre.
Fill the well with the egg, egg yolks, vanilla beans scraped from the pod, grated orange zest as desired, extra virgin olive oil, salt, milk and Strega liquor.
Use your fingers to break up the egg yolks, then turn the eggs in a circular motion with your fingers without spilling over the sides of the well. By doing this, the flour from the sides will be gradually incorporated into the egg mixture. But do not incorporate the flour too quickly or the dough will be lumpy.
Keep moving the eggs until the dough thickens, then use a fork to mix the dough thoroughly.
Run the dough through a pasta machine (or use a rolling pin to flatten the dough) to make long, thin stretches of pasta. Roll them up and wrap each roll in plastic film to keep the pasta moist.
Heat the butter in a pan until it softens. Cut out a chunk of pasta dough and keep the remaining dough wrapped in plastic film. Roll out the dough evenly until it is about 0.5-cm (0.02-inch) thick.
Brush some butter on the surface then fold the sheet of pasta into 2. Roll out the pasta again until it is 0.5-mm (0.02-inch) thick, then brush the surface with butter and fold into 2.
Repeat this process once more, then roll out the dough until is 0.5-cm (0.02-inch) thick and use a pasta cutter to cut 6-by-6-cm (2.4-by-2.4-inch) squares.
Roll up the squares diagonally and deep-fry until the pasta is cooked. Remove the cooked pasta from the oil with a strainer and place them on a plate line with kitchen tissue to absorb the excess oil.

Finishing
40 g/1⅜ oz/scant ¼ cup sugar

PRESENTATION
Sprinkle some sugar on the deep-fried pasta to serve.

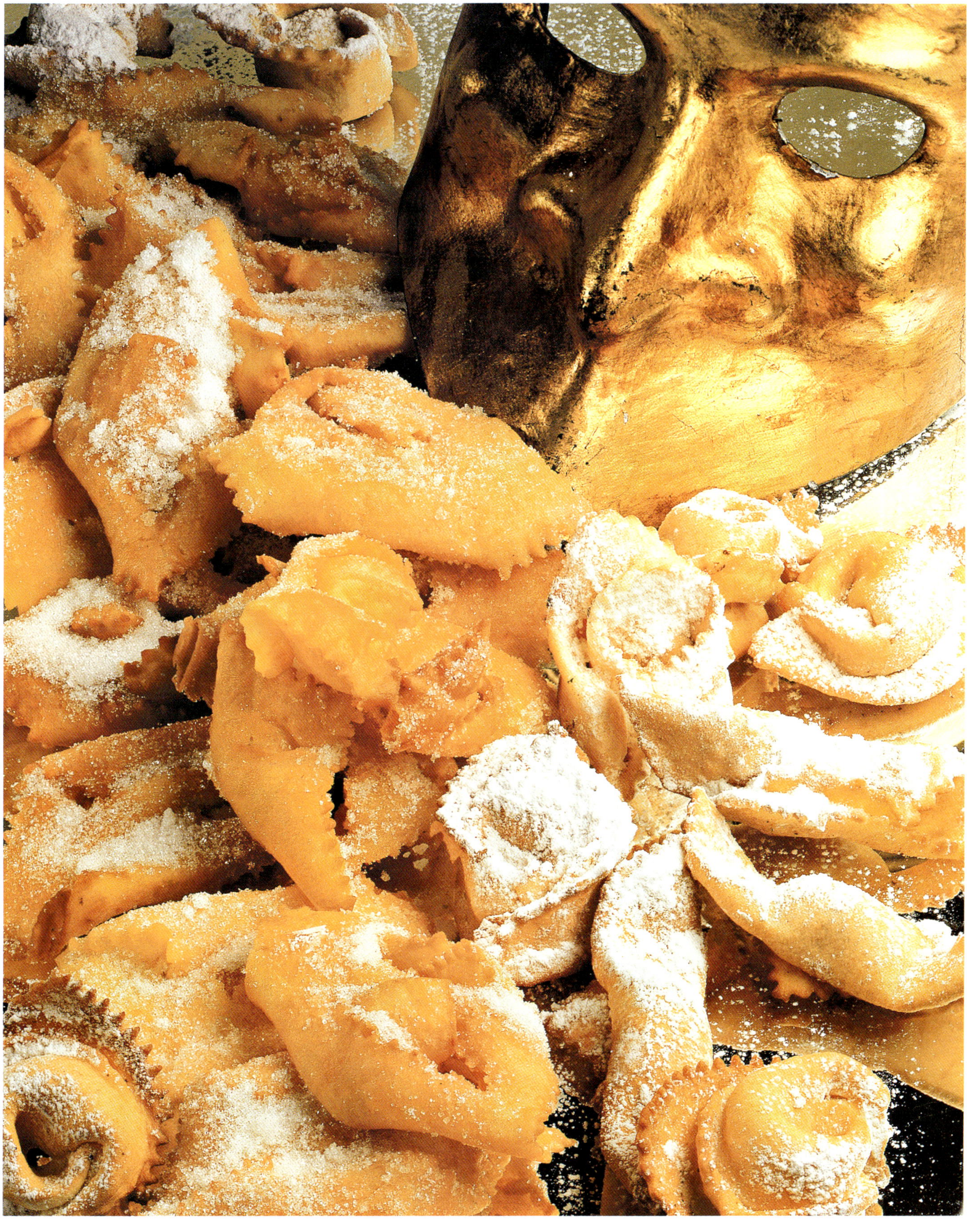

Celsius
Sydney

LEFT: Excellent food, superb wine and professional service are the hallmarks of Celsius, Peter Doyle's latest venture.
ABOVE: Double-clothed tables set with gleaming cutlery and top-end crystal and flatware are the perfect foils for Doyle's confident cooking.
ABOVE, LEFT: Decorated in bone and brown, Celsius' understated and conservative interior reinforces the restaurant's appeal to serious city diners.

Peter Doyle

Peter Doyle is a French-technique-inspired, Mediterranean-influenced Australian visionary who in the late seventies helped further his country's good-food revolution. Over the years he daringly stuffed ravioli with Tasmanian salmon slathered with a ginger butter sauce, sautéed baby octopus with balsamic vinegar, and put lamb wrapped in basil leaves on a shallot flan. For the previously complacent Australian diners this was a revelation.

A country boy who grew up on a farm, Doyle was working in the land-tax department when he had his first taste of fresh foie gras and warm brie, which helped put things into perspective. Hooked on surfing, he was also envious of his brother Greg's life as a chef, which permitted surfing between service periods. Hence his decision to spend his life in the kitchen. Now a busy jet-setting chef with a popular fine-dining restaurant and a briskly selling cookbook, Doyle is a much sought-after presence at food festivals and gourmet wine dinners all over the world. He confesses to using the freshest of seasonal native ingredients, cooked with care. But he is too modest. Above all he's a stickler who thrives on detail, who seeks out the finest supplier of curly leaf baby endive or Japanese mizuna, who willingly scrutinises piles of tiger prawns for just six pristine specimens…. Ditto for a handful of flawless figs. Or one perfectly formed porcini.

As one reviewer put it, 'Doyle's tastes and flavours dance on the tongue.'

▼ BRAISED WHITE RABBIT WITH SAUTÉED CHESTNUT MUSHROOMS, GREEN PEAS AND POTATO GALETTE Serves 6

INGREDIENTS

Potato Galette
3 desirée potatoes, peeled and cleaned;
clarified butter

Braised White Rabbit
2 white rabbit legs; sea salt; pepper;
200 ml/6¾ fl oz/⅞ cup olive oil;
1 carrot, peeled and sliced into rounds;
1 stick celery, cut into 2-cm (0.8-inch) lengths;
1 onion, peeled and sliced;
100 ml/3⅜ fl oz/⅜ cup dry white wine;
500 ml/1 pt 1 fl oz/2⅛ cup white stock (recipe on page 148);
1 clove garlic; 1 bouquet garni;
2 white rabbit racks, bones scraped and halved;
2 white rabbit saddles, deboned, trimmed and halved;
2 white rabbit kidneys, halved;
1 white rabbit liver, halved; clarified butter

Green Peas and Chestnut Mushrooms
4 tbsp chestnut mushrooms; sea salt; pepper;
clarified butter; 2 tbsp cooked pea purée;
4 tbsp green peas, blanched and refreshed

Herb Salad and Vinaigrette
20 ml/⅜ fl oz/4 tsp vinaigrette (1 part vinegar to 3 parts olive oil);
3 tbsp mixed herb salad

PREPARATION

Slice the potatoes with a mandoline fitted with the julienne blade. Heat some clarified butter in a small frying pan [8 cm (3.2 inches) in diameter] and add enough potato strips to cover the base of the pan in an even layer. Flatten the potatoes to form a disc. When the bottom layer of potatoes turns slightly golden brown in colour, flip the disc over carefully and pan-fry the other side until it is cooked.
Use a spatula to transfer the disc onto a plate lined with kitchen tissue to absorb the excess oil.
Prepare 5 more galettes with the remaining ingredients. Keep warm until required.

Preheat the oven at 160°C (320°F). Season the rabbit legs to taste with sea salt and pepper.
Heat half the olive oil in a pan over high heat and pan-fry the rabbit legs, carrot, celery and onion until they turn light brown in colour. Transfer the mixture onto a plate and set aside.
Discard the remaining olive oil from the pan and deglaze the pan with the white wine over high heat. Reduce the wine by half, then add the white stock and return the pan-fried rabbit legs and vegetables to the pan. Add the garlic clove and bouquet garni and lower the heat to a simmer. Cover the pan and place it in the pre-heated oven for 40 minutes. The braised meat should be tender and easily detached from the bone. Remove the legs from the stock and set aside to cool. Discard the vegetables, but retain the bouquet garni, and set the stock aside to settle for 5 minutes. Skim away the material floating on the stock's surface, then pour the stock into a clean pot and reduce by half. Once the legs are cool enough for handling, remove the meat from the bones in large pieces and add them to the reduced stock. Add the thyme leaves extracted from the bouquet garni and keep the stock warm until required. Season the white rabbit racks, saddles, kidneys and liver to taste with sea salt and pepper. Heat some clarified butter in a frying pan over medium heat and add the racks, saddles, kidneys and liver. Make sure the rabbit parts are cooked evenly and remove them (first the kidneys and liver, then the racks and lastly, the saddles) once they are cooked.

Season the chestnut mushrooms to taste with sea salt and pepper.
Heat some clarified butter in a pan, add the chestnut mushrooms and toss until they are cooked.
Add the cooked pea purée and green peas to the stock with chunks of rabbit leg meat and reheat.

Add the vinaigrette to the mixed herb salad and toss well.

PRESENTATION

Warm 6 dinner plates and place ½ tbsp of pea purée in the centre of each plate. Top the pea purée with equal portions of the braised rabbit leg meat. Place some chestnut mushrooms and green peas around and spoon a little braising stock over. Top each portion of meat with a potato galette.
Slice the saddle evenly, halve the kidneys, slice the liver pieces and cut the racks to make 6 portions. Arrange a few slices of saddle on top of each potato galette. Place the liver and kidney slices around the meat. Top each portion of saddle with a rack and garnish with a little mixed herb salad to serve.

GRILLED LANGOUSTINES WITH TROMPETTES DE MORT AND BARRAMUNDI WITH SAUTÉED VEGETABLES AND HERB SALAD Serves 6

INGREDIENTS

Langoustines with Trompettes de Mort
30 g/1 oz/⅓ cups dried trompettes de mort mushrooms, soaked in water;
1 tbsp extra virgin olive oil; 1 tbsp butter;
9 langoustines, heads removed, cleaned and halved lengthwise

Sautéed Vegetables
30 g/1 oz/⅓ cup dried trompettes de mort mushrooms, soaked in water;
150 ml/5 fl oz/⅔ cup clarified butter;
2 zucchinis, cleaned and diced;
50 g/1¾ oz/6¾ cups honshimeiji mushrooms;
1 tsp finely chopped garlic; sea salt; pepper;
½ tsp finely chopped thyme leaves

Barramundi
6 (each 50 g/1¾ oz) barramundi fillets, trimmed;
sea salt; pepper; extra virgin olive oil

Herb Salad
2 red jalapeno chillies,
4 tbsp curly endive leaves; 1 tbsp dill sprigs;
1 tbsp chervil sprigs; 4 tsp lemon juice;
100 ml/3¾ fl oz/⅔ cup extra virgin olive oil

PREPARATION

Squeeze the excess water from the soaked trompettes de mort mushrooms, then cut them into thin strips.
Warm the extra virgin olive oil in a pan over medium to high heat and sauté the mushrooms.
Add the butter just before they are cooked through and toss well.
Strain the mushrooms, discard the cooking juices, transfer the mushrooms onto a tray and set aside to cool.
When the mushrooms are cool, chop them finely and sprinkle a little over each langoustine.
Set aside until required.

Squeeze the excess water from the soaked trompettes de mort mushrooms and pat dry with kitchen tissue.
Heat 2 tbsp of clarified butter in a frying pan and add the diced zucchinis, trompettes de mort and honshimeiji mushrooms, and chopped garlic. Toss well and season to taste with sea salt and pepper.
About 1 minute before the ingredients are cooked, add the chopped thyme leaves and sauté over high heat.
When the ingredients are cooked through, strain the mixture and keep warm until required.

Season the barramundi fillets and prepared langoustines with sea salt and pepper.
Brush the barramundi fillets and langoustines with a little olive oil and cook over high heat on a grill (or under a salamander) quickly, taking care not to overcook the langoustines.

Remove the seeds from the red jalapeno chillies and chop finely.
Combine the chopped chillies with all the other ingredients in a mixing bowl and toss well.

PRESENTATION

Divide the sautéed vegetables among 6 plates and top each serving with a cooked barramundi fillet. Arrange 3 portions of langoustine on each barramundi fillet and top with a small mound of herb salad to serve.

RIGHT: Chinese calligraphy and handsewn lanterns in Jade's private dining rooms.
BELOW: The restaurant design combines colonial architecture and Oriental art with contemporary furnishing, creating an ambience befitting New Chinese Cuisine.
BOTTOM: An auspicious marble signage for Jade.

Jade
Singapore

Sam Leong

Chinese chefs aren't known just for being tough taskmasters. Older chefs are also infamous for their reluctance to share their special skills and secret recipes with their subordinates, unless the latter happen to be flesh and blood, and are being drilled to take over the family's business. For those who haven't had help from destiny but seek to pursue a career in the kitchen, an alternative approach is sneaking glances at the chefs when their backs are turned and memorising the 'extras', then quickly scribbling observations in a notebook.

Sam Leong, born to the owners of a modest but very popular Chinese diner in Johor Bahru, Malaysia, inherited his father's culinary genius and kitchen knowledge. He fondly recounts his late-night, after-service adventures as an apprentice sneaking into the forest with his mates to catch giant frogs for supper. Those were the highlights of typical workdays because life in the kitchen was hard; and being the sole heir to the business was even more gruelling as expectations of him were very high. Yearning to experience life outside his family's terrain, he packed his bags, headed for Singapore and hasn't looked back.

Bored with the classic presentation of Chinese food where huge servings, meant for all seated, are simultaneously placed on the lazy susan before the chopstick combat ensues, he experimented with plating the dishes individually, then serving them in succession with the appropriate cutlery. Ingredients and techniques previously unfamiliar to Chinese tradition began to surface in his cooking, and Leong's inventiveness soon found a worldwide following. Leong is now resident chef of Jade and Director of Kitchens for Tung Lok Restaurants, which is thriving on the popularity of New Chinese Cuisine. He makes regular guest appearances at international food festivals, cooking alongside fans and fellow chefs, Nobu Matsuhisa and Wolfgang Puck.

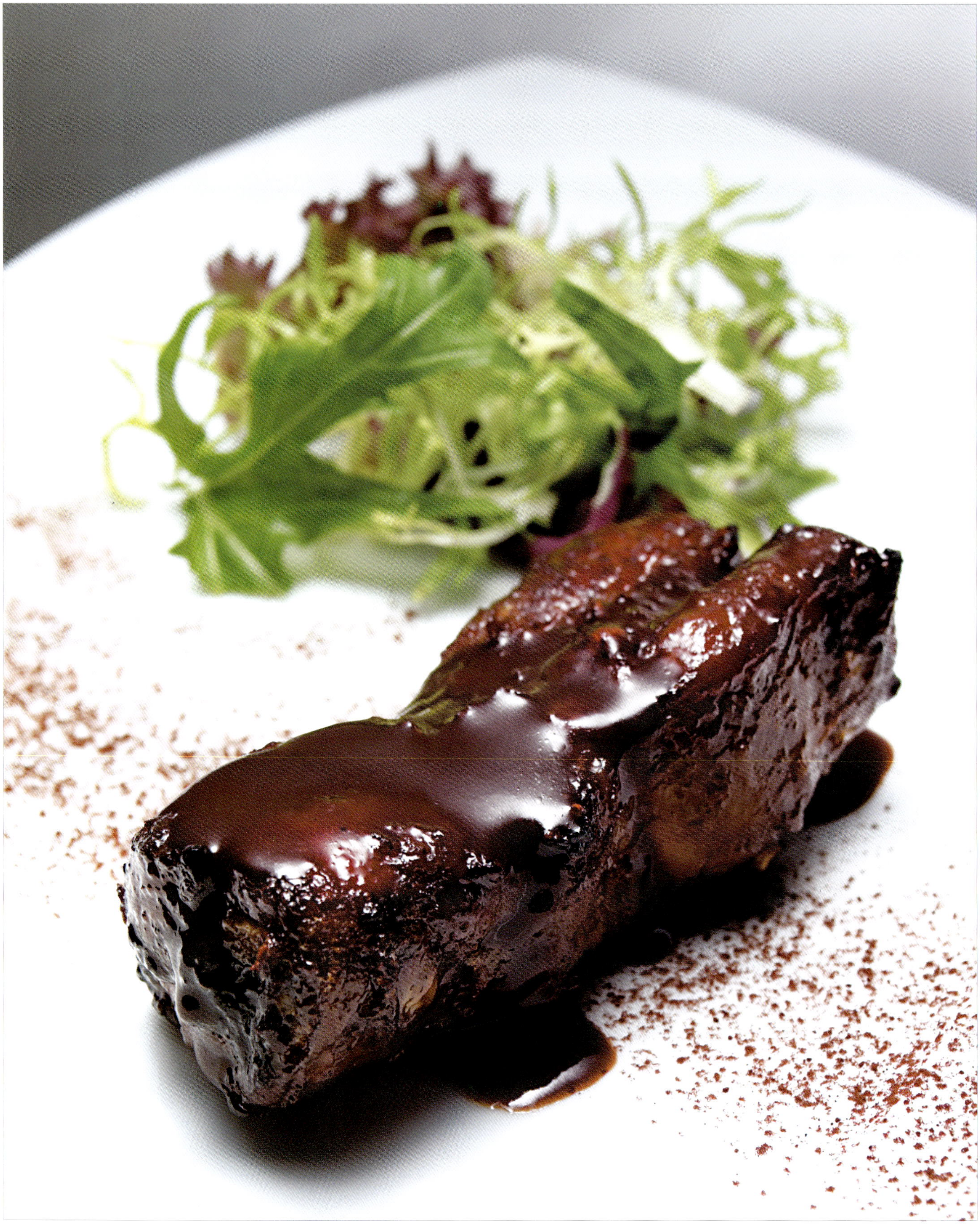

DEEP-FRIED COD WITH THAI CHILLI SAUCE, POMELO AND MANGO Serves 4

INGREDIENTS

Thai Chilli Sauce
120 ml/4 fl oz/½ cup Thai sweet chilli sauce;
80 ml/2¾ fl oz/⅓ cup tomato ketchup;
80 ml/2¾ fl oz/⅓ cup fresh lemon juice;
40 ml/1⅜ fl oz/⅛ cup white vinegar;
40 ml/1⅜ fl oz/⅛ cup honey or syrup;
80 ml/2¾ fl oz/⅓ cup water;
4 tsp minced garlic; 4 tsp minced shallots;
4 tsp minced red chilli;
20 g/¾ oz tomato flesh, shredded finely;
20 g/¾ oz coriander leaves, chopped finely

Deep-fried Cod
4 (100 g/3½ oz each) cod fillets; oil

Garnish
80 g/2⅞ oz/⅞ cup diced mango;
80 g/2⅞ oz/⅞ cup pomelo sacs;
4 tsp ebiko; 4 tsp bijih selesih

PREPARATION
Combine all the ingredients in a bowl and mix well.

Score the cod fillets diagonally and in opposite directions.
Deep-fry the fillets in very hot oil for 1 minute until they are cooked and turn golden brown in colour.
Transfer the fish to a plate lined with kitchen tissue to absorb the excess oil.

PRESENTATION
Place each fillet on a small plate and spoon the Thai chilli sauce over.
Garnish the fillets with diced mango, pomelo sacs, ebiko and bijih selesih to serve.

ROASTED PORK RIBS WITH MOCHA SAUCE Serves 4

INGREDIENTS

Roasted Pork Ribs
400 g/14⅛ oz pork ribs;
80 ml/2¾ fl oz/⅓ cup soya sauce;
120 g/4¼ oz/⅔ cup sugar; 3 tsp sesame oil;
2 egg whites; 4 tsp cornflour

Mocha Sauce
2 tsp mocha essence;
150 ml/5 fl oz/⅔ cup A1 sauce;
65 ml/2⅛ fl oz/¼ cup tomato ketchup;
80 ml/2¾ fl oz/⅓ cup plum oil;
90 g/3⅛ oz/⅔ cup marmalade;
90 g/3⅛ oz/⅔ cup apple jam;
2 tsp salt; 180 g/6⅜ oz/⅞ cup sugar;
48 g/1⅝ oz/scant ½ cup cocoa powder;
300 ml/10⅛ fl oz/1¼ cups water

Garnish
4 handfuls of mixed salad leaves;
2 tsp cocoa powder

PREPARATION
Mix the pork ribs with the soya sauce, sugar, sesame oil, egg whites and cornflour and marinate overnight in the refrigerator.
To serve, preheat the oven at 250°C (482°F). Bake the marinated pork ribs for 15 minutes until they are cooked and turn golden brown in colour.

Combine all the ingredients in a pot and whisk over low heat until they are well mixed.
Remove from the heat and set aside to cool.
Reheat the mocha sauce just before serving.

PRESENTATION
Divide the pork ribs among 4 plates and place a handful of salad leaves beside each portion.
Spoon the mocha sauce over the pork ribs and dust some cocoa powder over to serve.

RIGHT: Sergi Arola and team.
ABOVE: Sergi Arola's La Broche in Madrid has been called 'a shrine to modern cooking'.
ABOVE, RIGHT: The restaurant's stylishly understated entrance.
BELOW: La Broche's clientele outgrew the restaurant's capacity at Dr. Fleming Street, hence its move to the basement of Madrid's Miguel Ángel Hotel.

Sergi Arola

Sergi Arola's cooking is daring, modern and exciting, yet steeped in the authentic aromas and spirit of the Mediterranean. With diners such as the King and Queen of Spain at his table, it's obvious even Spanish royalty is tempted to take a walk on the wild side. Arola audaciously updates the classics. Sushi is served in a glass at La Broche, his restaurant in Madrid: a thin layer of soya-flavoured gelatine at the bottom of the glass is topped with cubes of tuna and avocado marinated in wasabi; a scoop of rice sorbet completes his tribute to the Japanese classic. But he would never dream up a creative combination just to shock. So every fortnight, he includes on the tasting menu items such as frog's legs stuffed with trout roe, or cream of bacon with blood sausage and egg-yolk ice cream, and takes votes. If his customers say 'no' to a particular dish, it's off for good.

By fine-tuning his bolder recipes, while maintaining originality without compromising on quality, and by dividing his menu into three categories, 'from the imagination, from the sea and from the mountains', he has managed to earn himself two Michelin stars in three years of operation. And he is currently nurturing ambitious plans for La Broche to open in Mexico and Miami. One of the more talented disciples of Ferran Adrià and Pierre Gagnaire—chefs known for their experimental styles, Arola has already proved a credit to his teachers.

▶ CRAYFISH WITH CHEESE, GRAPES, SUNNY-SIDE-UP EGG AND WALNUT PURÉE Serves 4

INGREDIENTS
Crayfish with Cheese
100 g/3½ oz Tupi del pillars or Munster cheese;
100 ml/3⅜ fl oz/⅜ cup pasteurised milk;
5 tsp water;
30 ml/1 fl oz/⅛ cup whipping cream, half-whipped;
4 big crayfish; olive oil

PREPARATION
Prepare the cheese 1 day ahead.
Combine the cheese, milk and water in a big bowl and place the bowl in a basin of warm water. Let it sit for 3 hours, then strain the mixture and retain the solid part. Keep refrigerated overnight.
The next day, mix the cheese with some half-whipped cream to smoothen its texture.
Peel the crayfish carefully and cut each tail into 5 medallions.
Just before serving, pan-fry the crayfish in some olive oil.

Walnut Purée
2 tsp walnut oil;
25 g/⅞ oz/¼ cup walnuts, peeled

Process the walnut oil and walnuts in a blender to obtain a smooth purée.

Grapes
20 sweet white grapes (Muscat grapes preferred)

Peel the grapes.

Sunny-side-up Egg
4 egg yolks

Preheat the salamander or oven at 200°C (392°F).
Divide the cheese mixture among 4 soup plates.
Place an egg yolk on each plate and arrange 5 peeled grapes next to each egg yolk to form a circle.
Drizzle some walnut purée over and place the plates under intense heat until a light brown crust forms on the sauce and the egg yolks are just cooked.

Garnish
4 dill sprigs; Maldon or sea salt;
extra virgin olive oil

PREPARATION
Place the pan-fried crayfish on top of the grapes. Sprinkle a little Maldon or sea salt on each egg yolk. Garnish with a drop of extra virgin olive oil on the egg yolk and a dill sprig to serve.

▼ ROYAL CONSOMMÉ WITH MUSHROOMS, FRIED SNAILS AND JABUGO HAM FOAM Serves 4

INGREDIENTS
Royal Consommé
500 g/1 lb ⅝ oz/5 cups trompettes de mort or morel mushrooms;
1 clove garlic, crushed;
1 litre/2 pts 1⅞ fl oz/4¼ cups chicken stock (recipe on page 148);
4 egg yolks, beaten; salt

PREPARATION
Preheat the oven at 160°C (320°F).
Sauté the mushrooms with the crushed garlic in a non-stick pot and add the chicken stock.
Bring to the boil, then lower the heat and simmer until the mixture reduces by half.
Strain, add the egg yolk to the consommé, and season to taste with salt.
Pour the consommé into 4 soup plates, place them on a shallow tray filled with water and heat in the oven for 10 minutes. Remove from the oven, then cover the plates with aluminium foil.

Jabugo Ham Foam
300 ml/10⅛ fl oz/1¼ cups milk;
200 ml/6¾ fl oz/⅞ cup cream;
250 g/8⅞ oz Jabugo ham, cut into pieces;
100 ml/3⅜ fl oz/⅜ cup egg white

Combine the milk, cream and Jabugo ham in a saucepan, mix well and bring to the boil.
Remove from the heat, cover the pan and set the mixture aside to cool (about 30 minutes).
When cool, strain and add the egg white to the liquid. Mix well.
Pour the liquid into a siphon and set aside.

Deep-fried Snails
200 g/7 oz/1½ cups flour;
75 ml/2½ fl oz/⅓ cup water; 10 g/⅜ oz royal yeast;
a pinch of salt; 16 cleaned snails; oil

Combine the flour, water, royal yeast and salt in a mixing bowl and mix into a smooth batter.
Dip the snails into the batter and deep-fry until golden brown and crispy.

PRESENTATION
Remove the aluminium foil from the plates and reheat the consommé under a salamander or in an oven. When the consommé is warm, arrange 4 deep-fried snails in the centre of each plate and top with Jabugo ham foam from the siphon to serve.

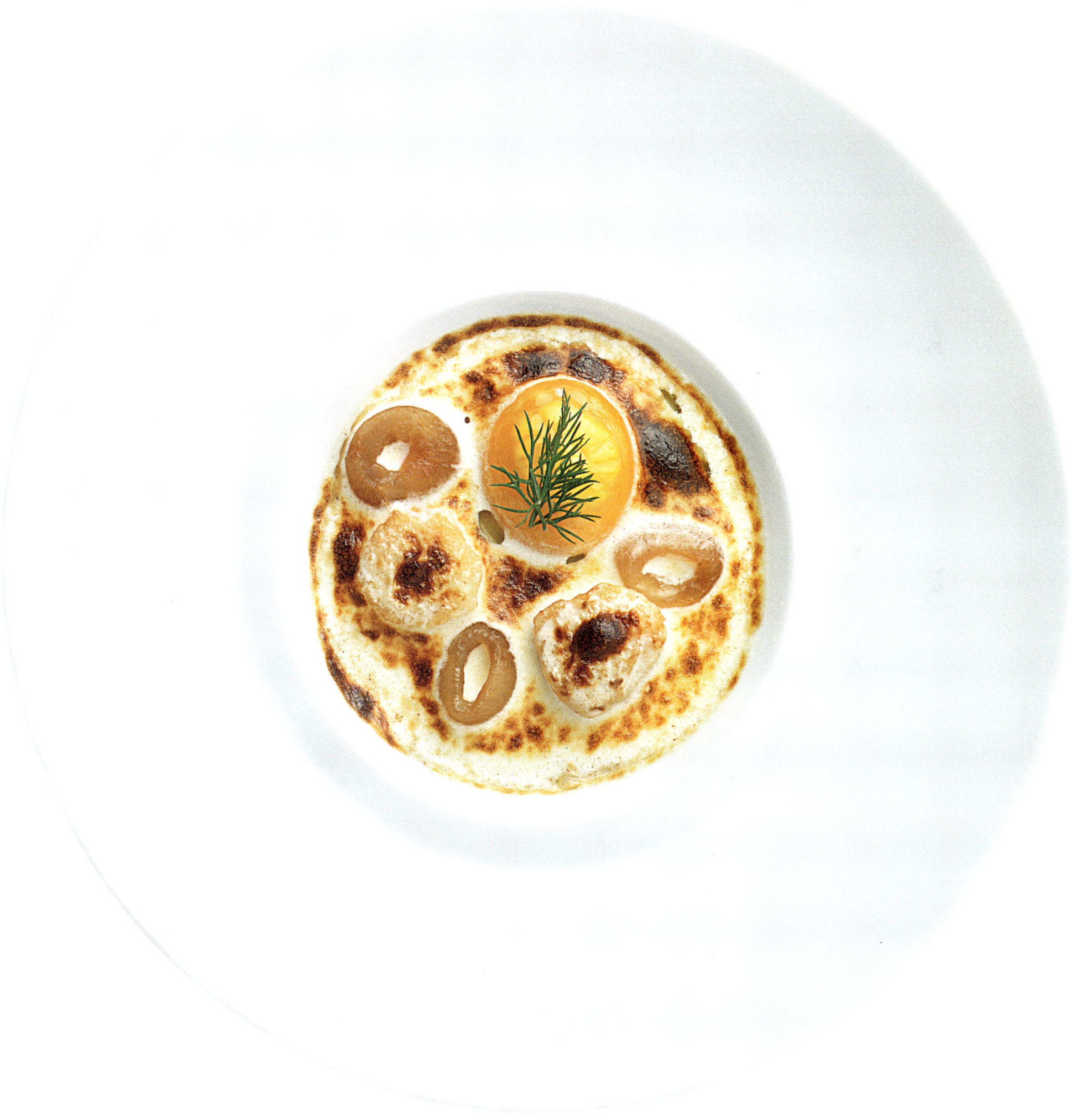

Susur
Toronto

BELOW: Miniature pop culture icons and the Stay-puffed Marshmallow Man are spotlighted at Toronto's hottest restaurant, Susur.

Susur Lee

Heads turn when Hong Kong-born Susur Lee walks by. His chiselled features, sleek black pony tail and slim build make him the perfect candidate for Hollywood. But when folks swoon in Toronto, it's because they recognise Lee for the culinary wizard he is and for turning Lotus, his tiny, unassuming restaurant, into one of Canada's leading establishments.

When he closed Lotus and moved to Singapore to consult for a large group of high-end Chinese restaurants, he stunned his loyal following. But though wooed in earnest by leading restaurateurs in New York for his original style of Asian-French fusion, he decided to return to the city he calls home. Now he has an exciting new place bearing his name, a state-of-the-art kitchen to manage and a large dining room to cater to, and everyone's happy.

Susur's basic snow-white interior subtly changes in both colour and mood—from a deep midnight blue to pale lavender and, as the evening progresses, a flattering shade of burnished gold. But it's the food that gets the gasps. Plump garlicky shrimp and wild mushrooms under a silken blanket of Japanese custard, cool smoked salmon mousse over hot smoked salmon fillet garnished with pickled daikon and ginger, lobster dumplings with slices of chorizo, venison awash in melted gorgonzola, intensely flavoured black raspberry sorbet in a pool of liquid caramel…his genius is evident on every plate.

▲ THOUSAND EAR TERRINE Serves 4

INGREDIENTS
Thousand Ear Terrine
700 g/1½ lb pigs' tongue; 4 pigs' ears;
700 g/1½ lb/8¾ cups mirepoix;
125 ml/4¼ fl oz/½ cup red Chinese rice wine;
20 g/⅛ oz cinnamon powder; 20 g/⅛ oz star anise;
20 g/⅛ oz cardamom; 20 g/⅛ oz pepper;
20 g/⅛ oz cloves; 20 g/⅛ oz Sichuan peppercorns;
20 g/⅛ oz wild ginger; 20 g/⅛ oz orange peel;
2 bay leaves; 20 g/⅛ oz sugar;
2 tbsp dark soya sauce; 2 tbsp light soya sauce;
1 tsp sesame oil;
8 litres/2 gallons 14 fl oz/34 cups water

PREPARATION
Combine all the ingredients in a big stockpot and bring to the boil. Keep boiling for 3 hours and add more water to prevent the ingredients from drying out and burning if necessary.
After 3 hours, remove the pot from the heat and set aside.
Line a medium-sized terrine with plastic film.
Arrange all the solid ingredients in the terrine in layers, then cover the contents with plastic film.
Refrigerate overnight.

PRESENTATION
Remove the terrine from the mould, cut 4 slices, and use a spatula to transfer each slice onto a plate.
Serve cold.

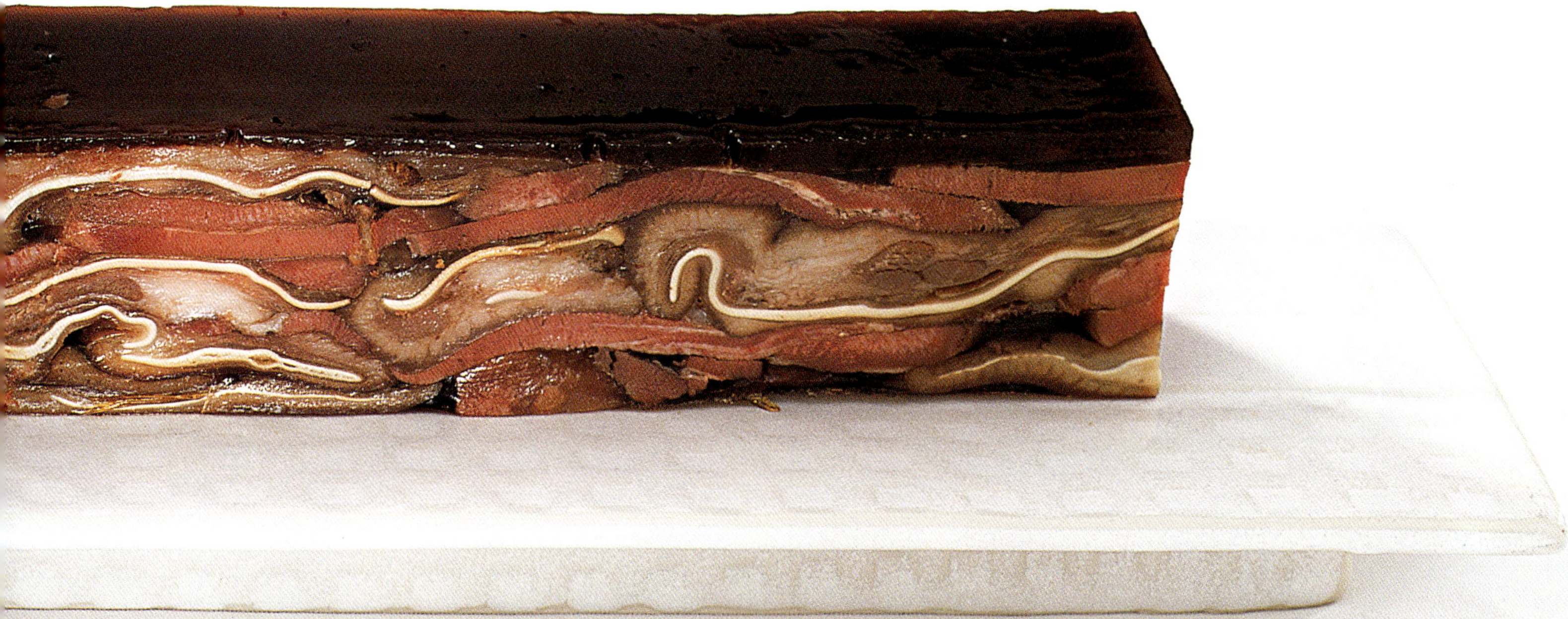

Tetsuya's
Sydney

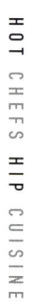

RIGHT: Tetsuya's, formerly cramped into a tiny compound on 'the other side of the bridge', now occupies a sprawling old Japanese house in Sydney's city centre.
ABOVE: Tetsuya indulges his passion for Danish design by filling his restaurant with Arne Jacobsen's leather chairs, skilfully crafted by Fritz Hansen.
ABOVE RIGHT: Guests in the main dining room look out to a quaint Japanese garden.

Tetsuya Wakuda

Since 1989, when he worked gastronomic miracles in the cramped kitchen of his restaurant in Sydney, Tetsuya Wakuda has been delighting fine food enthusiasts. His eponymous, inner-city restaurant—twice named Australia's 'Restaurant of the Year' and a member of the American Express Hall of Fame—was guilty of keeping a notoriously long waitlist, while the seemingly shy Tetsuya kept a low profile and toiled behind the scenes. Then came the millennium.

Abandoning his small, unstylishly located premises, he moved into the only private Japanese house in downtown Sydney. Sprawling over half-a-dozen dining areas including a bar and outer courtyards, the new Tetsuya's has a gleaming kitchen twice as big as his entire Darling Street restaurant and can feed five times as many diners. Nevertheless, bookings are taken up to six weeks ahead.

Tetsuya's Japanese side makes him assemble each dish into a miniature work of art, while his culinary side combines tantalising textures, tastes and flavours using French technique. In what is an exquisite dégustation rather than a normal meal, he rewards diners with an impressive parade of courses, each just two or three bites big. Fresh blue swimmer crab with wasabi mayonnaise, confit of ocean trout and marinated fennel, roasted lamb with chrysanthemum leaves and miso sauce, venison with braised morels, poached quail in truffle oil, orange-honey-pepper sorbet, crème brulee with ginger and lime. And that's only half of it.

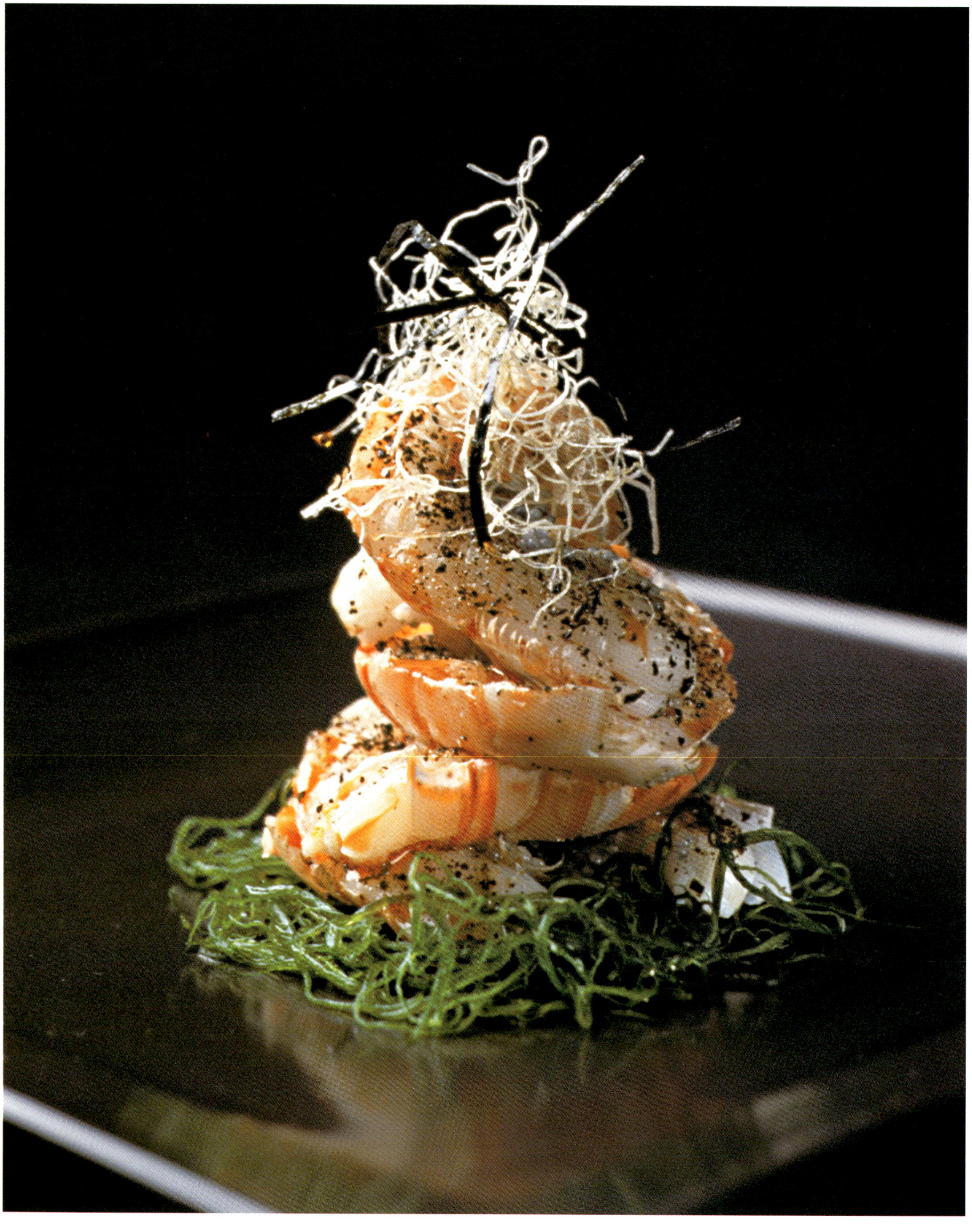

▶ GRANNY SMITH APPLE SORBET WITH SAUTERNES GELATINE

Serves 8 to 10

INGREDIENTS

Syrup
500 ml/1 pt 1 fl oz/2⅛ cups water;
250 g/8⅞ oz/1⅛ cups caster sugar;
100 g/3½ oz/ scant ¼ cup glucose

PREPARATION
Pour the water in a large saucepan and bring to the boil.
Slowly whisk in the sugar and glucose until they are completely dissolved. Bring the mixture to the boil for 30 seconds to 1 minute.
Remove from the heat and set aside to cool completely.
Pour the mixture into an airtight container and refrigerate until it is chilled. You should have about 500 ml/1 pt 1 fl oz/2⅛ cups of syrup.

Granny Smith Apple Sorbet
8 large Granny Smith apples, unpeeled, quartered and cored;
1 tbsp lemon juice

Process the apple quarters in a blender to obtain a smooth purée. Strain the apple juice through a fine-mesh sieve. You should have about 600 ml/1 pt 4¼ fl oz/2½ cups of apple juice.
Combine the apple juice, lemon juice and 150 ml/5 fl oz/⅝ cup of syrup in a big bowl and mix well.
Add a little more syrup to taste if necessary.
Process the mixture in an ice-cream machine set to sorbet specifications.
When ready, keep frozen until required.

Sauternes Gelatine
3½ sheets gelatine;
750 ml/1 pt 9⅜ fl oz/3⅛ cups Sauternes

Soak the gelatine in cold water to soften them.
Pour the Sauternes in a large saucepan and slowly bring it to the boil. Remove from the heat and set aside.
Squeeze out the excess water from the gelatine and stir it into the Sauternes until it has completely dissolved.
Pass the mixture through a fine-mesh sieve and pour it into a dish.
Cover the dish and refrigerate the mixture for 3 to 4 hours until the gelatine sets.

PRESENTATION
Spoon the gelatine into small shot glasses and top with the Granny Smith apple sorbet to serve.

◀ ROASTED LANGOUSTINE SEASONED WITH TEA AND LANGOUSTINE OIL   Serves 4

INGREDIENTS

Langoustine Oil
12 to 15 langoustine heads and shells;
300 ml/10⅛ fl oz/1¼ cups grapeseed or vegetable oil;
1 onion, chopped finely;
1 celery stick, chopped finely;
1 medium carrot, chopped finely;
1 clove garlic, chopped finely; 6 sprigs thyme;
300 ml/10⅛ fl oz/1¼ cups water;
4 to 5 tbsp tomato paste

PREPARATION
Place all the langoustine shells in a small pot and crush with a hammer.
Put a drop of grapeseed or vegetable oil in a pan and sauté the crushed shells over low heat until they are dry. Add the chopped onion, celery, carrot and garlic, and thyme and sauté until the onion is translucent.
Add the water followed by the tomato paste, taking care not to burn the ingredients. Dissolve the tomato paste in the water completely. Add the grapeseed or vegetable oil, stir well and bring to the boil.
Lower the heat and simmer for 1 hour to 1 hour 15 minutes.
Remove from the heat and set aside to cool slightly. Strain the mixture and discard the shells.
Allow the mixture to stand until the oil and water have separated. Skim off the oil into a clean bowl.
You should get about 300 ml/10⅛ fl oz/1¼ cups of langoustine oil. Strain the remaining liquid through an oil or coffee filter and into a bowl. The leftover liquid can be used as a soup or a sauce.

Roasted Langoustine
10 medium-sized langoustines, halved lengthwise;
salt; white pepper; 1 tsp Ceylon tea;
1 tbsp langoustine oil;
½ tsp Banyuls vinegar or sherry vinegar

Preheat the oven at 260°C (500°F). Season the langoustines with salt and white pepper.
Grind the tea into a powder and sprinkle on top of the langoustines. Arrange them on a baking tray and bake them for 3 minutes. As soon as the langoustines feel hot, they are ready. They should be just cooked and still slightly translucent. Overcooking will make the flesh mushy.
Combine the langoustine oil and vinegar and mix well.

Garnish
Ogonori or wakame;
deep-fried leek; shredded nori

PRESENTATION
Place a little ogonori or wakame on 4 plates and top with the cooked langoustines.
Drizzle the langoustine oil and vinegar mixture over.
Garnish with the deep-fried leek and shredded nori to serve.

LEFT: Yoshihiro Murata in his kitchen at Kikunoi.
BELOW: Dining in a ryotei enhances the traditional kaiseki experience.
RIGHT: The century-old Kikunoi.
BELOW RIGHT: Roan Kikunoi is Murata's personal showcase for modern Japanese cooking.

Kikunoi
Kyoto

Yoshihiro Murata

Japanese cuisine is one of the most exciting and varied. There are sushi and sashimi, tempura, yakitori and shabu shabu, soba, udon and unagi (exclusively eel dishes). On top of this, each category is interpreted in dedicated restaurants by specialist chefs who cook nothing but. Because the Japanese take their food very seriously, chefs often train for a decade before their food will reach a customer. From crockery, chopsticks, textures and colour of the table setting, to the dining room, the entire ambience plays as vital a role as the textures, flavours, shapes, sizes, colours and aroma of the seasonal ingredients. And nowhere are all of the above more crucial than in kaiseki, Japan's version of haute cuisine. In the opinion of Yoshihiro Murata, this meal alone is the epitome of his country's cultural and culinary heritage, and his lauded Kikunoi in Kyoto has been plying diners with traditional kaiseki for over a century.

Third generation restaurateur, world traveller, enthusiastic and outspoken TV personality, cookbook author, and culinary consultant to Singapore Airlines, Murata is multifaceted in his traditionalism. He maintains great respect for kaiseki, its rules and customs, in his family's restaurant, Kikunoi. At the same time he displays daring new concepts, which introduce into kaiseki ingredients and cooking techniques gleaned from his frequent trips abroad, at Roan Kikunoi, his personal showcase for what he calls 'New Wave Kyoto Cuisine'.

ABALONE AND SEA URCHIN BAKED IN SALT CRUST

Serves 10

INGREDIENTS

Abalone and Sea Urchin Baked in Salt Crust

10 abalones (with shells);
1 [8-cm- (3.2-inch-) long] daikon;
water; sake; 1 tbsp dark soya sauce;
1 kg/2 lb 3 $\frac{1}{4}$ oz salted wakame;
500 g/1 lb 1 $\frac{5}{8}$ oz sea urchin;
1 kg/2 lb 3 $\frac{1}{4}$ oz/scant 2 $\frac{1}{4}$ cups salt;
2 egg whites

PREPARATION

Remove the abalones from their shells and wash the shells with a brush to remove the grit completely.
Cut the daikon into 4 pieces, then combine them with the abalones in a pot.
Cover the abalones with 2 parts water and 1 part sake (e.g. if it takes 1 litre/2 pts 1 $\frac{7}{8}$ fl oz/4 $\frac{1}{4}$ cups of water to cover the abalone, you'll need 500 ml/1 pt 1 fl oz/2 $\frac{1}{8}$ cups of sake) and bring to the boil, keeping the pot covered. Lower the heat and add the dark soya sauce. Mix well and simmer the mixture for 1 hour until the abalones are cooked and tender. Remove from the heat and set aside to cool. Slice the abalones evenly.
Preheat the oven at 160°C (320°F). Wash the salted wakame in water and arrange them in the abalone shells. Arrange the sliced abalones and sea urchin alternately on the wakame. Cover the abalone and sea urchin with the remaining wakame and wrap each portion separately with aluminium foil.
Combine the salt and egg whites in a big bowl and mix well.
Cover the wrapped abalone shells with the salt crust mixture and bake them for 20 minutes.

Abalone Liver Sauce

10 abalone livers;
40 ml/1 $\frac{3}{8}$ fl oz/ $\frac{1}{8}$ cup dark soya sauce;
40 ml/1 $\frac{3}{8}$ fl oz/ $\frac{1}{8}$ cup sudachi juice

Combine the abalone livers, dark soya sauce and sudachi juice in an earthenware mortar and pound the ingredients with a wooden pestle until they are well-mixed.

Garnish

10 sudachi halves

PRESENTATION

Remove the abalones from the oven and remove the salt crust, taking care not to damage it.
Unwrap the abalones, discard the aluminium foil, then cover the shells with the salt crusts.
Arrange a salt-crusted abalone shell on a dish with half a sudachi on the side to serve.

SIMMERED PORK WITH BROAD BEAN PURÉE AND GOURD MELON

Serves 4

INGREDIENTS

Simmered Pork

1 kg/2 lb pork belly, cut into pieces; oil;
2 litres/4 pts 3 $\frac{5}{8}$ fl oz/8 $\frac{1}{2}$ cups rice water (water used to wash rice);
520 ml/1 pt 1 $\frac{5}{8}$ fl oz/scant 2 $\frac{1}{4}$ cups water;
520 ml/1 pt 1 $\frac{5}{8}$ fl oz/scant 2 $\frac{1}{4}$ cups sake;
50 ml/1 $\frac{3}{4}$ fl oz/ $\frac{1}{4}$ cups hatcho miso;
45 g/1 $\frac{1}{2}$ oz/scant $\frac{1}{4}$ cup brown sugar;
5 tsp dark soya sauce

PREPARATION

Fry the pork belly pieces in some oil until they are cooked and turn golden brown in colour.
Combine the pork and rice water and bring to the boil, then strain and rinse the pork in cold water.
Add some cold water to the pork and bring to the boil again.
When the water is boiling, remove the pork and rinse with cold water again.
Place the pork in a bamboo steamer and steam for 10 minutes.
Mix the water, sake, hatcho miso, brown sugar and dark soya sauce with the steamed pork and bring to the boil, then lower the heat and simmer for 1 hour.

Broad Bean Purée

100 ml/3 $\frac{3}{8}$ fl oz/ $\frac{3}{8}$ cup bonito stock;
1 tsp light soya sauce; scant $\frac{1}{2}$ tsp salt;
1 tsp arrowroot; 1 tsp water;
200 g/7 oz/1 $\frac{2}{3}$ cups broad beans

Combine the bonito stock, light soya sauce and salt in a saucepan and bring to the boil.
Dissolve the arrowroot in the water and use it to thicken the mixture. Set aside to cool.
Steam the broad beans until they are well-cooked, then mash them with a fork.
Pass the mash through a fine-mesh sieve to obtain a smooth purée.
Add the bonito stock mixture to the purée and mix well.

Gourd Melon

$\frac{1}{2}$ gourd melon

Slice the gourd melon into 10 long pieces and boil them in water until they are cooked.

Garnish

Sansho pepper; 4 tsp wagarashi mustard;
a handful of shiso flowers

PRESENTATION

Divide the broad bean purée among 4 dishes.
Arrange a few pieces of simmered pork on each portion and top with a slice of gourd melon.
Garnish with some sansho pepper, 1 tsp of wagarashi mustard and shiso flowers on the side to serve.

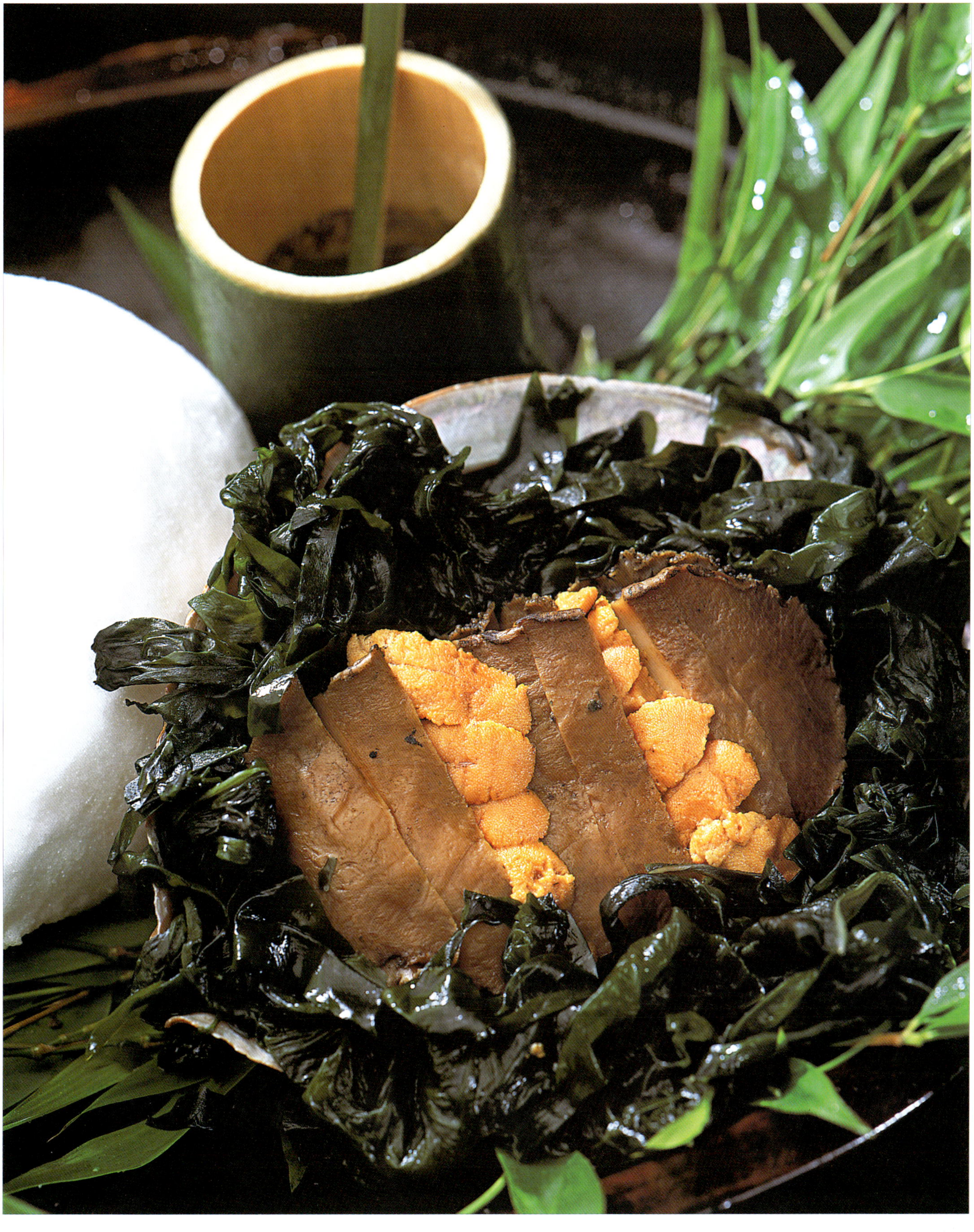

FISH STOCK Makes 1.9 litres/4 pts/8 cups

INGREDIENTS

455 g/1 lb bones from white-fleshed, non-oily fish; 1 leek (white part only), halved lengthwise and sliced; 2 shallots, chopped finely; 1½ tbsp olive oil; 240 ml/8⅛ fl oz/1 cup dry white wine; 1.9 litres/4 pts/8 cups water; 2 sprigs fresh thyme; 2 sheets dried kelp

PREPARATION

Clean the fish bones under cold running water. Pat them dry with kitchen tissue. Chop them roughly.
Sauté the sliced leek and chopped shallots in the olive oil in a stockpot over medium to high heat for 1 minute. Add the fish bones and sauté for 2 minutes. Deglaze with the dry white wine and cook until most of the wine has evaporated. Add the water, followed by the thyme and dried kelp. When the mixture is almost boiling, lower the heat and simmer for 5 minutes. Remove from the heat and let the mixture sit for 1 hour.
Pass the mixture through a muslin strainer and set aside to cool.
Keep refrigerated for up to 2 days, or frozen for up to 3 months, until required.

LOBSTER STOCK Makes 1.9 litres/4 pts/8 cups

INGREDIENTS

2 carrots; 2 shallots; 2 cloves garlic; 1 [7.5-cm- (3-inch-)] pc ginger; 1 tbsp olive oil; 2 tbsp tomato paste; lobster shells from 4 to 6 lobsters, chopped roughly; 130 ml/4⅓ fl oz/½ cup port; 130 ml/4⅓ fl oz/½ cup Cognac; 1.9 litres/4 pts/8 cups fish stock (recipe above)

PREPARATION

Peel the carrots, shallots, garlic and ginger and chop them roughly.
Sauté them in the olive oil in a stockpot over medium to high heat for 2 to 3 minutes until they soften slightly. Add the tomato paste and chopped lobster shells, and sauté for 2 minutes.
Add the port and Cognac, increase the heat to high, and cook the mixture until it is almost dry.
Add the fish stock and bring to the boil. Remove from the heat and let the mixture sit for 40 minutes.
Pass the mixture through a muslin strainer and set aside to cool.
Keep refrigerated for up to 2 days, or frozen for up to 3 months, until required.

CHICKEN STOCK Makes 3 litres/6 pts 5½ fl oz/12⅔ cups

INGREDIENTS

3 kg/6 lb 9⅞ oz chicken bones and joints; 5 litres/10 pts 9⅛ fl oz/21⅛ cups water; 4 sticks celery; 2 leeks (white part only); 3 large onions, peeled; 3 large carrots; ½ head of garlic, unpeeled; 1 sprig thyme; 25 g/⅞ oz/scant ⅛ cup rock salt

PREPARATION

Combine the chicken bones and joints, and water in a stockpot or large saucepan and bring to the boil.
Skim away the material that floats to the surface. Chop the celery, leeks, onions and carrots coarsely.
Add the remaining ingredients and make sure they are completely submerged.
Return to the boil and simmer for about 4 hours 30 minutes, skimming frequently.
Pass the mixture through a muslin strainer and set aside to cool.
Keep refrigerated for up to 2 days, or frozen for up to 3 months, until required.

BEEF STOCK Makes 1.4 litres/3 pts/6 cups

INGREDIENTS

4.6 kg/10 lb beef bones; 2 carrots; 2 sticks celery; 1 yellow onion, peeled; 1 leek, cleaned; 1 head of garlic, halved and peeled; 2 tbsp grapeseed oil; 40 g/1⅜ oz/½ cup tomato concassée; 960 ml/2 pts/4 cups red wine

PREPARATION

Preheat the oven at 230°C (446°F). Place the beef bones in a roasting pan and roast them in the oven for 2 hours until they are golden brown in colour. Chop the carrots, celery, yellow onion and leek coarsely.
In a large stockpot, caramelise them and the garlic in the grapeseed oil. Add the tomato concassée and cook for 5 minutes. Deglaze with the red wine and cook until most of the wine has evaporated. Add the browned bones and cover with cold water. Bring to the boil, lower the heat and simmer over medium heat for 8 hours, skimming away the material that floats to the surface. Pass the mixture through a muslin strainer and set aside to cool. Keep refrigerated for up to 2 days, or frozen for up to 3 months, until required.

WHITE STOCK Makes 1 litre/2 pts 1⅞ fl oz/4¼ cups

INGREDIENTS

1 kg/2 lbs 3¼ oz veal bones, cut into pieces; 200 g/7 oz veal trimmings; 50 g/1¾ oz onion, peeled; 2 cloves; 100 g/3½ oz carrots, peeled and chopped coarsely; 1 leek (white part only), chopped coarsely; 1 stick celery, chopped coarsely; 1 clove garlic, peeled; 1 bouquet garni

PREPARATION

Wash the veal bones and trimmings. Place them in a stockpot and cover them with cold water, then slowly bring to the boil. Skim away the material that floats to the surface and simmer for 2 minutes.
Pour away the water and rinse the bones and trimmings with cold water. Stud the onion with the cloves, then place it and the carrots, leek, celery, garlic and bouquet garni in a clean stockpot. Add the bones and trimmings and cover the ingredients with cold water. Bring to the boil and simmer for between 2 hours 30 minutes and 3 hours, skimming away the surface material occasionally. Pass the mixture through a muslin strainer and set aside to cool. Keep refrigerated for up to 2 days, or frozen for up to 3 months, until required.

MUSHROOM STOCK Makes 350 ml/11⅞ fl oz/1½ cups

INGREDIENTS

25 g/⅞ oz/¼ cup chopped Spanish onion; 2 cloves garlic, peeled; 680 g/1 lb 8 oz/5¼ cups assorted wild mushrooms (such as shiitake, portobello or cremini); 700 ml/1 pt 7⅝ fl oz/3 cups water

PREPARATION

Combine all the ingredients in a medium saucepan and simmer over medium heat for 40 minutes.
Pass the mixture through a fine-mesh sieve.
Return the liquid to the saucepan and simmer for 20 minutes until 350 ml/11⅞ fl oz/1½ cups of stock remain.
Keep refrigerated for up to 2 days, or frozen for up to 3 months, until required.

VEGETABLE STOCK Makes 1.5 litres/3 pts 2¾ fl oz/6⅓ cups

INGREDIENTS

1 leek (white part only), chopped coarsely; 3 carrots, peeled and diced; 1 clove garlic, peeled; ½ onion, peeled; 1 shallot, peeled; 1 bouquet garni; 200 ml/6 ¾ fl oz/⅞ cup dry white wine; 2 litres/4 pts 3⅝ fl oz/8½ cups water

PREPARATION

Combine all the ingredients in a stockpot and bring to the boil.
Lower the heat and simmer for 35 minutes, skimming away the material that floats to the surafce.
Pass the mixture through a muslin strainer and set aside to cool.
Keep refrigerated for up to 2 days, or frozen for up to 3 months, until required.

BASIC RECIPES

VEGETABLE NAGE Makes 1.5 litres/3 pts 2¾ fl oz/6⅓ cups

INGREDIENTS
3 onions, peeled; 1 leek; 2 sticks celery;
6 carrots; ½ head of garlic, peeled;
1 lemon, cut into 6 wedges; ¼ tsp white peppercorns;
¼ tsp pink peppercorns; ½ bay leaf; 4 pcs star anise;
2 litres/4 pts 3⅝ fl oz/8½ cups water;
200 ml/6¾ fl oz/⅞ cup dry white wine;
1 sprig tarragon; 1 basil leaf; 1 sprig coriander;
1 sprig thyme; 1 sprig parsley; 1 sprig chervil

PREPARATION
Chop the onions, leek, celery and carrots coarsely.
Combine them with the garlic, lemon wedges, peppercorns, bay leaf, star anise and water in a stockpot or large saucepan and bring to the boil. Lower the heat and simmer for 10 minutes.
Remove from the heat and add the dry white wine and submerge the fresh herbs in the stock.
Set aside to cool and allow the herbs to infuse the stock with their flavours.
When cool, pour the stock into jars and refrigerate. Continue the steeping process for another 24 hours.
Pass the mixture through a muslin strainer.
Keep refrigerated for up to 2 days, or frozen for up to 3 months, until required.

CONSOMMÉ Makes 2.5 litres/5 pts 4½ fl oz/10⅝ cups

INGREDIENTS
1 onion, peeled; 1 stick celery;
50 g/1¾ oz leek (white part only);
50 g/1¾ oz carrots; 1 sprig parsley;
500 g/1 lb 1⅝ oz meat from beef shin, minced;
1 tomato; 2 egg whites;
1.5 litres/3 pts 2¾ fl oz/6⅓ cups beef stock
(recipe on facing page)

PREPARATION
Chop the onion, celery, leek, carrot, parsley and tomato roughly.
Combine all the ingredients, except the beef stock, in a stockpot and mix well.
Add the beef stock and mix well. Warm the mixture over medium heat and keep stirring until it is almost boiling. When it starts to boil, lower the heat and simmer for 1 hour 30 minutes without stirring.
Remove from the heat and let the mixture sit for 40 minutes.
Pass the mixture through a muslin strainer and set aside to cool.
Keep refrigerated for up to 2 days, or frozen for up to 3 months, until required.

SHELLFISH OIL Makes 120 ml/4 fl oz/½ cup

INGREDIENTS
4 lobster heads;
1 tsp tomato paste;
240 ml/8⅛ fl oz/1 cup corn oil

PREPARATION
Preheat the oven at 200°C (392°F). Place the lobster heads in a roasting pan and roast them in the oven for 40 minutes until they are bright red in colour.
Break up the heads and place them in a small saucepan with the tomato paste and corn oil.
Heat the mixture for 10 minutes, then remove from the heat and set aside to cool.
Refrigerate for 2 days, then pass the oil through a muslin strainer.
Keep refrigerated until required or for up to 2 weeks.

MUSTARD OIL Makes 120 ml/4 fl oz/½ cup

INGREDIENTS
1½ tsp mustard seeds;
⅛ tsp turmeric powder;
120 ml/4 fl oz/½ cup grapeseed oil

PREPARATION
Preheat the oven at 180°C (356°F). Roast the mustard seeds in the oven for 5 minutes.
Grind the mustard seeds and turmeric powder in a spice grinder. Process the spices and oil in a blender on high until the spices are completely incorporated. Store, covered, for 1 day in the refrigerator.
Pass the oil through a muslin strainer and refrigerate for more than 1 day before use.
Keep refrigerated until required or for up to 2 weeks.

VEAL JUS Makes 1 litre/2 pts 1⅞ fl oz/4¼ cups

INGREDIENTS
100 g/3½ oz carrots; 50 g/1¾ oz onion; 1 shallot;
1 kg/2 lb 3¼ oz veal knuckles, cut into pieces;
1 kg/2 lb 3¼ oz veal bones;
200 g/7 oz veal trimmings; 50 g/1¾ oz butter;
1 clove garlic, peeled and crushed;
500 ml/1 pt 1 fl oz/2⅛ cups dry white wine;
1 bouquet garni; 4 litres/8 pts 7¼ fl oz/17 cups water

PREPARATION
Peel and cut the carrots, onion and shallot into cubes.
In a pot, sauté the veal knuckles, bones and trimmings in the butter until they turn brown in colour, then add the carrots, onion, shallot and garlic, and sauté for 10 minutes.
Remove the excess fat and deglaze the mixture with the dry white wine.
Add the bouquet garni and reduce until dry. Add the water, cover the pot and simmer for 2 hours, skimming away the material that floats to the surface occasionally.
Pass the mixture through a muslin strainer and return to the heat.
Reduce until about 1 litre/2 pts 1⅞ fl oz/4¼ cups of veal jus remain.

BRAISED VEAL TONGUE Makes 1 veal tongue

INGREDIENTS
1 veal tongue; salt; pepper; 2 tbsp grapeseed oil;
3 large carrots, cut into 2-cm- (0.75-inch-) thick slices;
150 g/5¼ oz/1½ cups chopped Spanish onion;
2 leeks, chopped; 1.9 litres/4 pts/8 cups beef stock
(recipe on facing page); 1 tsp black peppercorns;
1 head of garlic, halved; 8 sprigs thyme;
2 bay leaves; 2 sprigs rosemary;
240 ml/8⅛ fl oz/1 cup sherry

PREPARATION
Preheat the oven at 120°C (248°F). Season the tongue with salt and pepper.
In a hot braising pan, sear the veal tongue in the grapeseed oil over medium-high heat for 3 minutes on each side until it turns golden brown in colour. Remove the tongue from the pan.
Add the carrot slices, and chopped Spanish onion and leek, and cook for 5 to 7 minutes until they turn golden brown in colour. Return the tongue to the pan and add the beef stock, black peppercorns, garlic, thyme, bay leaves, rosemary and sherry. Bring the mixture to a simmer and cover.
Transfer the pot to the oven and braise the tongue for 4 to 5 hours until tender.
Remove the tongue from the braising liquid and set aside to cool. When cool, peel off the skin before using.

SHALLOT CONFIT Makes 100 g/3½ oz shallot confit

INGREDIENTS
100 g/3½ oz shallots, peeled;
80 ml/2¾ fl oz/⅓ cup olive oil or duck fat

PREPARATION
Combine the shallots and olive oil or duck fat in a thick-based saucepan and cook over low heat for 1 hour until they are soft. Remove from the heat and set aside to cool.

GLOSSARY

A

Aioli A type of mayonnaise sauce originating from the Provençal region. The name is formed from the words 'ail' (garlic in the Provençal dialect) and 'oli' (oil). It can be served as a garnish or dressing.

Allspice Also called 'Jamaican pepper' and 'pimento', it is used whole in pickles and marinades or as a seasoning for puddings, cakes and meats when ground.

Annatto seed Used as a food colouring, this is the scarlet seed of the Bixa Orellana, a tree native to America. It is also ground and used as a spice.

Aquitaine caviar Caviar from the province of Aquitaine in France. Aquitaine is the leading producer of caviar today and its caviar is reputed to be as good as that from Russia and Iran.

Armagnac Brandy made from wine from a region in Gascony and produced mainly in Bas-Armagnac.

B

Barramundi A popular table and angling fish, found naturally in the fresh and salt waters of Northern Australia. It is silver in colour and has the potential to grow up to a length of 1.5 m (6 inches) and weigh more than 30 kg (66 lb).

Bavarois A French dessert made of an egg custard mixed with whipped cream and set in a mould with gelatin.

Belachan Dried fermented shrimp paste. It has a pungent odour and is used as a flavouring in many Southeast Asian dishes.

Bijih selesih The small, oval seed of the lemon-scented basil. It is commonly used in cold dessert drinks and is believed to relieve stomach ailments. To use, soak in water until it develops a translucent coat.

Bird's eye chilli A long, thin red or green chilli grown mainly in Asia and California. It is very hot, and has a thin flesh and many seeds.

Blanch To partially cook an ingredient in boiling water.

Bone marrow A soft fatty, nutritious substance found in the cavities of animal bones. Beef marrow is commonly used in cooking. Marrow is eaten on its own or it can be used as a filling and for flavouring sauces and soups.

Bouquet garni A collection of aromatic plants used to add flavour to stocks and sauces. It usually consists of two or three sprigs of parsley, a sprig of thyme and one or two dried bay leaves, but celery, leek and sage may also be added. While cooking they are tied together in a small bundle, generally within a small muslin bag to prevent from dispersing in liquid. The bag is removed prior to serving.

Brunoise Both a method for dicing vegetables and a term used to describe the resulting diced vegetables.

C

Calvados A type of brandy produced in the Normandy region of France and formed by the distillation of cider.

Carcass The body of an animal after it has been slaughtered and processed for food.

Cardamom Also called 'cardamon'. A pungent plant originally from the Malabar region in the southwest of India. It has capsules which contain seeds that are dried and used as a spice. It is most common in India where it is used to flavour rice, cakes, omelettes, meatballs and noodles. In Scandinavian countries it is used to spice mulled wines, stewed fruit and flans.

Carnevale The Italian word for 'carnival', this refers to the period before Ash Wednesday and the start of the 40-day Lenten fasting period, when traditional processions, masquerades and riotous revelry take place. Carnevale is mostly celebrated in Roman Catholic countries in Europe and Central and South America, and lasts from a day to a week, depending on where it is celebrated. Special foods are normally prepared during this time.

Casserole A covered heat-proof cooking utensil that allows for long, slow cooking and most are attractive enough to be employed as serving dishes. It also refers to the kind of food cooked in a casserole.

Cayenne pepper A spice made from the seeds of the chilli pepper and produced in Asia and Africa.

Cèpe The edible varieties of the boletus mushroom, of which there are over 20. It is distinguished by a large swollen stalk and the more famous varieties include the Bordeaux cèpe and the bronzed cèpe grown in southwestern France, Sologne and Alsace. Cèpes are better eaten young as older specimens are often infested by maggots. Can be eaten raw in salads or cooked in omelettes.

Chanterelle An edible mushroom shaped like a curved trumpet, which grows in Europe, the United States and Africa. Often used in omelettes and as a garnish for meat, it should be cooked slowly over low heat as they tend to get hard if cooked too quickly.

Chénopode Bon Henri Sometimes known as 'wild spinach'. Originally from Iran, it is an annual plant with small, green flowers which acquire a red tint when the seeds mature. Mature seeds resemble little black discs.

Chervil A herb of the parsley family, its aromatic leaves are used to flavour soups and salads.

Chiffonade A preparation of cutting herbs and vegetables, such as parsley, lettuce, sorrel or endive, into strips.

Citronelle Also called 'pepper of the bees' and 'tea of France'. Originally from the Mediterranean basin, it can now be found in both the United States and Europe. Its small sheets resemble basil in appearance. It emits a citronnelle essence and maintains flavour after drying. Although traditional uses include calming of the nervous system and relief for indigestion, it can also be used to flavour salads, soups, ragouts, desserts, sorbets and various marinades.

Confit A piece of preserved meat, usually duck, goose, pork or turkey, cooked in its own fat, then stored in a pot and covered in the fat, which preserves it. It can be eaten hot or cold and is used to flavour many dishes.

Coulis A thin purée made from vegetables or fruit, it is used to flavour sauces and soups and sometimes used as a sauce on its own.

Couverture chocolate Very pure chocolate with a high percentage of cocoa, which gives it excellent flavour. It is often used in handmade chocolates and as decoration.

Cremini mushroom Closely related to the common white mushroom, the cremini mushroom has a stronger flavour. The larger varieties of the cremini mushroom are called 'portobello mushrooms'.

D

Daikon Also known as 'Japanese radish' or 'satsuma radish', this white radish is grown in the Far East. In Japan, it is eaten raw, as a garnish for sashimi, salads and soups, or pickled in salt.

Dover sole A flatfish fish with an excellent flavour, the Dover sole is fished from the English Channel and the Atlantic. It is oval in shape and has an eye only on its right side. Its superb flavour makes it suitable for many preparations, including deep-frying, grilling and baking.

E

Emulsion A preparation where one liquid is evenly dispersed in another liquid though the two liquids do not mix. Common emulsions used in cooking include butter, cream and milk and sauces such as mayonnaise and hollandaise.

Endive A vegetable with bitter leaves, it is also called 'chicory'. Its leaves may be eaten either raw in salads, or it may be cooked and used as an accompaniment to a meat dish.

F

Foie gras Goose or duck liver that has been enlarged by force-feeding the bird. This delicacy can be eaten hot or cold, and the foie gras from southwestern France and Strasbourg are best known.

GLOSSARY

Fricassee This is a preparation of chicken, and occasionally veal or lamb, in a white sauce. The meat is sliced into pieces, then the garnish is added. The ingredients are then sautéed over low heat so as to prevent browning.

G

Galangal A plant that is similar to root ginger in appearance and can be found in two forms: greater and lesser galangal. Greater galangal, also known as 'lengkuas', originates from Java and Malaysia while lesser galangal comes from Hainan Island and the southeastern coasts of China. Both are used to enhance and add flavour.

Garden peas There are two types of white-flowered garden peas: green peas which have round, smooth seeds and are often kept frozen and preserved, and marrowfat which have wrinkled skins and are used in broths and soups.

Gastronome A connoisseur of fine food and drink.

Girolle A tube-shaped mushroom generally picked between the months of June and October. It is found in both hardwood and coniferous forests, and comes in several varieties. The two most common varieties are the fragile and cockscomb girolles. The fragile girolle is both delicate and sumptuous, while the cockscomb girolle tends to be thicker, shorter and slightly less flavourful.

Glucose The simplest form of carbohydrates and the form in which the body uses sugar. During digestion, complex carbohydrates are broken down into glucose. Industrially, glucose is manufactured by heating starch with acids. This process does not produce pure glucose but contains dextrin. Glucose is used to sweeten wine and beer, as well as syrup and jam.

Gravlax A style of salmon preparation from Scandinavia. The preparation process includes cleaning, scaling, bisecting and deboning of the fish. Prior to serving, the fish is drained and brushed clean, then sliced into thin slivers. Traditionally, the arrangement of the gravlax was specifically a man's duty.

H

Hatcho miso Miso is formed from the natural fermentation of soya beans and grains. Hatcho is the most famous variety of miso. It comes from and is named after the '8th street' in Okazaki, a town in the Japanese province of Aichi. Hatcho miso's savoury aroma and flavour have led to an international fascination with miso. Initially introduced to the West as a medicinal soup base, it has since become a highly sought-after ingredient. It can be used as a substitute for both salt and beef stock, and combines well with soups, stews or baked and simmered dishes.

Heart of palm The heart of the Sabal Palmetto, a tall, tough-barked but graceful palm that is the state tree of Florida. Formerly called 'swamp cabbage' by the natives of Florida, it is now seen as a delicacy. It is extremely tender, has no cholesterol and hardly any fat content. It is also an excellent source of fibre.

Honshimeiji mushroom Also known as 'beech mushroom', it has a short, thick steam with either brown or white caps. Its firm texture and mildly sweet and nutty flavour make it good for soups and stir-fries.

J

John Dory A thin-bodied fish with a large head and jaw. It is characterised by a large black spot on each side of its body. Its firm white flesh makes excellent fillets and it is commonly used in the preparation of bouillabaisse.

Juniper berry A dark-coloured berry from the juniper tree. Used in both the manufacture of wines and spirits as well as in cooking. It is strongly pungent and somewhat resinous in flavour. Can be used in either whole or ground form. Particularly popular in Scandinavian cooking. Commonly used in marinades, court-bouillon, game dishes and sauerkraut.

Jus In French cookery, jus refers to gravy made from roast, where the pan juices are diluted with liquid, such as water or clear stock, then boiled again. It also refers to a brown stock, especially veal stock (jus de veau) and juice extracted from fruit and raw vegetables.

K

Konbu A seaweed featured in many Japanese dishes, especially soups. Also used as a garnish.

L

Langoustine Closely resembling a crayfish, the langoustine is a marine crustacean commonly found in Western Europe. It is unable to survive long out of water and as a result, is often sold in cooked form on a bed of ice to maintain freshness. It is often served poached and whole. When purchasing, note that the eyes are shiny and black, and the shell is pink in colour.

Linseed Also known as 'flaxseed', this plant originated from Great Britain and France, and is found in the wild, mainly in fields. It has narrow leaves with flowers ranging from blue, violet, pink and off-white. The seeds are contained within a capsule and each capsule holds less than 10 seeds. The oil extracted from the seeds has been used for medicinal purposes for centuries.

M

Macerate To soften an ingredient by immersing it in either a hot or cold liquid.

Mandoline A vegetable slicer with adjustable blades used to slice cabbage, carrots, turnips and potatoes in varying degrees of thickness.

Mirepoix A French term for a mixture of diced vegetables usually consisting carrots, onions and celery. It enhances the flavour of stocks and sauces.

Mizuna This hardy plant has dark, shiny green leaves. It is adaptable to both hot and cold environments and grows in the shape of a large rosette. It thrives best in moist, wet environments. Although mizuna is generally grown in spring and autumn, if provided with sufficient shade it can be cultivated during the summer months as well. It can grow in various soil types but prefers rich high water retention soils.

Munster A flat round cheese made from the milk of cows from the Vosges mountains in Munster in Alsace. It was created by Irish monks in the 7th century; the name is derived from monastère, meaning 'monastery'.

Muscat A white grape used widely in Alsace, the south of France, Italy and many other countries for winemaking. Muscat wines can be sweet or dry.

Muscovado Raw or unrefined sugar extracted from the juice of sugar cane. Its dark colouring and moistness is caused by high levels of impurity.

N

Niçoise Refers to dishes typical to the region around Nice, where key ingredients include anchovies, garlic, olives, French beans and tomatoes.

Noilly Prat The most well-known of French dry vermouth.

O

Ogonori A fine seaweed which is available fresh or dried. Rinse well before use to get rid of excess salt.

P

Parmentier Antoine Augustin Parmentier was a military pharmacist, French agronomist and avid proprietor of the potato. He helped during the famine by promoting the nutritional value of the potato and was awarded in 1773 for his efforts. In light of his achievements, the potato was known as 'parmentière' for some time and various potato dishes—in particular chopped beef topped with potato purée and baked in the oven—were named in his honour.

Pernod A potent drink consisting of either extracts of absinthe or aniseed.

Potato galette Galette refers to a round, flat cake which comes in various sizes. Traditionally made from oats,

GLOSSARY

wheat and rye. When prepared with potato, the potatoes are either finely diced or puréed.

R

Reine des Prés Known as the 'Queen of meadows', it can be found in North America, Europe and parts of Asia. It is a large, leafy plant ranging from 10 to 120 cm (4 to 48 inches) in height. Its medicinal properties were first discovered in the Renaissance era. It is primarily used for fighting obesity, cellulite and as an anti-inflammatory drug. Because of its medicinal characteristics, it is often associated with garlic, blackcurrant and ginseng. Its flowers generally have five petals, are cream in colour and protrude from long stalks. The flowering period for the Reine des Prés is during the summer months from June to August.

Rempah Freshly ground spices which can be made into a paste; common to Asian regions.

Risotto A rice dish which originated in Italy, where medium or long grain rice is sautéed in butter, then cooked in stock. The rice absorbs the flavours of the stock and other ingredients that are added to it.

Rocket Also known as 'arugula' or 'white mustard' due to its similarity to the mustard plant. It young leaves are used to add spiciness to salads.

S

Salamander A type of oven within which heat is directed down from the roof. Used professionally for glazing, browning and caramelising sweet or savoury dishes.

Salsify Also called 'oyster plant' or 'vegetable oyster'. This is a root vegetable with tender flesh and slightly bitter taste. The root is generally baked or boiled and can be used to make a cream soup. It is best to cook it after peeling. The easiest way to do so is to first cut it into large pieces, then proceed to remove the skin.

Sambal oelek Also called 'sambal ulek', this is a hot relish made from chilli, salt and vinegar or tamarind.

Sansho pepper Sansho is a shrub that grows in Japan, Korea and China. The berries are dried and ground to make a spice called 'sansho pepper', or 'Japanese pepper'. More tangy than hot, the spice is used in many Japanese dishes.

Sauternes A highly aromatic and delectable white wine from Sauternes in Bordeaux.

Scorzone truffle Derived from 'scorza' (Italian for 'black exterior'). This black summer truffle is mostly found in Italy, the South of France and in Northern Spain. Although both outer colour and size resemble its more sought-after counterpart, the black winter truffle, its interior is light beige and white. High quality Scorzone truffle has a somewhat nutty and woody mushroom taste. Its soft aroma, good flavour and relatively inexpensive price makes it ideal for meals.

Sedum Also called 'white stonecrop'. Although wild in America, many varieties of this perennial plant can also be found in Europe and Asia. Sometimes known as the 'coral carpet' or 'crested form', this variety of the stonecrop family has dark, green, succulent, spear-shaped leaves and grows in clusters of tiny star-shaped white or pale-pink flowers. While it prefers to be in the sun, it can tolerate partial shade and thrives best in dry soil environments.

Shiso Also known as 'oba', both the head and leaves of this plant are edible. Shiso is used in tempura, vinegar dishes and in Japanese pickles. It is also commonly used as a garnish.

Siphon A bottle made of aluminium or thick glass filled with carbonated water. Its screwed-on lid has a lever, which when depressed, allows the liquid to flow through a tube in the bottle.

Spelt A whole-grain wheat that has had a place in the creation of grain products for centuries. Rich in protein, it is also known to prevent blood clots and stabilise the immune system.

Star anise A Far Eastern fruit shaped like an eight-pointed star. Its seeds are slightly spiced with a hot aniseed flavour. It was first imported into Europe during the Renaissance by the English. It is commonly used in the preparation of liqueurs but can also be added during pastry and biscuit-making as is done in Scandinavian countries. In China, it is used as a meat seasoning, while in India, it is added to all ground spice mixtures. When chewed, it can work as a breath freshener.

Strega liquor A golden Italian liqueur made from herbs and flowers and has a sweet and slightly floral flavour.

Sudachi A small, green citrus fruit from Japan. With the exception of size (sudachi is smaller) it is similar to the lemon. Generally used when eating fish.

Swiss chard Also known as 'spinach beet', Swiss chard is a variety of beet whose leaves are edible. It is usually prepared in the same way as spinach.

T

Taro A type of potato from Southeast Asia found in both large and small varieties. Generally barrel-like in shape with a hairy, brown exterior, the flesh of the vegetable is white with some flecks of purple. If not well cooked, it can emit high levels of acridity and cause nausea or severe throat irritation.

Timbale A utensil used to mould items into small round shapes. Generally used on custards and rice mixtures.

Tomato concassée Tomato flesh which has been peeled, deseeded and finely chopped.

Trompettes de mort A member of the chanterelle group of mushrooms. It is known as the "trumpet of death" by the French because of its large, frilled cap and black colour. While fairly bland in taste, it can be mixed with other varieties of mushroom to enhance a dish. It is easily dried and can be used as a condiment.

Truffle A fungus that grows underground in a symbiotic relationship with certain trees, mainly the oak, beech, chestnut and hazel. An expensive delicacy, the black truffle from Périgord in France and the white truffle from Piedmont in Italy are the best known. Truffle cultivation has declined due to deforestation and other reasons so truffle is used sparingly in most dishes and often only as a garnish.

Tuile A thin and crisp biscuit moulded in the shape of a curved tile. The dough consists of sugar, almonds (either shredded or ground), eggs and flour. Vanilla and butter may be added to the baking sheet if desired.

Turbot An Atlantic and Mediterranean dwelling flatfish. The meat is both tender and tasty, making it a highly sought-after meal item and therefore quite expensive.

V

Vermouth Wine incorporating herbs, spices, barks and peels first made in the 18th century for medicinal purposes. The best vermouth is produced in Italy and France. Vermouth is often used in stuffings, sauces and stocks because of its herbal properties.

W

Wagarashi This yellow-coloured mustard is from Japan. Its bright colour and spicy taste make it ideal for seasoning. In place of the traditional powder, a tube paste form has become increasingly popular. It goes well with Japanese meals such as Oden and Tonkatsu. To maintain flavour, avoid exposure to air.

White flour '0' Also a hard wheat flour, this is dark and contains a high level of protein. It is used as a base for the production of rye bread.

White flour '00' A strong, all purpose hard wheat flour that is used to make breads, buns, puff pastry and rolls.

RESTAURANTS

ASIA	Japan	**BELFRY GARDEN** 8-11 Yaga 2 Chome, Higashiku-Ku, 732-0042 Hiroshima, +81.82.2837077 **HOTEL DE MIKUNI** 1-18 Wakaba, Shinjuku-ku, 160-0011 Tokyo, +81.3.33513810, www.oui-mikuni.co.jp **KIKUNOI** 459 Makuzugahara Shimokawaramachi, Maruyama Higashiyama-ku, Kyoto, +81.75.5610016
	Singapore	**JADE** The Fullerton Singapore, 1 Fullerton Square, +65.68778188, www.tunglok.com **SENSO** 21 Club Street, 01-01, +65.62243534 **THE ORIENTAL HOTEL** 5 Raffles Avenue, Marina Square, +65.63380066, www.mandarin-oriental.com
AUSTRALIA	Australia	**CELSIUS** 27 O'Connell Street, Sydney NSW 2000, +61.2.82140496 **TETSUYA'S** 529 Kent Street, Sydney NSW 2000, +61.2.92672900 **THE GRANGE** Adelaide Hilton Hotel, 233 Victoria Square, Adelaide, +61.8.82172000, www.hilton.com
EUROPE	England	**RESTAURANT GORDON RAMSAY** 68 Royal Hospital Road, London, +44.20.73524441, www.gordonramsay.com
	France	**ARPÈGE** 84 Rue de Varenne, 75007 Paris, +33.1.47050906, www.alain-passard.com **LE GRAND VÉFOUR** 17 Rue du Beaujolais, 75001 Paris, +33.1.4296.5627, www.relaischateaux.fr **LE PRÉ CATELAN** Bois de Boulogne, 75016 Paris, +33.1.44144117 **LES ELYSÉES** Hotel Vernet, 25 Rue Vernet, 75008 Paris, +33.1.44319800 **RESTAURANT GUY SAVOY** 18 Rue Troyon, Paris 75017, +33.1.43804061, www.guysavoy.com **AUBERGE DE L'ERIDAN** 13 Vielle Route des Pensières, 74290 Veyrier du Lac, +33.4.50602400, www.marcveyrat.com **LA BASTIDE SAINT ANTOINE** 48 Rue Henri-Dunant, 06130 Grasse, +33.4.93709494, www.jacques-chibois.com **LES JARDIN DES SENS** 11 Avenue Saint Lazare, 34000 Montpellier, +33.4.99583838, www.relaischateaux.fr **TROISGROS** Place de la Gare, 42300 Roanne, +33.4.77716697, www.troisgros.fr
	Germany	**RESIDENZ HEINZ WINKLER** Kirchplatz 1 D-83229 Aschau, +49.80.52 17990, www.residenz-heinz-winkler.de
	Italy	**DAL PESCATORE** Località Runate 17 Canneto S/O 1, 46013 Mantova, +39.0376.723001, www.dalpescatore.com
	Spain	**EL BULLI** Cala Montjoi, AP. 30 Roses, 17480 Girona, +34.972.150457, www.elbulli.com **LA BROCHE** Miguel Angel 29-31, 28010 Madrid, +34.91.3993437, www.labroche.com **MARTIN BERASATEGUI** 4 Loidi Kalea, 00160 Lasarte Guipuzcoa, +34.943.366471, www.martinberasategui.com **RESTAURANTE MUGARITZ** 20 Caserío Otzazulueta, 20100 Errentería, +34.943.522455, www.mugaritz.com
	Switzerland	**DIE FISCHERZUNFT** 8202 Schaffhausen, +41.52.6253281, www.fischerzunft.ch
NORTH AMERICA	Canada	**SUSUR** 601 King Street West, Toronto, Ontario, +1.416.5339539
	USA	**AQUAVIT** 13 West 54th Street, New York, 10019 New York, +1.212.3077311, www.aquavit.org **JEAN GEORGES** Central Park West, New York, 10023 New York, +1.212.2993901, www.jean-georges.com **CHARLIE TROTTER'S** 816 West Armitage Avenue, Chicago, 60614 Illinois, +1.773.2486228, www.charlietrotters.com **JOËL** The Forum, 3290 Northside Parkway, Atlanta, 30327 Georgia, +1.404.2333500, www.joelrestaurant.com
SOUTH AMERICA	Brazil	**CLAUDE TROISGROS** Avenue Alexandre Ferreira, 66 Lagoa, 22470-220 Rio de Janeiro, +55.21.5390033, www.claudetroisgros.com.br

PHOTO CREDITS

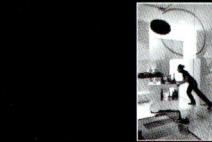

Photographs 1, 2 and 3 by Françesc Guillamet, courtesy of Sergi Arola; photographs 4, 5 and 6 by Jörg Sundermann and Lai Choon How; photograph 7 courtesy of Les Jardin Des Sens; photograph 8 by Quentin Bacon, courtesy of Jean-Georges Vongerichten; photograph 9 and 10 by Shimon and Tammar Rothstein, courtesy of Marcus Samuelsson.

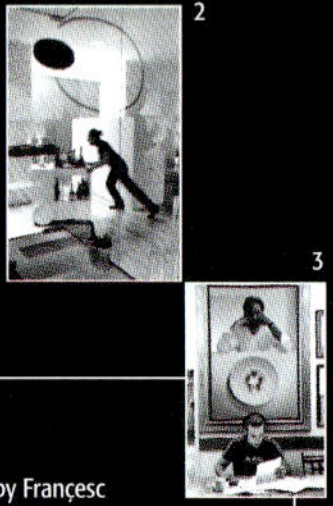

ALAIN PASSARD
Restaurant and chef's photographs by Eric Cuvillier; food photographs by Philippe Schaff.
All photographs courtesy of Alain Passard.

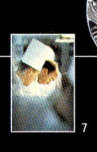

ALAIN SOLIVÉRÈS
All photographs courtesy of Alain Solivérès.

ALBERT ADRIÀ
All photographs by Françesc Guillamet, courtesy of Albert Adrià.

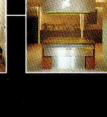

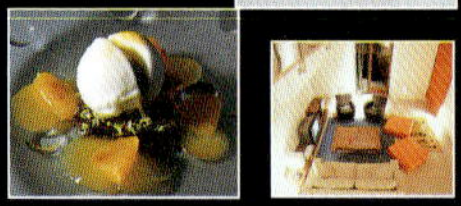

ANDONI LUIS ADURIZ
All photographs by Lopez de Zubiria, courtesy of Andoni Luis Aduriz.

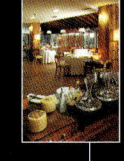

ANDRÉ JAEGER
All photographs by Pierre-Michel Delessert, courtesy of André Jaeger.

CHARLIE TROTTER
All photographs by Tim Turner, courtesy of Charlie Trotter.

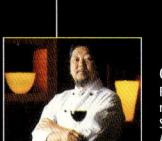

CHEONG LIEW
Food and chef's photographs by Adam Bruzzone; restaurant photographs courtesy of the South Australian Tourism Commission.
All photographs courtesy of Cheong Liew.

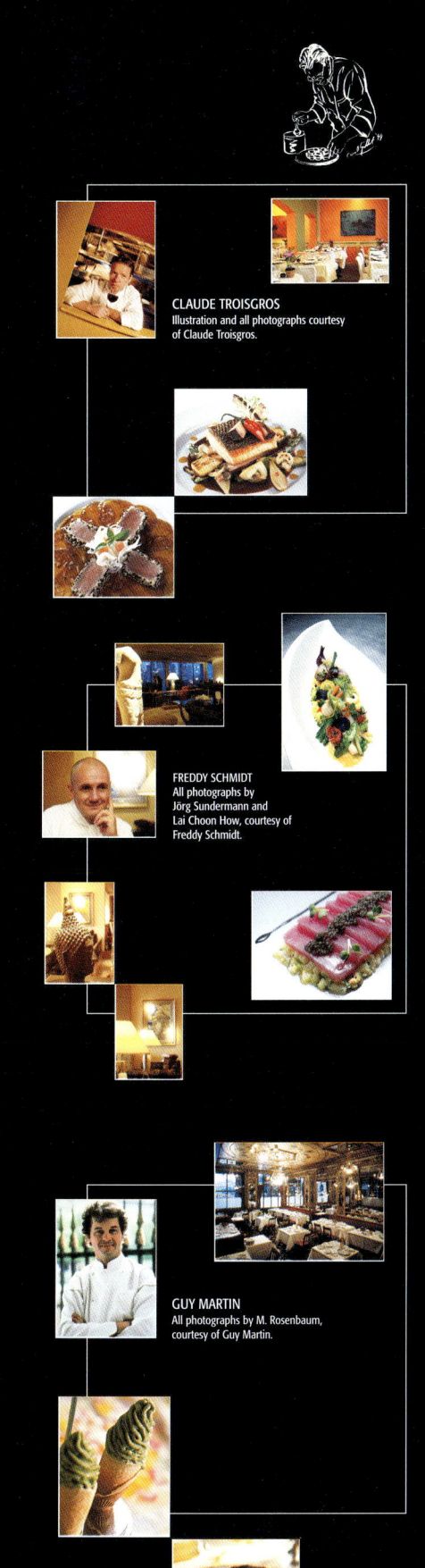

CLAUDE TROISGROS
Illustration and all photographs courtesy of Claude Troisgros.

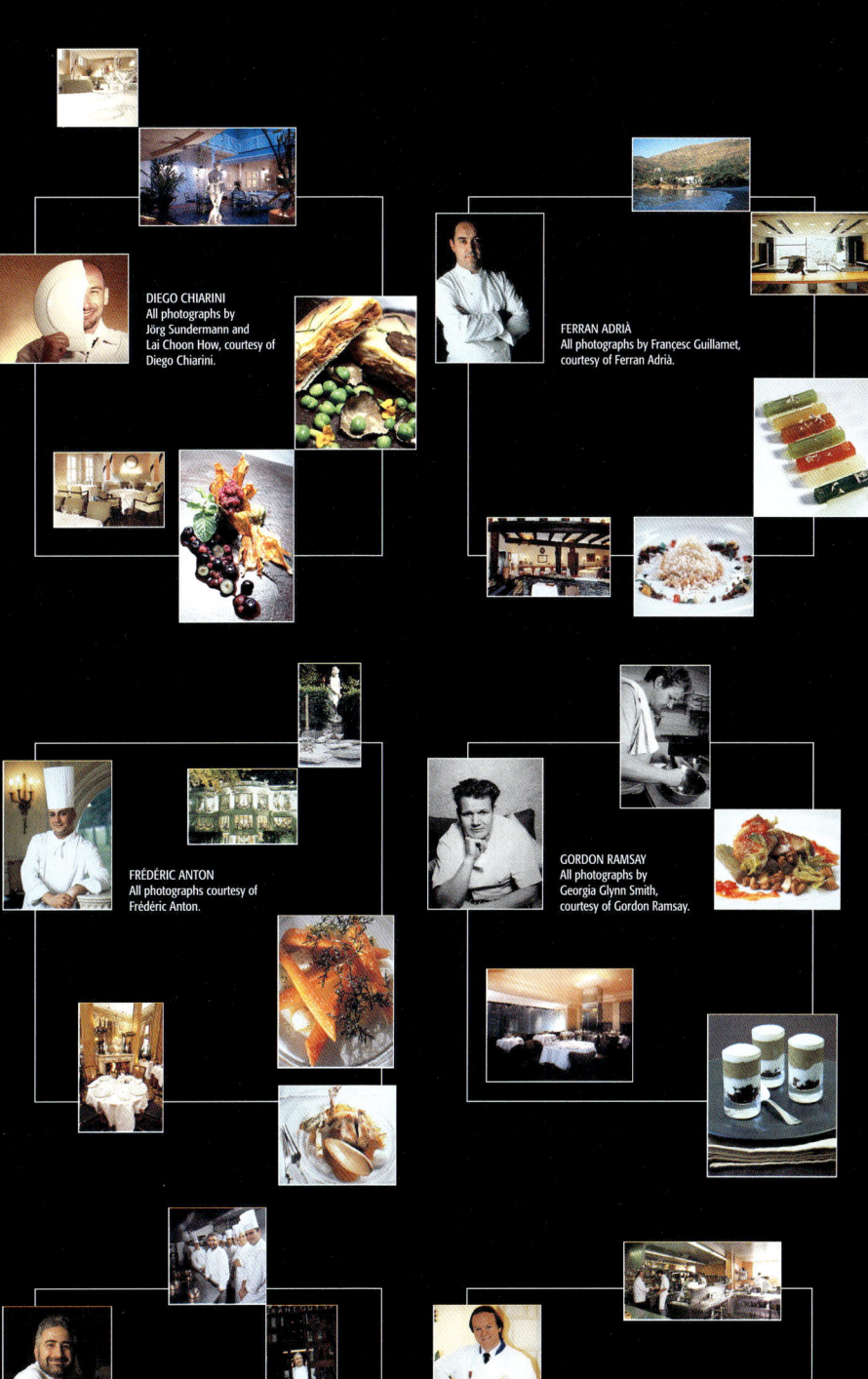

DIEGO CHIARINI
All photographs by Jörg Sundermann and Lai Choon How, courtesy of Diego Chiarini.

FERRAN ADRIÀ
All photographs by Francesc Guillamet, courtesy of Ferran Adrià.

FREDDY SCHMIDT
All photographs by Jörg Sundermann and Lai Choon How, courtesy of Freddy Schmidt.

FRÉDÉRIC ANTON
All photographs courtesy of Frédéric Anton.

GORDON RAMSAY
All photographs by Georgia Glynn Smith, courtesy of Gordon Ramsay.

GUY MARTIN
All photographs by M. Rosenbaum, courtesy of Guy Martin.

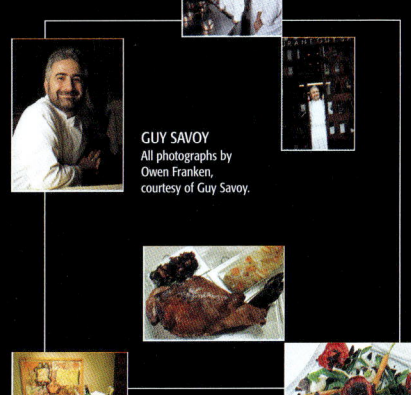

GUY SAVOY
All photographs by Owen Franken, courtesy of Guy Savoy.

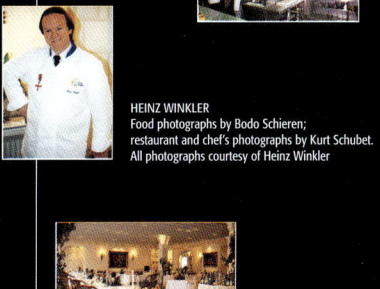

HEINZ WINKLER
Food photographs by Bodo Schieren; restaurant and chef's photographs by Kurt Schubet. All photographs courtesy of Heinz Winkler

PHOTO CREDITS 155

JACQUES CHIBOIS
All photographs by Fabienne Kreisse and Bergoend Eric, courtesy of Jacques Chibois.

JACQUES AND LAURENT POURCEL
All photographs courtesy of Les Jardin Des Sens.

JEAN-GEORGES VONGERICHTEN
Chef's photograph by Patrick Demarchelier; restaurant photographs by Peter Paige; food illustrations by Daniel Del Vecchio. All photographs and illustrations courtesy of Jean-Georges Vongerichten.

JOËL ANTUNES
Food photographs by Tim Rider; terrace photograph by Chris Thomas; kitchen photograph by Thomas Birdwell; restaurant photograph by Nathan Feder. All photographs courtesy of Joël Antunes.

KIYOMI MIKUNI
All photographs by Noboru Morikawa, courtesy of Kiyomi Mikuni.

MARCUS SAMUELSSON
Restaurant and chef's photographs by Paul Brissman; food photographs by Shimon and Tammar Rothstein. All photographs courtesy of Marcus Samuelsson.

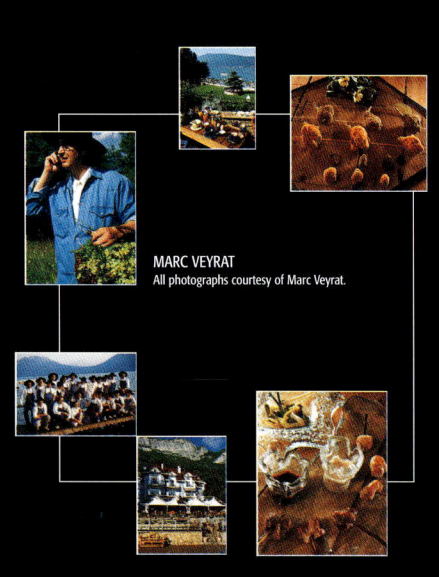

MARC VEYRAT
All photographs courtesy of Marc Veyrat.

MARTIN BERASATEGUI
All photographs by Lopez de Zubiria, courtesy of Martin Berasategui.

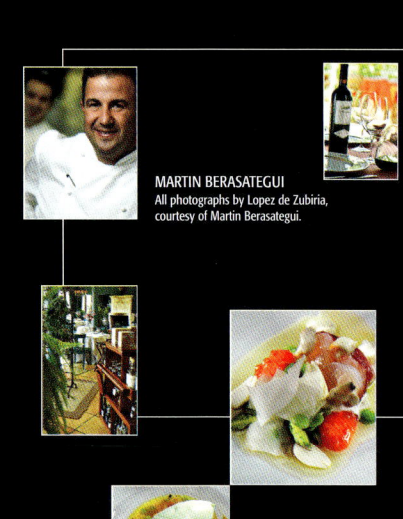

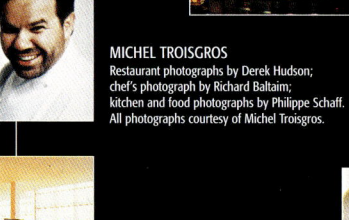

MICHEL TROISGROS
Restaurant photographs by Derek Hudson; chef's photograph by Richard Baltaim; kitchen and food photographs by Philippe Schaff. All photographs courtesy of Michel Troisgros.

156 HOT CHEFS HIP CUISINE

MITSUHIRO ODA
Food photographs by Hitoshi Kobatake;
restaurant and chef's photographs by Takashi Nagao.
All photographs courtesy of Mitsuhiro Oda.

NADIA SANTINI
Restaurant and chef's photographs by
Maurice Rougemont; food photographs by
Giovanni Gerardi.
All photographs courtesy of Nadia Santini.

PETER DOYLE
All photographs by Rodney Weidland,
courtesy of Peter Doyle.

SAM LEONG
All photographs by Jörg Sundermann and
Lai Choon How, courtesy of Sam Leong.

SERGI AROLA
All photographs by Françesc Guillamet,
courtesy of Sergi Arola.

SUSUR LEE
Food and chef's photographs by Anthony Luke.
All photographs courtesy of Susur Lee.

TETSUYA WAKUDA
Granny Smith Apple Sorbet photograph by
Takashi Morieda; Roasted Langoustine
and restaurant photographs by Louise Lister;
chef's photograph by Jennifer Soo.
All photographs courtesy of Tetsuya Wakuda.

YOSHIHIRO MURATA
All photographs by Ei Oiwa,
courtesy of Yoshihiro Murata.

MELISA TEO
Portrait by Nina Nolte.

SANDI BUTCHKISS
Photograph by Cliff Shaffran.

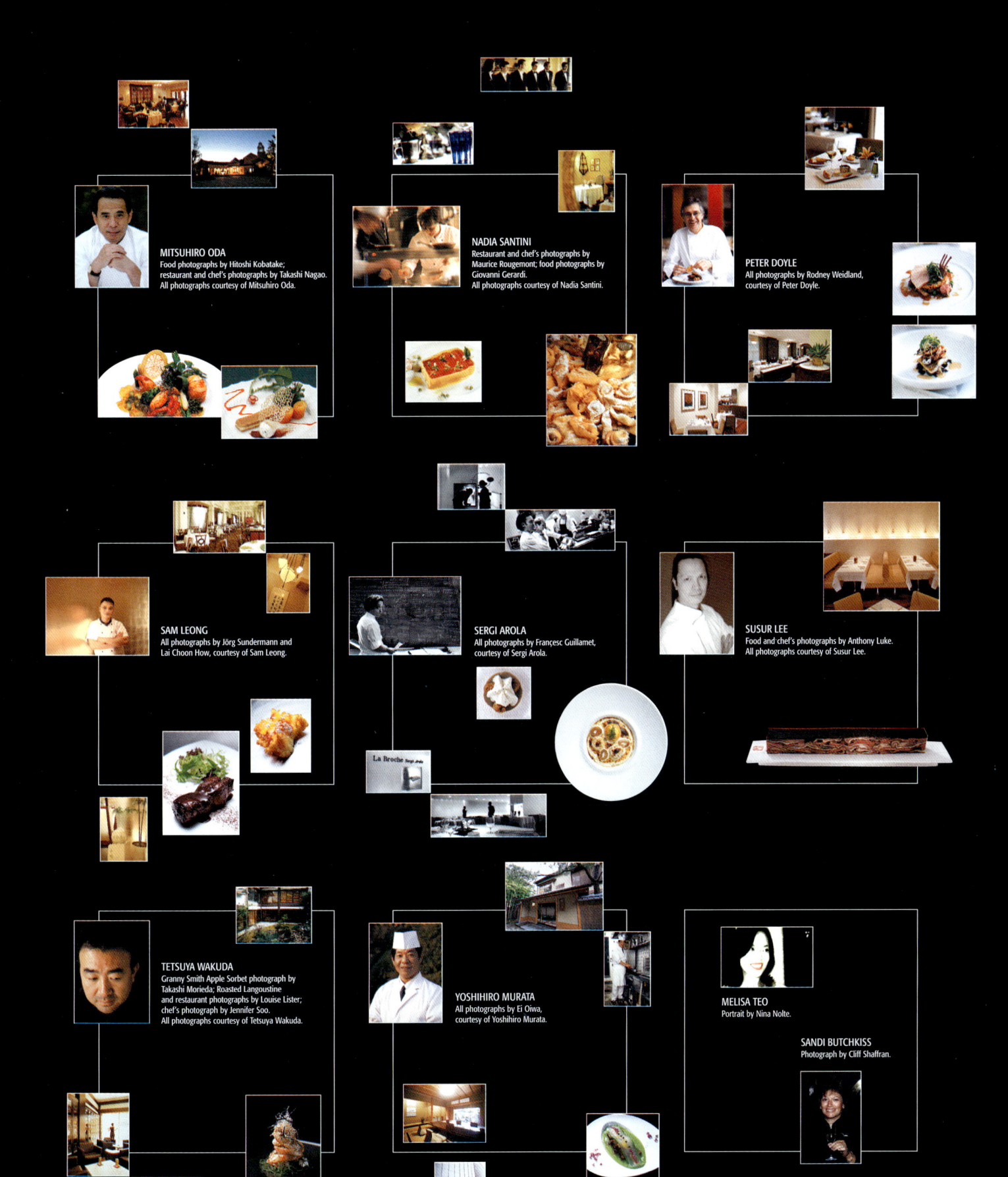

157 PHOTO CREDITS

RECIPE INDEX

A
Abalone and Sea Urchin Baked in Salt Crust, 146
Aioli, 150
in Four Dances of the Sea, 40
Allspice, 150
in Spice Island Lobster, Salsify Purée and Fig-date Chutney, 91
Annatto seed, 150
in Spice Island Lobster, Salsify Purée and Fig-date Chutney, 91
Appetisers
Abalone and Sea Urchin Baked in Salt Crust, 146–147
Avocado Bavarois and Langoustine and Caviar Tarama with Pistachio Oil, 17
Black and Blue Tuna with Marinated Daikon and Sesame Oil Vinaigrette, 44–45
Carpaccio of Yellow Fin Tuna with Three Mustards, 98–99
Carrot Purée with Orange and Lemon Confit, and Spinach with Sesame Oil, 16–17
Cauliflower Couscous, 54–55
Composition of Tomato, Eggplant, Basil Flowers and Olive Oil, 122
Crayfish with Cheese, Grapes, Sunny-side-up Egg and Walnut Purée, 134–135
Deep-fried Cod with Thai Chilli Sauce, Pomelo and Mango, 131
Foie Gras Torchon on Brioche with Truffle Ice Cream and Sauternes-consommé Gelatine, 118
Four Dances of the Sea, 40–41
Liquorice Flavoured Frogs' Legs with Spring Salad and Field Flowers, 106
Lobster and Tomato Juice Gelatine with Warm Salad of Asparagus, Cauliflower Stems and Vegetables, 110–111
Melon and Tomatoes with Lemon and Olive Oil Emulsion and Poppy Seeds, 83
Parfait of Smoked Salmon and Tomato Jelly with Cucumber Sauce, 79
Poached Eggplant and Lime Gelatine with a touch of Cumin, 114
Roasted Langoustine Seasoned with Tea and Langoustine Oil, 142–143
Savoyard-style Chicken Nuggets with Peanut and Reine des Prés Sauces, 106–107
Thousand Ear Terrine, 138–139
Tuna Tartare with Tomato Pulp, Tomato Dressing and Micro Basil, 94–95
Vegetable Potée and Beetroot and Black Truffle Mille Feuille with Foie Gras Sauce, 74
Vegetables on the Grill, 52–53
Yellow Fin Tuna with Caviar Dressing and Cucumber Lemon Salsa, 59
Young Carrot Confit Caramelised with Gingerbread Sauce, 62
Young Vegetable Casserole with Orange and Sichuan Pepper Emulsion, 58–59
Apple
and Prune, Butterscotch and Yoghurt Compote, 67
Granny Smith, in Cauliflower Couscous, 54
Granny Smith, Sorbet, with Sauternes Gelatine, 143
Green, Sorbet, and Vinegar and Pea Tuile, with Pea and Banana Soup, 111
jam, in Roasted Pork Ribs with Mocha Sauce, 131
Aquitaine caviar, 150
in Avocado Bavarois and Langoustine and Caviar Tarama with Pistachio Oil, 17
Armagnac, 150
in Apple, Prune, Butterscotch and Yoghurt Compote, 67
in Foie Gras Torchon on Brioche with Truffle Ice Cream and Sauternes-consommé Gelatine, 118
Asparagus
green, in Pan-fried Salmon, Sautéed Vegetables and Hearts of Palm with Sweet and Sour Red Wine Sauce, 45
green, in Young Vegetable Casserole with Orange and Sichuan Pepper Emulsion, 59
tips, in Braised Veal Tongue with Sweet Corn Emulsion, 37
warm, gelatine, in Vegetables on the Grill, 53
Warm Salad of, Cauliflower Stems and Vegetables, with Lobster and Tomato Juice Gelatine, 111
white and green, in Roasted Lobster and Vodka Sorbet with Crabmeat and Coral, 119
and Orange, with Yoghurt Sorbet, 25
Avocado
Bavarois, and Langoustine and Caviar Tarama with Pistachio Oil, 17
in Four Dances of the Sea, 40

B
Barramundi, 150
with Sautéed Vegetables and Herb Salad, and Grilled Langoustines with Trompettes de Mort, 127
Bavarois, 150
Avocado, and Langoustine and Caviar Tarama with Pistachio Oil, 17
Belachan, 150
in Four Dances of the Sea, 40
Bijih selasih, 150
in Deep-fried Cod with Thai Chilli Sauce, Pomelo and Mango, 131
Bird's eye chilli(es), 150
in Lobster Roll with Hot and Sour Broth, 103
Blanch, 150
Bone marrow(s), 150
in Spelt Risotto with Black Truffles, 21
Bouquet garni, 150
in Braised White Rabbit with Sautéed Chestnut Mushrooms, Green Peas and Potato Galette, 126
in Parmentier of Oxtail and Black Truffles, 70
in Poached Eggplant and Lime Gelatine with a touch of Cumin, 114
in Savoyard-style Chicken Nuggets with Peanut and Reine des Prés Sauces, 106
in Veal Jus, 149
in Vegetable Stock, 148
in White Stock, 148
in Young Vegetable Casserole with Orange and Sichuan Pepper Emulsion, 59
Brunoise, 150

C
Calvados, 150
in Apple, Prune, Butterscotch and Yoghurt Compote, 67
Carcass(es), 150
duck, in Poached Eggplant and Lime Gelatine with a touch of Cumin, 114
Cardamom, 150
black, seed, in Roasted Chilean Sea Bass, Tomato and Lemon Grass Broth, 94
in Thousand Ear Terrine, 138
Carnevale, 150
Lettuce of, 122
Carrot(s)
brunoise, in Carpaccio of Yellow Fin Tuna with Three Mustards, 99
in Beef Stock, 148
in Braised White Rabbit with Sautéed Chestnut Mushrooms, Green Peas and Potato Galette, 126
in Consommé, 149
in Duck Breast and Leg Confit topped with Cracked Jordan Almonds, Young Radishes, Sautéed Foie Gras and Honey Wine Jus, 90
in Lobster Stock, 148
in Madras Curry Marinated Lamb Chops in Filo Pastry with Lamb Gravy, and Green Papaya Salad and Boutique Greens with Thai Vinaigrette, 32
in Milk-fed Lamb Leg, Vegetable Casserole, Spinach and Sautéed Lamb Neck, 75
in Oven-baked Vegetarian Ravioli-stuffed Bread, Green Pea and Black Summer Scorzone Truffle Sauce, 49
in Oxtail-stuffed Baby Squid, Roasted Cremini Mushrooms and Salsify Purée with Oxtail Braising Juices and Mustard Oil, 37
in Parfait of Smoked Salmon and Tomato Jelly with Cucumber Sauce, 79
in Parmentier of Oxtail and Black Truffles, 70
in Poached Eggplant and Lime Gelatine with a touch of Cumin, 114
in Roasted Lobster and Vodka Sorbet with Crabmeat and Coral, 119
in Savoyard-style Chicken Nuggets with Peanut and Reine des Prés Sauces, 106
in Veal Jus, 149
in Vegetable Nage, 149
in Vegetable Potée and Beetroot and Black Truffle Mille Feuille with Foie Gras Sauce, 74
in Vegetable Stock, 148
in White Stock, 148
large, in Braised Veal Tongue, 149
large, in Chicken Stock, 148
medium, in Roasted Langoustine Seasoned with Tea and Langoustine Oil, 143
Purée, with Orange and Lemon Confit, and Spinach with Sesame Oil, 17
warm, gelatine, in Vegetables on the Grill, 53
Young, Confit Caramelised with Gingerbread Sauce, 62
young, in Young Vegetable Casserole with Orange and Sichuan Pepper Emulsion, 59
Casserole, 150
Young Vegetable, with Orange and Sichuan Pepper Emulsion, 59
Cauliflower
Couscous, 54
in Oven-baked Vegetarian Ravioli-stuffed Bread, Green Pea and Black Summer Scorzone Truffle Sauce, 49
Stems, and Vegetables, with Lobster and Tomato Juice Gelatine with Warm Salad of Asparagus, 111
Caviar
and Langoustine Tarama, with Pistachio Oil, and Avocado Bavarois, 17
Aquitaine, 150
Dressing, and Cucumber Lemon Salsa, with Yellow Fin Tuna, 59
eggplant, in Roasted Chilean Sea Bass, Tomato and Lemon Grass Broth, 94
in Carpaccio of Yellow Fin Tuna with Three Mustards, 99
Keta, in Parfait of Smoked Salmon and Tomato Jelly with Cucumber Sauce, 79
Sevruga, in Lobster Roll with Hot and Sour Broth, 103
Cayenne pepper, 150
in Spice Island Lobster, Salsify Purée and Fig-date Chutney, 91
Cèpe(s), 150
and Potato Raviolis, with Roasted Sea Bass with Swiss Chard, Artichokes, 20
in Oven-roasted Partridge with Gratinated Macaroni and Stuffing on Toast, 63
Chanterelle(s), 150
young, in Duck Breast and Leg Confit topped with Cracked Jordan Almonds, Young Radishes, Sautéed Foie Gras and Honey Wine Jus, 90
Cheese
Comté, in Oven-roasted Partridge with Gratinated Macaroni and Stuffing on Toast, 63
grated Parmesan, in Roasted Sea Bass with Swiss Chard, Artichokes, Cèpes and Potato Raviolis, 20
grated Parmesan, in Spelt Risotto with Black Truffles, 21
ricotta and Parmesan, in Oven-baked Vegetarian Ravioli-stuffed Bread, Green Pea and Black Summer Scorzone Truffle Sauce, 49
with Crayfish, Grapes, Sunny-side-up Egg and Walnut Purée, 134
Chénopode Bon Henri, 150
in Liquorice Flavoured Frogs' Legs with Spring Salad and Field Flowers, 106
Chervil, 150
chopped, in Young Carrot Confit Caramelised with Gingerbread Sauce, 62
in Roasted Lobster and Vodka Sorbet with Crabmeat and Coral, 119
leaves, in Cauliflower Couscous, 54
leaves, in Parfait of Smoked Salmon and Tomato Jelly with Cucumber Sauce, 79
sprigs, in Carpaccio of Yellow Fin Tuna with Three Mustards, 99
sprigs, in Four Dances of the Sea, 40
sprigs, in Grilled Langoustines with Trompettes de Mort and Barramundi with Sautéed Vegetables and Herb Salad, 127
sprig, in Vegetable Nage, 149
Chiffonade, 150
Citronelle, 150
and Linseed Sauce, with John Dory and Niçoise Zucchini, 83
Confit, 150
Orange and Lemon, and Spinach with Sesame Oil, with Carrot Purée, 17
orange and lemon zest, in Young Vegetable Casserole with Orange and Sichuan Pepper Emulsion, 59
Leg, topped with Cracked Jordan Almonds, Young Radishes, Sautéed Foie Gras and Honey Wine Jus, and Duck Breast, 90
Shallot, 149
shallot, in Oven-roasted Partridge with Gratinated Macaroni and Stuffing on Toast, 63
Young Carrot, Caramelised with Gingerbread Sauce, 62
Consommé, 149
jelly, in Roasted Lobster and Vodka Sorbet with Crabmeat and Coral, 119
Royal, with Mushrooms, Fried Snails and Jabugo Ham Foam, 134
Sauternes-, gelatine, with Foie Gras Torchon on Brioche with Truffle Ice Cream, 118
Couscous, Cauliflower, 54
Crayfish
in Braised Veal Tongue with Sweet Corn Emulsion, 37
with Cheese, Grapes, Sunny-side-up Egg and Walnut Purée, 134

D
Daikon(s), 150
cress, in Yellow Fin Tuna with Caviar Dressing and Cucumber Lemon Salsa, 59
in Abalone and Sea Urchin Baked in Salt Crust, 146
Marinated, and Sesame Oil Vinaigrette, with Black and Blue Tuna, 45
warm, gelatine, in Vegetables on the Grill, 53
Desserts
Apple, Prune, Butterscotch and Yoghurt Compote, 66–67
Candied Zucchini Flowers with Mixed Berry Sorbet and Sauce, 49
Chocolate with Apricot Sauce, 24–25
Green Pea Ice Cream, 70
Lettuce of Carnevale, 122–123
Pea and Banana Soup with Green Apple Sorbet and Vinegar and Pea Tuile, 110–111
Pineapple Ravioli with Raspberries, 86–87
Platinum of Fresh Mint–Kiyomi Mikuni, 99
The Apple for Sweet Dreams at Night, 115
Yoghurt Sorbet with Asparagus and Orange, 25
Dover sole(s), 150
in Pan-fried Fillet of Sole with Saffron-shellfish Fricassee, 86
Duck
Breast, and Leg Confit topped with Cracked Jordan Almonds, Young Radishes, Sautéed Foie Gras and Honey Wine Jus, 90
carcasses, in Poached Eggplant and Lime Gelatine with a touch of Cumin, 114
fat, in Shallot Confit, 149
-ling breast, in Savoyard-style Chicken Nuggets with Peanut and Reine des Prés Sauces, 106
meat from, legs, in Foie Gras Torchon on Brioche with Truffle Ice Cream and Sauternes-consommé Gelatine, 118

E
Emulsion, 150
Lemon and Olive Oil, and Poppy Seeds, with Melon and Tomatoes, 83
Orange and Sichuan Pepper, with Young Vegetable Casserole, 59
Sweet Corn, with Braised Veal Tongue, 37
Endive, 150
curly, leaves, in Grilled Langoustines with Trompettes de Mort and Barramundi with Sautéed Vegetables and Herb Salad, 127
curly, leaves, in Pan-fried Salmon, Sautéed Vegetables and Hearts of Palm with Sweet and Sour Red Wine Sauce, 45

F
Foie Gras, 150
Char-grilled, with Rice 'Bomba' and Seaweed Stock, 28
in Oven-roasted Partridge with Gratinated Macaroni and Stuffing on Toast, 63
Liquorice, and Pear Crisps with Pear and Black Bean Chutney, with Cinnamon Pigeon, 33
Sauce, with Vegetable Potée and Beetroot and Black Truffle Mille Feuille, 74
Sautéed, and Honey Wine Jus, with Duck Breast and Leg Confit topped with Cracked Jordan Almonds, Young Radishes, 90
Torchon, on Brioche with Truffle Ice Cream and Sauternes-consommé Gelatine, 118
Fricassee, 151
Saffron-shellfish, with Pan-fried Fillet of Sole, 86
Frogs' Legs, Liquorice Flavoured, with Spring Salad and Field Flowers, 106

G
Galangal, 151
fresh, in Four Dances of the Sea, 40
in Spice Island Lobster, Salsify Purée and Fig-date Chutney, 91
Garden peas, 151
Gelatine
Campari, in Cauliflower Couscous, 54
leaves, in Grilled Turbot with Warm Citric Vinaigrette and Crystallised Zest, 28
leaves, in Pea and Banana Soup with Green Apple Sorbet and Vinegar and Pea Tuile, 111
leaves, in Roasted Lobster and Vodka Sorbet with Crabmeat and Coral, 119
Lime, with a touch of Cumin, and Poached Eggplant, 114
Muscat, in Yoghurt Sorbet with Asparagus and Orange, 25
Sauternes-consommé, and Foie Gras Torchon on Brioche with Truffle Ice Cream, 118
Sauternes, with Granny Smith Apple Sorbet, 143
sheets, in Parfait of Smoked Salmon and Tomato Jelly with Cucumber Sauce, 79
Tomato Juice, with Warm Salad of Asparagus, Cauliflower Stems and Vegetables, and Lobster, 111
vegetable, in Composition of Tomato, Eggplant, Basil Flowers and Olive Oil, 122

RECIPE INDEX

warm red capsicum, warm green capsicum, warm onion, warm celery, warm daikon, warm carrot, warm asparagus in Vegetables on the Grill, 53
Girolle(s), 151
  in Summery Quails with Tomato Tarragon Dressing, 67
Glucose, 151
  in Candied Zucchini Flowers with Mixed Berry Sorbet and Sauce, 49
  in Cauliflower Couscous, 54
  in Chocolate with Apricot Sauce, 25
  in Granny Smith Apple Sorbet with Sauternes Gelatine, 143
  in Pea and Banana Soup with Green Apple Sorbet and Vinegar and Pea Tuile, 111
  in The Apple for Sweet Dreams at Night, 115
  in Yoghurt Sorbet with Asparagus and Orange, 25
Green Pea(s)
  and Black Summer Scorzone Truffle Sauce, with Oven-baked Vegetarian Ravioli-stuffed Bread, 49
  and Potato Galette, with Braised White Rabbit with Sautéed Chestnut Mushrooms, 126
  Ice Cream, 70
  small, in Pea and Banana Soup with Green Apple Sorbet and Vinegar and Pea Tuile, 111

H
Hatcho miso, 151
  in Simmered Pork with Broad Bean Purée and Gourd Melon, 146
Heart(s) of Palm, 151
  in Kobe Beef Ravioli with Truffle Tea, 103
  with Sweet and Sour Red Wine Sauce, with Pan-fried Salmon and Sautéed Vegetables, 45
Honshimeiji mushroom(s), 151
  in Grilled Langoustines with Trompettes de Mort and Barramundi with Sautéed Vegetables and Herb Salad, 127
  in Pan-fried Salmon, Sautéed Vegetables and Hearts of Palm with Sweet and Sour Red Wine Sauce, 45

I
Ice Cream
  Green Pea, 70
  Truffle, and Sauternes-consommé Gelatine, with Foie Gras Torchon on Brioche, 118
  walnut, in The Apple for Sweet Dreams at Night, 115

J
John Dory, 151
  and Niçoise Zucchini with Citronelle and Linseed Sauce, 83
Juniper berry(ies), 151
  in Cauliflower Couscous, 54
  in Parmentier of Oxtail and Black Truffles, 70
Jus, 151
  duck, in Duck Breast and Leg Confit topped with Cracked Jordan Almonds, Young Radishes, Sautéed Foie Gras and Honey Wine Jus, 90
  Honey Wine, and Duck Breast and Leg Confit topped with Cracked Jordan Almonds, Young Radishes, Sautéed Foie Gras, 90
  Veal, 149
  veal, in Spelt Risotto with Black Truffles, 21

K
Konbu, 151
  in Spice Island Lobster, Salsify Purée and Fig-date Chutney, 91

L
Langoustine, 151
  and Caviar Tarama, with Pistachio Oil, and Avocado Bavarois, 17
  Grilled, with Trompettes de Mort and Barramundi with Sautéed Vegetables and Herb Salad, 127
  Roasted, Seasoned with Tea and Langoustine Oil, 143
Linseed, 151
  and Citronelle Sauce, with John Dory and Niçoise Zucchini, 83
Liquorice
  Flavoured Frogs' Legs, with Spring Salad and Field Flowers, 106
  Foie Gras, and Pear Crisps with Pear and Black Bean Chutney, with Cinnamon Pigeon, 33
  stick, in Savoyard-style Chicken Nuggets with Peanut and Reine des Prés Sauces, 106
Lobster
  and Tomato Juice Gelatine, with Warm Salad of Asparagus, Cauliflower Stems and Vegetables, 111
  heads, in Shellfish Oil, 149
  Roasted, and Vodka Sorbet with Crabmeat and Coral, 119
  Roll, with Hot and Sour Broth, 103
  Spice Island, Salsify Purée and Fig-date Chutney, 91
  Stock, 148

M
Macerate, 151
Main Courses
  Braised Veal Tongue with Sweet Corn Emulsion, 37
  Braised White Rabbit with Sautéed Chestnut Mushrooms, Green Peas and Potato Galette, 126
  Char-grilled Foie Gras with Rice 'Bomba' and Seaweed Stock, 28
  Cinnamon Pigeon, Liquorice Foie Gras and Pear Crisps with Pear and Black Bean Chutney, 33
  Duck Breast and Leg Confit topped with Cracked Jordan Almonds, Young Radishes, Sautéed Foie Gras and Honey Wine Jus, 90
  Foie Gras Torchon on Brioche with Truffle Ice Cream and Sauternes-consommé Gelatine, 118
  Grilled Langoustines with Trompettes de Mort and Barramundi with Sautéed Vegetables and Herb Salad, 127
  Grilled Turbot with Warm Citric Vinaigrette and Crystallised Zest, 28–29
  John Dory and Niçoise Zucchini with Citronelle and Linseed Sauce, 82–83
  Kobe Beef Ravioli with Truffle Tea, 102–103
  Lobster Roll with Hot and Sour Broth, 103
  Madras Curry Marinated Lamb Chops in Filo Pastry with Lamb Gravy, and Green Papaya Salad and Boutique Greens with Thai Vinaigrette, 32
  Milk-fed Lamb Leg, Vegetable Casserole, Spinach and Sautéed Lamb Neck, 75
  Oven-baked Vegetarian Ravioli-stuffed Bread, Green Pea and Black Summer Scorzone Truffle Sauce, 48–49
  Oven-roasted Partridge with Gratinated Macaroni and Stuffing on Toast, 63
  Oxtail-stuffed Baby Squid, Roasted Cremini Mushrooms and Salsify Purée with Oxtail Braising Juices and Mustard Oil, 36–37
  Pan-fried Fillet of Sole with Saffron-shellfish Fricassee, 86
  Pan-fried Salmon, Sautéed Vegetables and Hearts of Palm with Sweet and Sour Red Wine Sauce, 44–45
  Parmentier of Oxtail and Black Truffles, 70–71
  Roasted Chilean Sea Bass, Tomato and Lemon Grass Broth, 94
  Roasted Lobster and Vodka Sorbet with Crabmeat and Coral, 119
  Roasted Pork Ribs with Mocha Sauce, 130–131
  Roasted Sea Bass with Swiss Chard, Artichokes, Cèpes and Potato Raviolis, 20
  Simmered Pork with Broad Bean Purée and Gourd Melon, 146
  Spelt Risotto with Black Truffles, 21
  Spice Island Lobster, Salsify Purée and Fig-date Chutney, 91
  Summery Quails with Tomato Tarragon Dressing, 67
Mandoline, 151
Mirepoix, 151
  in Foie Gras Torchon on Brioche with Truffle Ice Cream and Sauternes-consommé Gelatine, 118
  in Thousand Ear Terrine, 138
Mizuna, 151
  in Liquorice Flavoured Frogs' Legs with Spring Salad and Field Flowers, 106
Munster, 151
  in Crayfish with Cheese, Grapes, Sunny-side-up Egg and Walnut Purée, 134
Muscat, 151
  gelatine, in Yoghurt Sorbet with Asparagus and Orange, 25
  grapes, in Crayfish with Cheese, Grapes, Sunny-side-up Egg and Walnut Purée, 134
Muscovado, 151
  sugar, in Cauliflower Couscous, 54

N
Niçoise, 151
  Zucchini, with Citronelle and Linseed Sauce, and John Dory, 83
Noilly Prat, 151
  in Chilled Tomato Soup with Devilfish Medallions, 79
  in John Dory and Niçoise Zucchini with Citronelle and Linseed Sauce, 83
  reduced, in Parfait of Smoked Salmon and Tomato Jelly with Cucumber Sauce, 79

O
Ogonori, 151
  in Roasted Langoustine Seasoned with Tea and Langoustine Oil, 143

P
Parmentier, 151
  of Oxtail and Black Truffles, 70
Pernod, 151
  in Parfait of Smoked Salmon and Tomato Jelly with Cucumber Sauce, 79
Potato Galette, 151–152
  and Braised White Rabbit with Sautéed Chestnut Mushrooms, Green Peas, 126

R
Reine des Prés, 152
  and Peanut Sauces, with Savoyard-style Chicken Nuggets, 106
Rempah, 152
  in Four Dances of the Sea, 40
Risotto, 152
  Spelt, with Black Truffles, 21
Rocket, 152
  in Liquorice Flavoured Frogs' Legs with Spring Salad and Field Flowers, 106

S
Salamander, 152
Salsify, 152
  Purée, and Fig-date Chutney, with Spice Island Lobster, 91
  Purée, with Oxtail Braising Juices and Mustard Oil, and Oxtail-stuffed Baby Squid, Roasted Cremini Mushrooms, 37
Sambal oelek, 152
  in Lobster Roll with Hot and Sour Broth, 103
Sansho pepper, 152
  in Simmered Pork with Broad Bean Purée and Gourd Melon, 146
Sauternes, 152
  -consommé Gelatine, and Foie Gras Torchon on Brioche with Truffle Ice Cream, 118
  Gelatine, with Granny Smith Apple Sorbet, 143
Scorzone truffle, 152
  Black Summer, and Green Pea Sauce, with Oven-baked Vegetarian Ravioli-stuffed Bread, 49
Sea Urchin, and Abalone, Baked in Salt Crust, 146
Sedum, 152
  in Liquorice Flavoured Frogs' Legs with Spring Salad and Field Flowers, 106
Sesame
  oil, in Four Dances of the Sea, 40
  oil, in Madras Curry Marinated Lamb Chops in Filo Pastry with Lamb Gravy, and Green Papaya Salad and Boutique Greens with Thai Vinaigrette, 32
  oil, in Roasted Pork Ribs with Mocha Sauce, 131
  oil, in Thousand Ear Terrine, 138
  Oil Vinaigrette, and Black and Blue Tuna with Marinated Daikon, 45
  Oil, with Spinach, and Carrot Purée with Orange and Lemon Confit, 17
Shiso, 152
  flowers, in Simmered Pork with Broad Bean Purée and Gourd Melon, 146
Siphon, 152
Sorbet
  chocolate, in Chocolate with Apricot Sauce, 25
  Granny Smith Apple, with Sauternes Gelatine, 143
  Green Apple, and Vinegar and Pea Tuile, with Pea and Banana Soup, 111
  mint, in Platinum of Fresh Mint–Kiyomi Mikuni, 99
  Mixed Berry, and Sauce, with Candied Zucchini Flowers, 49
  verbena, in Pineapple Ravioli with Raspberries, 86
  Vodka, with Crabmeat and Coral, and Roasted Lobster, 119
  Yoghurt, with Asparagus and Orange, 25
Soups
  Chilled Tomato Soup with Devilfish Medallions, 78–79
  Pea and Banana Soup with Green Apple Sorbet and Vinegar and Pea Tuile, 110–111
  Royal Consommé with Mushrooms, Fried Snails and Jabugo Ham Foam, 134
Spelt, 152
  Risotto with Black Truffles, 21
Star anise, 152
  in Pan-fried Salmon, Sautéed Vegetables and Hearts of Palm with Sweet and Sour Red Wine Sauce, 45
  in Thousand Ear Terrine, 138
  in Young Vegetable Casserole with Orange and Sichuan Pepper Emulsion, 59
Stock
  Beef, 148
  Chicken, 148
  Fish, 148
  Lobster, 148
  Mushroom, 148
  red wine, in Pan-fried Salmon, Sautéed Vegetables and Hearts of Palm with Sweet and Sour Red Wine Sauce, 45
  Rice 'Bomba' and Seaweed, with Char-grilled Foie Gras, 28
  Vegetable, 148
  vegetable, in Savoyard-style Chicken Nuggets with Peanut and Reine des Prés Sauces, 106
  White, 148
Strega liquor, 152
  in Lettuce of Carnevale, 122
Sudachi, 152
  juice, in Abalone and Sea Urchin Baked in Salt Crust, 146
Swiss chard, 152
  and Artichokes, Cèpes and Potato Raviolis, with Roasted Sea Bass, 20
  in Milk-fed Lamb Leg, Vegetable Casserole, Spinach and Sautéed Lamb Neck, 75
  in Spelt Risotto with Black Truffles, 21

T
Taro, 152
  mash filling, in Kobe Beef Ravioli with Truffle Tea, 103
Timbale, 152
Tomato concassée, 152
  in Beef Stock, 148
Truffle(s), 152
  Black, and Beetroot Mille Feuille, with Foie Gras Sauce, and Vegetable Potée, 74
  Black, and Parmentier of Oxtail, 70
  black, in Roasted Sea Bass with Swiss Chard, Artichokes, Cèpes and Potato Raviolis, 20
  black, in Young Vegetable Casserole with Orange and Sichuan Pepper Emulsion, 59
  Black Summer Scorzone, and Green Pea Sauce, with Oven-baked Vegetarian Ravioli-stuffed Bread, 49
  Black, with Spelt Risotto, 21
  Ice Cream, and Sauternes-consommé Gelatine, with Foie Gras Torchon on Brioche, 118
  Tea, with Kobe Beef Ravioli, 103
Tuile, 152
  Vinegar and Pea, and Pea and Banana Soup with Green Apple Sorbet, 111
Turbot, 152
  Grilled, with Warm Citric Vinaigrette and Crystallised Zest, 28

V
Vermouth, 152
  in John Dory and Niçoise Zucchini with Citronelle and Linseed Sauce, 83
  see also Noilly Prat.
Vinaigrette
  and herb salad, in Braised White Rabbit with Sautéed Chestnut Mushrooms, Green Peas and Potato Galette, 126
  balsamic, in Carpaccio of Yellow Fin Tuna with Three Mustards, 99
  cider, in Lobster and Tomato Juice Gelatine with Warm Salad of Asparagus, Cauliflower Stems and Vegetables, 111
  orange, in Liquorice Flavoured Frogs' Legs with Spring Salad and Field Flowers, 106
  port, in Duck Breast and Leg Confit topped with Cracked Jordan Almonds, Young Radishes, Sautéed Foie Gras and Honey Wine Jus, 90
  Sesame Oil, and Black and Blue Tuna with Marinated Daikon, 45
  Thai, with Green Papaya Salad and Boutique Greens, and Madras Curry Marinated Lamb Chops in Filo Pastry with Lamb Gravy, 32
  Warm Citric, and Crystallised Zest, with Grilled Turbot, 28

W
Wagarashi, 152
  mustard, in Simmered Pork with Broad Bean Purée and Gourd Melon, 146
White flour '0', 152
  in Oven-baked Vegetarian Ravioli-stuffed Bread, Green Pea and Black Summer Scorzone Truffle Sauce, 49
White flour '00', 152
  in Oven-baked Vegetarian Ravioli-stuffed Bread, Green Pea and Black Summer Scorzone Truffle Sauce, 49

PAGE 160: Rare-seared Tuna Scallop with Potato Chips and Soya Sauce by Marcus Samuelsson of Aquavit in New York.

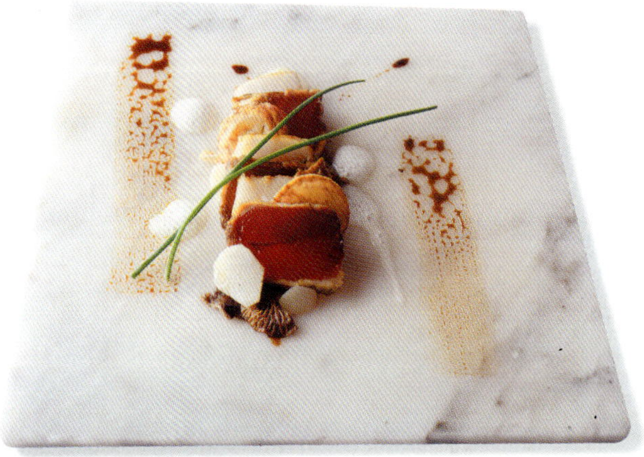